Desiring Donne

Desiring Donne

POETRY, SEXUALITY,
INTERPRETATION

BEN SAUNDERS

HARVARD UNIVERSITY PRESS
Cambridge, Massachusetts, and London, England   2006

Library of Congress Cataloging-in-Publication Data

Saunders, Ben, 1968–
    Desiring Donne : poetry, sexuality, interpretation / Ben Saunders.
      p. cm.
    Includes bibliographical references and index.
    ISBN-13: 978–0–674–02347–5 (alk. paper)
    ISBN-10: 0–674–02347–1 (alk. paper)
    1. Donne, John, 1572–1631—Criticism and interpretation. 2. Love
poetry, English—History and criticism. 3. Poetry—Psychological aspects.
4. Desire in literature. I. Title.

PR2248.S28 2006
821'.3—dc22   2006043593

*This book is dedicated to my teachers,
and to the wider interpretive community of
Donne's readers, past, present, and future*

Acknowledgments

I owe a special debt to Stanley Fish, whose antipathy toward Donne is well known, but who nevertheless welcomed the challenge of disagreement. It is mere self-flattery for me to say that his influence is apparent in the pages that follow. I am grateful, above all, for his intellectual generosity, for the example of his critical acumen, and for his remarkable sense of humor.

I owe an additional debt to the following individuals, all of whom read and commented upon portions of this work, or else provided invaluable help and advice as interlocuters, at different times over the last ten years: Nigel Alderman, Sarah Beckwith, Roger Beebe, Matthew Biberman, Louise Bishop, Charles Daniel Blanton, Lara Bovilsky, Andrew "Hiscane" Cole, James Crosswhite, A. Leigh DeNeef, Greg Dobbins, James Earl, Karen Ford, Lisa Freinkel, Denise Fulbrook, Amanpal Garcha, Daniel Juan Gil, Warren Ginsberg, Kevin Haynes, Trent Hill, Austin Kelly, Aaron Kunin, Katherine Little, Jack Murnighan, Mark Owens, Paul Peppis, Joseph A. Porter, Forrest "Tres" Pyle, Maureen Quilligan, George Rowe, Eva Star Sayre, Deep Singh, Jennifer Snead, and Peter Terpinski. My friends, colleagues, and highly esteemed fellow-travelers: I simply do not have the words to convey my respect, affection, and gratitude.

I would also like to extend a more general thanks to Drew Bruce, Jean Cottel, Kyle Debord, Larisa Devine, Lisa Freinkel, Rich Gaston, Daniel Mackay, Jim Thomas, Ezra Tishman, and the entire Q.B. family, for the gifts of community and fellowship.

Lindsay Waters, my editor at Harvard University Press, has been more than supportive; his passionate commitment to the truth of experience has been inspirational. Thank you, Lindsay, for your help and your example.

Thanks are also due to my anonymous readers at the Press, both for their kind remarks and for their criticisms. Their generous service has surely helped to improve and strengthen this work overall.

Finally, I must express gratitude to my family: my smart, funny, and talented brother, Josh Saunders; and my parents, Jill and David Saunders, who first taught me to value the arts. Because of those early lessons, "appreciation" will never be a pejorative term in my critical vocabulary.

Contents

Desiring Donne

The Desire of Criticism
and the Criticism of Desire (Part I)

John Donne was well acquainted with the costs and consequences of desire. He wanted a courtly career badly enough to renounce the Catholicism of his childhood, and he came close to achieving it, landing a good job as private secretary to Queen Elizabeth's Lord Keeper. Then he wanted a woman badly enough to gamble that same career for her sake. He lost, then spent the next ten years vainly striving to reopen the door he had closed on himself before finally acknowledging that the opportunity was gone for good. He pursued philosophical and theological questions with a passion to match his courtly and romantic ambitions, remarking in one of his gloomier moments that these academic inclinations actually betrayed "the worst voluptuousnes" on his part; he felt that he had failed to "contribute something" to the world at large because he had been "diverted," in his words, by "an Hydroptique immoderate desire of humane learning and languages."[1] When the priesthood finally provided the public position denied him at court, Donne took off after the souls of his parishioners with the same fervent zeal he had displayed in every other arena, if we can judge by his sermons. Indeed, he was not above addressing God Himself in tones of "immoderate desire," variously adopting the postures of demand, seduction, desperation, fidelity, and abjection in his poetic prayers.

He wrote constantly about the desires that racked and delighted him. Frustration taught him the worst curse he knew—"Itching desire, and no abilitie"—but he also knew that satisfaction came with its own double bind and that fantasy could never be entirely transcended, even in the achievement of a dream: "Hee that hath all can have no more," he wrote; and also: "all our joyes are but fantasticall."[2]

Death became the ultimate object of Donne's passionate attention. He prepared for that final date with assiduous care, posing for a portrait in his funeral shroud, keeping the resulting ghastly image by his bedside like a lover's picture, and roundly declaring, "I were miserable if I might not dye." The devoutly wished for consummation came on March 31, 1631; Donne closed his eyes, breathed his last, and knew desire no more.

We have been pursuing the knowledge of his desire ever since.[3]

Whether we have found such knowledge is open to debate. But sometimes, in the process of searching, we have discovered our own desires, although we have not always recognized them as such. In *Desiring Donne,* I tell some stories of this almost 400-year-long pursuit, beginning with one of Donne's earliest readers and ending with some of his most recent poststructuralist and feminist critics. I explore Donne's verse in its contemporary bibliographic, social, literary-historical, and theological contexts and also in the contexts of present-day critical theory. I challenge the conclusions reached by some of his most influential readers during the last twenty-five years, and, in the process, I offer some new readings of his love poetry and new interpretations of several key arguments within the tradition of Donnean criticism. But I also attempt something more: to shed light not only on the specific nature of Donnean desire, but also on the role played by readerly desire within interpretive practice.

Over the course of this introduction, I explicate the intellectual principles that unify the disparate materials of my subsequent chapters, elaborating upon my central concept of "interpretive desire." However, my argument can be reduced to three basic positions, which, as here laid out, also describe the trajectory of the book as a whole:

1. Literary criticism is shaped as much by desire as by historical, cultural, and institutional contexts. Although a good deal of recent work in the humanities has focused on the significance of the latter three terms for critical epistemology, and psychoanalytic criticism has offered some powerful conceptualizations of desire and its vicissitudes, the role played by desire in interpretive practice remains worthy of more sustained investigation.

2. Donne's poetry and the responses it has inspired together provide a uniquely appropriate site for such investigation. Donne's reception history exposes the dynamic of desire within interpretation, and Donne's poems are themselves interpretations of desire: meditations on affect that reveal the interconnections between history, sexuality, and knowledge. While his work cannot be approached in the manner of a philosophical treatise, Donne is one of the greatest theorists of desire to write in English, and he repays scrutiny as such.

3. The unique challenges of the Donnean text also demonstrate the necessity of formulating a critical practice self-conscious about the destabilizing effects of its own desire, which at the same time refuses to subsume aesthetic questions entirely into the categories of the social and historical. The problems raised by Donne and Donne criticism can help us to understand the function and value of literary criticism in a poststructuralist universe. It is only by asking the difficult question, "What does the literary critic want?" that we can begin to understand what criticism actually does and what it can hope to do in the future.

I

> Quotations have a special interest, since one is not apt to quote what is not one's own words, whoever may have written them. The "whoever" is the quoter in another guise, in another age, under other circumstances.
>
> —WALLACE STEVENS, LETTER TO ELSIE VIOLA KACHEL

I begin with the desire to be Donne. The pun resolutely asserts itself, like it or not, and so I shall make the best use of it that I can. As with all puns, it cuts in several directions. To begin with the desire to be Donne is to admit that by the time I'm done with Donne, I hope to have persuaded you that my Donne is the right Donne, the most convincingly "Donnean" Donne, to proffer a deliberate re-donne-dancy. So we might say that my desire, at some basic level, is to be Donne for you once you are done with me.

Before I am accused of self-indulgence (literary critics, not generally noted for their humor, are often most amusing when trying their best not to be), I should quickly add that this desire to be Donne is not mine alone. I am also speaking of a more generalized interpretive longing: the desire of the critic. After all, is there not a sense in which all of Donne's interpreters can be said to begin with the desire to be Donne *for* each other (even if we sometimes end only with the desire to be done *with* each other)? But the logic of desire leads inexorably to the critic's undoing. To begin with the desire to be Donne is, *ipso facto*, not to be Donne; it is to be un-Donne, to know that one can never be Donne. We cannot close that endlessly productive gap of nonidentity. There will always be more.

To conceive of literary interpretation as an expression of desire is to open a large can of bookworms; a deceptively simple proposition, it raises profound questions about the ontological principles that secure (or fail to secure) critical judgments. Of course, in recent years, the various methodologies of historicism, poststructuralism, political criticism, psychoanalysis, and reader-response criticism, in their differently inflected ways, have made us wary of saying that the text "speaks for itself." But the profession has been more reluctant to consider some corollary positions.[4] For if the text does not speak for itself, it follows that at some level we must make it speak for us, of our desires, and not only our desires as individuals but also the collective desires that percolate and bubble within the osmotic boundaries of interpretive communities, desires that we sometimes call "ideological." By raising questions about the nature of critical authority, the scandal of interpretive desire touches not only on the way we write about literature in the present, but also on the way we understand the criticism of the past. The stakes are high; as Vincent Crapanzano has written, the question of how the human sciences articulate themselves can produce nothing less than "conceptual anguish."[5]

Against this background, the injunction to "always historicize" and the concept of the interpretive community can both be construed as evasions. Despite the valuable work they generate, such notions also divert the critic away from a direct confrontation with the wild card of his or her desire. Although the profession at large is at least superficially comfortable with the idea that interpretation involves an element of creative projection (witness the general acceptance of shibboleths like the suggestion that "all reading is also misreading"), we continue to invoke the protocols of the interpretive community and/or the limitations of historical context to contain or constrain the more perverse and willful readerly responses. But the logic of the return of the repressed cannot be denied. The perverse and willful readings of today often turn out to be the paradigm-shaping interpretations of to-morrow—and the partial, conservative, or reductionist perspectives of next week. Historical contexts are endlessly subject to revision and transformation, while the bitter internecine squabbles that notoriously characterize "progress" in the humanities indicate that the interpretive community is not a clean and well-swept institutional space with pro-scribed rules of procedure and engagement, but an agonistic, seething mass of competing impulses, dominated as much by accident and affect as it is by reason and intellect.

I do not pretend that a self-reflexive awareness of interpretive desire will ultimately help anyone escape its dialectical clutches, thus allowing the text (at last!) to speak for itself. However, I think that if we take seriously the proposition that interpretations are always words chosen out of desire, in Wallace Stevens's phrase, we can at least raise the prospect of an alternative approach to critical disagreements and to the texts that inspire them. This approach would involve asking whether different structures of interpretive desire can account for the production of utterly contradictory readings of the same texts (and if so, what structures), rather than struggling to settle the question in favor of one reading or another. Perhaps more provocatively, it might allow us to name different interpretive desires not according to chilly institutional and professional categories (such as "formalist," "deconstructivist," "humanist," "feminist," or "historicist") but as fundamentally emo-tional and affective responses (acts of identification, admiration, mourning, nostalgia, lust, disgust, and so on). Most important, this approach would entail a partial recuperation of the maligned category of the aesthetic, even in the wake of the strong sociological and his-toricist impulses of much recent criticism. By reminding us of the dy-namic and affectively oriented component of a critical response, the concept of interpretive desire also reminds us that, at its most philo-sophically bold, the aesthetic refers less to the practice of making for-mally evaluative distinctions between types of "art-object" than to the project of describing a complex, creatively mediated relationship be-tween human subjects.

If my discussion thus far has a melodramatic air, this may only be appropriate. Questions of critical epistemology often display a dis-tinctly "whodunit?" quality ("His account is plausible, but can we think of it as *true?*" "How can we distinguish the textual facts from our interpretive desires?" "Who killed the author, and was it murder or justifiable homicide?" "Who are the meaning police?" and so on).

I have begun by evoking such questions because they arise naturally out of the obvious association between desire and emotion, which, since the Middle Ages (at least), we have been inclined to see as antithetical to reasoned thought: traditionally, and commonsensically, reason opposes emotion. *Desiring Donne* questions this commonsense opposition, blurring the boundary between reason and emotion. For desire resides in that psychological shadow land where thought and feeling meet and touch, as Donne understood; and, like Donne, I, too, desire to understand desire and the relation of desire to understanding. But Donne's own treatment of desire goes well beyond this hermeneutic horizon, addressing desire in its broadest senses: sexual desire, of course, but also spiritual desire and the desire for fame, social success, and renown. (Although the fact that sexual desire, spiritual desire, and the desire for fame can all be figured as forms of knowing or being known suggests that at some level we may still be in epistemological territory.)

Can we begin to speak of the intersection of these broader desires with interpretive desire? The point of the question is not simply that our thoughts and interpretations are shaped by disavowed impulses of the flesh, the spirit, or the narcissistic ego (though of course they are) but to raise the hermeneutic problem from the other side, as it were, and ask to what degree those primal impulses themselves are *already* forms of thought, *already interpretations*.

It may be overly portentous to say that *Desiring Donne* attempts to draw together the discourses of literature, criticism, psychoanalysis, and the history of sexuality, to weave a textual veil through which, paradoxically, we can better see reason *as* emotion, knowledge *as* fantasy, interpretation *as* desire; but the metaphor of the veil that unveils— a resonant image of desire from the English Renaissance to modern pop lyrics—is apt. In fact, if my use of the term "desire" in the pages that follow sometimes seems imprecise, I hope it will not sound disingenuous to say that this is the nature of the beast. How frequently is it the case, after all, that we are most aware of our desires when we are least able to verbalize them? Desire, at some level, is the name we give to feelings that cannot easily be named, feelings that are, precisely, *felt*. When it must be articulated, desire tends to impress us impressionistically: when it is partially descried, almost uncovered, simultaneously veiled and revealed by allegories, analogies, and images, by metaphors that border on tautologies, exposing at once the bridge and the void between word and world.

Indeed, it is axiomatic at this moment in our culture that named desires are also diminished desires or, at least, more manageable desires. The ability to articulate powerful and painful feelings is presumed of a piece with taming and controlling those feelings, and with the process of emotional growth. Conversely, it is said that to live with unspoken or unacknowledged desire is to live in bad faith; worse still, it can make one sick, hysterically symptomatic or neurotically obsessive and compulsive. Freud was not the first astute observer of human behavior to note that "it's good to talk," though he may have been among the first to charge a fee for listening, and he must take some credit, or blame, for secularizing the confessional sacrament as the basis of modern therapy and self-help literature. Today, basic tenets of psychoanalytic and existentialist thought about the nature of desire recirculate and coagulate in unexpected and sometimes alarming ways in the no-man's land of daytime television, from the reactionary trailer parks of Jerry Springer to the liberal suburbs of Oprah Winfrey (with Dr. Phil as a kind of roving Jean-Paul Sartre for the postmodern masses, constantly castigating us for our failure to live according to the truth of our being). In the seventeenth century, too, Donne was familiar with the idea that desire expressed hurts less than desire repressed, but he also saw that there were dangers in saying too much, dangers that he linked, intriguingly, to knowing too much:

The triple Foole
I am two fooles, I know,
For loving, and for saying so
    In whining Poëtry;
But where's that wiseman, that would not be I,
    If she would not deny?
Then as th'earths inward narrow crooked lanes
Do purge sea waters fretfull salt away
    I thought, if I could draw my paines,
Through Rimes vexation, I should them allay,
Griefe brought to numbers cannot be so fierce,
For, he tames it, that fetters it in verse.

    But when I have done so,
Some man, his art and voice to show,
    Doth Set and sing my paine,
And by delighting many, frees againe
    Griefe, which verse did restraine.
To Love, and Griefe tribute of Verse belongs
But not of such as pleases when 'tis read,

> Both are increased by such songs;
> For both their triumphs so are published,
> And I, which was two fooles, do so grow three;
> Who are a little wise, the best fooles bee.[6]

In two stanzas, this deceptively simple poem conveys the effect of desire upon the individual in its grip, the significance for the desiring subject of both prohibition and approval, the difficulty of representing desire formally in language, and the complex relationship between desire, aesthetic form, interpretation, and pleasure—all before bringing us back to epistemology with its final ambiguous claim about the desirability of knowledge. It therefore provides a neat platform from which to say a little more about desire as a keyword in my own discourse.

First, Donne's poem reminds us that the desiring subject is a divided subject; the tendency of the first-person pronoun to instantiate the illusion of a single, univocal (Cartesian) self, much mooted in recent philosophy, is brought up short in just three words: "I am *two*." Early modernists will hear this opening as a variant on a familiar (if paradoxical) Renaissance formula for identity: "I am not I." But the splintering of this particular self is swiftly provided with an etiology. "I am two fools" for two reasons: desire ("loving") and language ("Poëtry"). Thus the illusion of the single, whole, univocal self is reinstated with the same breath that it was denied, implicitly posited as the speaker's *prior* state, the condition of life before desire and language came along, or came together. In the next two lines, the speaker raises the possibility of a conditional return to that integrated state, imagining the singular, enviable "I" that he would surely become if access to the beloved object were not prohibited: "But where's that wiseman, that would not be I / If she would not deny?" This suggestion that the prize of a reintegrated ego will be awarded to the subject on the successful possession of his or her desired object (a belief expressed in contemporary culture by the Hollywood formula of "you complete me") has, of course, been identified within psychoanalytic theory as one of humankind's most primal fantasies—something that Donne also recognizes here. More recent variations on this theory have emphasized that such fantasies of reintegration necessarily require an admiring Other, for it is only from a perspective outside itself that the self can even imagine itself whole; and strikingly, Donne's rhetoric confirms this postmodern version of psychoanalysis when he claims that everyone of good judgment would like to be in his (subject) position, if he could only get what he wants. "I am not I," the poet concedes, "but if I had my desire, I would be, and everyone else would want to be, too."

The short story of desire in the first five lines of this poem, then, runs as follows: Desire divides the self from itself through the agency of language but is also imagined as that which can reintegrate the self through the possession of a desired object, even as it throws into relief the constitutively social character of subjectivization. This conception of desire as the equivocatory fiend that lies like truth, at once the false ground of the univocal self and the true origin of the split subject, is one that I will test, explicate, and elaborate, through and against Donne's own meditations on the relation between desire and selfhood, in subsequent chapters.

However, the poem goes on to anticipate several other problems that attend upon a sustained discussion of desire and its vicissitudes, not least being the impossibility of its direct articulation. Donne's elaborate metaphor for poetic production as the filtration of salt from seawater complicates what is nowadays a banally familiar literal point (though probably new and daring in the seventeenth century): that the bitterness of frustrated desire can be alleviated not in prayer but in art. The metaphor indirectly emphasizes the difficulty of this process, both in its substance and in its formal deployment; as the seawater trickles slowly along "th'earth's inward narrow crooked lanes," so the reader's eye, too, must travel the entire length of the first pair of successive pentameter lines in the poem before discovering what the metaphor actually describes, creating a sense of effort and delay. The laboriousness of the task is further compounded by the absence of the kind of alliteration that made the first, isolated pentameter line skip along at a relatively rapid rate ("But where's that wiseman, that would not be I"). Thus, the literal argument of lines six through eleven is that by giving a form to desire we gain some control over it; but the formal structure of the verse undercuts this stated faith in formal structures by stressing the challenges involved. As events unfold in the second stanza, this (already formally compromised) promise of form will be recognized as false. The speaker's belief that he can ease the pain of desire by articulating it as verse turns out to be mistaken; his pain returns when he hears his own words sung in the voice of another. This return precipitates further reflection on the relationship between desire and representation.

We can read this literally resonant moment as emblematic of a common intellectual error in discussions of desire: the tendency to think of desire, and particularly sexual desire, as having an essentially formless or "natural" state, prior to the "civilizing" influence of society and symbolization. What often gets left out of such accounts is the way in which the socializing and symbolizing of our supposedly natural impulses will change the *content* of those impulses with their form. To illustrate this point, consider the ritualized (and hence formalized) aspects of dining. Nothing could seem more natural than the urge to satisfy hunger. However, with a concept like the appetizer, we actually disconnect food from this impulse and instead *eat in order to become more hungry.* The formal "laws" of etiquette, as they are tellingly known, produce still more complicated forms of bodily response, or embodied thinking. For example, one may sit down at the table with a considerable appetite but then be so disgusted by the presence of a person with poor manners as to be unable to eat. "Nature" obviously has little to do with this last reaction; instead, it is a function of what postmodern psychoanalysis refers to as the Symbolic order, but (and this is the key point) it is no less visceral and no more inherently manageable for being so.

These affective effects of symbolization are exactly what the speaker of "The triple Foole" stumbles across. The poet imagined that he could mitigate the painful sensations associated with an essentially "natural" (pre-Symbolic) desire by pressing it through the filter of formalized language ("Rimes vexation"). He did not consider the possibility that he was in fact changing the content of his desire by imposing poetic form upon it, thereby creating a new desire structured around something other than the original cause—but this is indeed what he does. Before, his desire was activated by an unattainable woman, but now his desire is activated by poetry itself. In a revision of our common-sensical notions, then, this poem suggests that we do not simply release bottled-up desires and frustrations when we articulate them, thereby rendering them more manageable (although this may be one possible effect of such articulation), nor do we somehow tame those desires and frustrations by imposing the formal discipline of language upon our impulsive drives (although, again, it may sometimes feel like this is what is happening). We also change and even *create* our desires in their formal articulation. The speaker of "The triple Foole" starts out believing, reasonably enough, that the pangs of desire generate the need for form. By the end of the poem, however, he has learned that the truth of the case is just the opposite: *form produces desire.* This productive relation of form to desire, the fact that desire and form are inextricably bound together, is also something that I have attempted to keep in the forefront of my thinking in the pages that follow.

But we have not learned all that we can about the limits of representation and the problem of desire from "The triple Foole." For as anyone conditioned by the procedures of deconstructive reading will note, Donne has not actually given us the poem that first tames and later activates his desire here. He has instead given us a poem *about* the poem that tames and activates his desire. Although "The triple Foole" concerns both the wished-for and the actual consequences of articulated desire, that desire itself is never articulated. We might say, again drawing upon well-known deconstructive principles, that the unspoken poem—or, more accurately, the unsung song that both is and is not at the center of "The triple Foole"—is the necessary, self-referential element of the text that must be suppressed in order for the poem to constitute itself. By positing the existence of a prior poem possessed of an almost sublime affective power, "The triple Foole" thereby comes to partake of that affective power, but the enabling condition of this participation in sublimity is the erasure of the original and putatively sublime poem.

The virtue of this deconstructive reading lies in its complication of what, ever since Plato, has generally been conceived as "the problem of representation": that there will always be some aspect of "real" experience that inevitably falls out of representation, because experience is infinite and our capacity for symbolization finite. The slightly more subtle point, which "The triple Foole" illustrates vividly and succinctly, is that the act of representation itself produces this unrepresentable element. The sublime poem that expresses, tames, and then reawakens the poet's desire not only lies behind "The triple Foole," temporally located in the past of the speaker; it is also posited by "The triple Foole," called into existence by it. Thus, the unsingable song of desire that inspires "The triple Foole" is also and in a fundamental sense the *product* of "The triple Foole." It is both post and prior: in Hegelian terms, it is both presupposed and posed; in Lacanian terms, it is a piece of the Real. As Lacan's great explicator Slavoj Žižek has written: "We have the Real as the starting point, the basis, the foundation of the process of symbolization . . . the Real which in a sense precedes the symbolic order and is subsequently structured by it. . . . But the Real is at the same time the product, remainder, leftover, scraps of the process of symbolization, the remnants, the excess which escapes symbolization and is as such produced by the symbolization itself."[7] However, within the internal narrative of "The triple Foole," the unsymbolizable Real that prompts Donne's act of failed but unexpectedly productive symbolization is the Real of his desire. It is Donne's desire itself that, like the unknowable poem of the Real, turns out to be at once impossible to attain and also impossible to escape. Thus, "The triple Fool" lays bare the logic of desire at its most basic, as at once self-perpetuating and self-defeating or, better, self-perpetuating because self-defeating.

This logic becomes particularly clear if we simply attempt to plot the movement of desire through the text. At the outset, Donne's desire is to restrain desire in a poem; however, the poem that he writes only ends up reproducing the initial desire that prompted his desire to restrain desire in a poem. The result is a poem about the desire to write a poem to restrain desire that results in a poem that reproduces the initial desire to write a poem to restrain desire, which in turn produces a poem about the desire to write a poem to restrain desire that reproduces the initial desire, and so on, *ad infinitum*. Donne's desire is therefore sustained precisely by its perpetual failure to achieve its aim. "The triple Foole" achieves a perfect, self-reflexive loop describing the paradoxical ideal of desire, which is *not* to reach its goal but, rather, to reproduce itself endlessly.

This central paradox of desire as infinite regression is inevitably one to which I shall return. But for now I want to note another counter-intuitive but important idea implied by this paradoxical logic: namely, that to the extent that desire evades satisfaction, desire and pleasure are *opposed* concepts. This idea has received much elaboration in post-modern psychoanalysis in recent years; but, again, Donne seems to have anticipated the theorists, making it part of the argument of his second stanza, which is worth reproducing a second time (after all, if my argument is correct, the poem is designed to catch the mind's eye and encourages repeated—indeed, literally *recursive*—reading):

> But when I have done so,
> Some man, his art and voice to show,
>   Doth Set and sing my paine,
> And by delighting many, frees againe
>   Griefe, which verse did restraine.
> To Love, and Griefe tribute of Verse belongs
> But not of such as pleases when 'tis read,
>   Both are increased by such songs;
> For both their triumphs so are published,
> And I, which was two fooles, do so grow three;
> Who are a little wise, the best fooles bee.

Pleasure Donne had not, or so it would seem, before he wrote his sublime poem. Instead, he possessed, or more accurately was possessed by, a painful desire; his speech, though self-mocking in its self-recrimination, was full of "paine" and "Griefe." But now pleasure *is* introduced into the discursive world of the poem, and Donne's artistic agency is the primary cause. Still, this pleasure largely passes *him* by. All he gets to enjoy is bittersweet knowledge that the pain that once was his alone is now "delighting many." Fascinatingly, the power of form is further emphasized, as Donne's necessarily unreadable poem-within-the-poem becomes a necessarily silent song, "Set" to music in what Donne scornfully implies is a narcissistic artistic exercise by "*Some* man." Each consecutive upping of the formalist ante seems to increase the affective reach, so to speak, of Donne's initial and painful experience of desire. As the "vexations" of rhyme, the "fetters" of meter, and the uniquely arresting motion of music are applied to this experience, the amount of pleasure to be had from it grows for everyone in the interpretive circle—everyone, that is, except for the poet himself. In a complicated double movement, Donne's subjective pain is dissolved in the pleasure of public art and at the same time confirmed as the origin of that art. The pain-pleasure nexus implied by this doubled dissolution and reconstitution of subjectivity is more often linked to the practices of religious asceticism or sadomasochism than artistic production, but as "The triple Foole" shows, poetry can engage similar psychic structures. Indeed, the kinky fun of literary formalism was already hinted at in the first verse; Donne's impulse there to bind desire with metrical links and torment it with echoing combinations of sound obviously evokes the illicit thrill of bondage (in this context, it may be worth noting that the literal root of "vexation," as in "Rimes vexation," is the Latin *vexare,* meaning to harass or agitate).

Donne's conclusion confirms that different modalities characterize the logic of desire and the logic of satisfaction when he insists that the only appropriate "tribute of Verse" due to the twin representatives of desire, "Love, and Griefe," is a perverse verse that does *not* give pleasure "when 'tis read." "Pleasurable poems about the pain of love only produce more pain for me," the argument goes. "Therefore, it is better to write poems that don't please anybody." Belied by its own bitter wit, the position is, of course, self-consciously self-canceling. We can't fail to note the structural irony of taking up a position against poetry in a poem. But Donne is also indirectly foregrounding the fact that some element of pleasure is produced even in the renunciation of pleasure. Trapped within the reflexive loop of the Real of desire that seeks to sustain itself in the refusal of satisfaction, Donne manages nevertheless to squeeze a minimal satisfaction out of that very refusal. In this respect, "The triple Foole" might be instructively compared to the Rolling Stones' classic "(I Can't Get No) Satisfaction"; not only do the protagonists of both texts portray themselves as permanently frustrated fools of desire, but the unstated and yet palpable satisfaction produced by publicly declaring oneself unsatisfied is rhetorically equivalent to the unstated and yet palpable pleasure Donne produces when he declares himself against poetic pleasure. The (anti) truth effect is the same in both cases, too. We didn't quite believe Mick, and we don't quite believe Donne, either.

The delicate balance of this exquisite poem, in which desire is sustained by denial, and pleasure produced by renunciation, is epitomized by the poised ambiguity of the final line. This last statement is self-deprecation offered with a sly wink, an admission of foolishness that nevertheless may take some pride in folly, the confession of a loser who knows that the biggest mistake you can make when it comes to desire is to try to win. On the one hand, the line simply reworks the cliché that a little knowledge can be a dangerous thing, but on the other hand, to be one of the "best fooles" is still to be good at something, even if it is only foolishness. The familiar Christian notion of the Holy Fool, and the concept of Trinitarianism, may also lend a positive spin to the ostensibly negative charge of multiplied foolishness; the connection is surely not too far-fetched, given the association between three-selves-in-one and the doctrine of the Trinity that Donne directly employs in sexual contexts elsewhere in his work (most famously in the seduction scene of "The Flea"). Certainly, it does not require much hermeneutic effort to note the resemblance between Donne's "foolish" suffering for the sake of an art that brings delight to many and the sacred folly of Christian martyrdom. Donne himself was well versed (as it were) in such strategies of typological exegesis.

Of course, to read Donne's conclusion as (perhaps) advocating martyrlike suffering for the conjoined causes of love and art will strike some as wrongheadedly Romantic, as if Donne were a sort of seventeenth-century Shelley. However, the association between the speaker and Christ need not be sincerely meant. Donne's ironic mode allows us to hear the allusion to the Trinity without assuming that the speaker of the poem literally imagines himself performing the secular equivalent of the *imitatio Christi* by delighting many in his "paine." But merely to hint at a parallel between himself and Christ would be bold enough—and, as I will show, this is a repeated provocation in Donne's writing.

I could continue to say more about this little poem of Donne's, unpacking themes and questions that speak to the general nature of my argument, but you may already feel like an unfortunate wedding guest, trapped on the threshold of the church by an excessively loquacious ex-mariner. Indeed, the pages of interpretation that I have generated from "The triple Foole," independent of their actual content, bear tragicomic witness to the epistemophillic desire of the compulsive literary hermeneut—the very desire I am supposed to be investigating—raising the concern that I may be too close to the project of close reading to do the job properly.

Nevertheless, I cannot move on without making one last observation about this poem: my own concept of interpretive desire, like so much else, has also been anticipated here by Donne. Along with the void that shapes and is shaped by desire and representation, Donne has managed to enfold the position of the interpreter into his poem, through his invocation of the musician-singer who literally re-in-forms Donne's formalist poem as a song. According to Donne, the interpretive desires of this singer are entirely selfish. He may have a good voice, but he does what he does simply in order to show off his talent, without interest in, shall we say, the historical circumstances of the life that lies behind the poem he has so thoughtlessly plucked out of context: without regard for the experiential truth of the poet's pain. He is, in short, a ready emblem of the critic as artistic parasite. However, the apparent disregard of this musical interpreter for the poet who provided him with the primary materials for his narcissistic display also turns out to be an *enabling* condition of artistic pleasure for others.

Now, I don't necessarily mean to imply that all literary critics can be placed in the interpretive position of "Some man," here—at least, not without pointing out that Donne's depiction of the singer's desire is self-consciously and amusingly grumpy (indeed, when it comes to relations between artists and their interpreters, we might add that it is has ever been thus). But I do think that, in an ambivalent way, Donne's poem reveals that the relation of artist to interpreter can be one of *mutual* benefit and gratification; and, moreover, it attests to a more complex symbiotic relationship between artists and critics than the reduction of interpretation to mere narcissistic display would imply. In "The triple Foole," Donne may overtly dismiss the complex nature of the interpreter's desire, insisting instead on its secondary, belated, and even parasitic status. But, at the same time, he implicitly concedes the power of the gifted interpreter to increase the capacity of art to delight. Insofar as interpretive desires go, that is one, at least, that I am proud to own.

II

> But whatsoever is the object of any mans Appetite or
> Desire; that is it, which he for his part calleth Good:
> And the object of his Hate and Aversion, Evill. . . .
> For these words . . . are ever used with relation to the
> person that useth them: There being nothing simply
> and absolutely so; nor any common Rule of Good
> and Evil, to be taken from the nature of the objects
> themselves.
>
> —THOMAS HOBBES, *LEVIATHAN*

At this juncture, someone might point out that my focus on interpretive desire is all very well, but why pin so much on Donne—an author for whom critical ardor may once have burned but toward whom feelings lately seem to have cooled? Why posit Donne as an author-subject especially suited to an inquiry into the operations of interpretive desire, ahead of numerous other possible candidates, when at the present moment in critical history he seems to hold rather less fascination than he once did for us?

Admittedly, critical desire for Donne is not what it used to be. In fact, it has become a reflex move within the shrinking borders of Donne studies to cop to the fact of diminished professional interest early in the game. For example, Barbara Everett begins a recent (2001) essay on the poet by observing that "[i]t's a quiet time just now in Donne criticism" before going on to remark that "[i]t's a quiet time, perhaps, in anything criticism" (a statement of dubious comfort if one is disposed to think it accurate!). Still, Everett has a point, one made previously by Elizabeth D. Harvey and Katherine Eisaman Maus in the introduction to their important essay collection *Soliciting Interpretation* (1990), where they note that Donne has been subject to a "striking" degree of marginalization since the days of New Criticism, when he was by contrast "absolutely central." Ronald Corthell cites Harvey and Maus on the first page of his own (1997) book-length study of Donne and is moved to ask whether, since "Donne has been done and undone," we should not "be done with him" altogether (the pun once again proving irresistible).[8] Although Corthell obviously answers this question in the negative, his sense that he must address it bespeaks an awareness that nowadays a passion for Donne can be a professionally embarrassing affair. As in the eighteenth century, Donne seems almost to have become an "improper" object of literary desire, thereby turning those of us who love him into literary fetishists, forced to adopt the Freudian logic of "I know, but . . ." Corthell's status as an engaged reader of Donne puts him on the defensive from the very beginning.

When our desires threaten to become a source of anxiety and embarrassment, the object of both internalized and institutional acts of surveillance, we do not need to be card-carrying Foucauldians to realize that we have run up against the disciplinary operation of power. Now it is quite understandable that, most of the time, we prefer not to acknowledge the acts of exclusion upon which our agendas are founded when we attempt to establish the proper objects of interpretative desire (as in, say, debates about the canon) or the nature of proper interpretations (as in debates that oppose, say, formalism to explicitly political reading strategies such as Marxism). But as Judith Butler observes in a perceptive and preventatively oriented commentary on the potential for conflict between feminist and queer theoretical strategies, "[T]he institution of the 'proper object' takes place . . . through a mundane sort of violence"[9]—sometimes so mundane in fact as to be barely recognizable as violence. Consequently, to regard the cooling of critical desire for Donne ruefully, as a sign of the times, like Everett, or neutrally, as an inevitable consequence of a prior period of overvaluation, like Harvey and Maus, is to mistake disciplinary violence, however mundane, for a natural process. Donne's marginalization is not merely a neutral fact of professional life to be acknowledged reluctantly or casually noted; rather, it needs to be critically examined for what it reveals about the institutional and ideological processes that govern the determination of appropriately desirable literary objects. Thus, the diminished critical interest in Donne that we have seen in recent years actually makes him *more* rather than less appropriate as a subject for study.

This argument has wider implications if we take a step back and consider the shape of critical desire for Donne over a longer period. For Donne has been subject to the "mundane violence" of which Butler speaks throughout his entire interpretive history. Of course, given my earlier remarks about the nature of interpretation as "words chosen out of desire," certain acts of critical exclusion, if not downright violence, are unavoidable. Moreover, such acts of exclusion have undoubtedly been fundamental to Donne's periods of success on the canonical stock market as well as his periods of failure. Nevertheless, it is fair to say that Donne has attracted a striking amount of negative criticism over the last 400 years. In fact, I would go so far as to claim that Donne has inspired more hostile commentary from more powerful and respected tastemakers and critics than any author of equivalent stature in the annals of English literary historiography and, furthermore, that the implications of this claim for our understanding of both Donne and literary criticism have not been realized, for all that the general contours of Donne's reception history are well known.

The larger pattern of critical hostility toward Donne may require demonstration before I can expound upon its unrecognized significance. Although Donne was popular in his own lifetime as a manuscript poet, the first signs of his fall from favor appear in the late seventeenth century. Among his earliest significant detractors we can name John Dryden, who allowed Donne a measure of wit, while generally adopting a posture of sniffy disdain toward his work. Without elaborating fully upon Dryden's position, the degree to which his criticism turns upon the "unnatural" quality of Donne's style is worth emphasizing. For example, he notoriously charges Donne with "affecting the metaphysics . . . in his amorous verses where nature should only reign."[10] Dryden's ambivalence toward Donne was subsequently echoed by many literary figures of the eighteenth century, including Pope and, most famously, Samuel Johnson. I will return to both of these authors, but for now Johnson's judgment that the reader of Donne's verse, "though he sometimes admires, is seldom pleased," may be taken as representative of eighteenth-century views in general.[11] Johnson ultimately advises against reading too much Donne, and the literate public of the day was content to follow the doctor's orders.

The nineteenth century saw a revival of interest in Donne, although, as Deborah Aldrich Larson's useful reception history shows, Donne's "romantic" biography appears to have held as much interest as his writing. When it came to specific commentary on the poetry, "at least as many nineteenth-century writers objected to Donne's style as approved of it."[12] Larson further suggests that interest in Donne during this period can appear greater than it was because, generally speaking, figures who continue to excite readers today, such as Coleridge, the Brownings, de Quincey, and Rossetti, expressed admiration for Donne, while more obscure authors like Hazlitt and Southey, along with numerous and now largely forgotten writers and critics such as James Montgomery, Francis Cunningham, Henry Hart Milman, and Edwin Percy Whipple, expressed much more negative sentiments. However, from the perspective of what was once called the general reader, Palgrave's decision to severely limit the selection of Donne poems in his enormously popular *Golden Treasury*, on both moral and aesthetic grounds, was probably more significant than the commentary of either a Coleridge or a Cunningham. Despite effectively adopting a policy of censorship by omission, Palgrave's personal response to Donne was revealingly complex; he claimed to find Donne " 'almost equally fascinating and repellant,' " a phraseology that neatly emblematizes the polarized attitude the poet characteristically provoked within the emergent institutions of modern "Eng. Lit."[13]

Overall, the rehabilitation of Donne's writerly reputation seems very gradual prior to the publication of T. S. Eliot's early essays on the poet; in fact, without Eliot's intervention, and the subsequent elevation of Donne by the New Critics, I am uncertain that we would now interpret the occasional crumb of praise from Coleridge, and others as part of a rising curve. The impact of Eliot's Donne criticism cannot be overestimated, inseparable as it is from the impact of Eliot's own poetry; and the canonical fortunes of the two poets have arguably been intertwined ever since. But, significantly, even during the peak of his newfound fame throughout the 1930s and 1940s, Donne was harshly attacked by some of the most respected voices in Renaissance studies, including Douglas Bush, C. S. Lewis, and E. M. W. Tillyard. Perhaps in reaction to the reverential New Critical approach, castigations of Donne from this period can appear almost comically shrill, exceeding the supposed norms of critical decorum. Just consider the following sample of the most vituperative repudiations of Donne from 1903 to 1952: "No one has injured English writing more than Donne" (Richard Garnett and Edmund Gosse); he is "the worst kind of bore—the hoteyed, unescapable kind" (C. S. Lewis); "an egregious and offensive coxcomb" (J. E. V. Crofts) whose lyrics are "no more poetical than anagrams" (A. E. Housman); Donne is "twisted, angry, and . . . tortured" (Louis Untermeyer), "bordering on the freakish" (Karl Shapiro).[14]

With the decline of the New Criticism, the weight of critical opinion has come down against Donne yet once more, more firmly than at any time since the eighteenth century; among the multiple competing methodologies of the poststructuralist era, less than laudatory assessments of Donne have been proffered by important exponents of almost every major critical perspective, including Marxism (David Aers and Gunther Kress), deconstruction (Thomas Docherty, Stanley Fish), New Historicism (Arthur Marotti, Jonathan Goldberg), and feminism (Janel Mueller, Janet Halley).[15] To this list we must add John Carey's hostile, judgmental, superbly written critical biography, *John Donne: Life, Mind, Art* (1980); although Carey's work prompted one reviewer to speculate about the kind of Donne scholarship an academic Iago would produce, his book remains the most influential single text on Donne to have been published in the last thirty years. With the notable exception of Fish (who begins his essay by declaring that "Donne is sick"), these critics tend to eschew the vehement rhetoric of their Donne-bashing predecessors, adopting a calmer but still more-or-less moralized tone of disapproval toward aspects of his sexual politics or personal character.

Even from this necessarily selective history, then, we can see it is misleading to speak of the recent decline of critical interest in Donne exclusively in relation to the peak of his twentieth-century popularity. Such relative marginalization looks far less striking when we realize that the cycle of boom and bust thought to describe Donne's critical fortunes during the last eighty years is really only the standard readerly response to Donne, writ diachronically large. For Donne has always divided his readers, and not just against one another but against themselves. The seeds of the critical back and forth over Donne's worth that I have sketched are readily discernible in the earliest recorded reactions to the work, as, for example, when Ben Jonson told William Drummond that he thought Donne was "the first poet in the world for some things" and then immediately added that Donne, "for not being understood, would perish."[16] Lest I myself be misunderstood: the point is not, absurdly, that Donne has never been appreciated. Obviously he has had and continues to have his share of important, interesting, and influential defenders. The point is, rather, that Donne's reception history, from Ben Jonson to the present, is characterized less by a linear progression through neglect to overvaluation and back again and more by constant oscillation—less by a cycle of boom and bust, more by a continual and profound ambivalence. About Donne, we might say, the institution of criticism appears always already conflicted; or, to describe the matter in terms appropriate to my emphasis on interpretive desire, what we have here is a classic "love-hate relationship."[17]

If critical desire for Donne must be weighed against an equal and opposite critical desire to be done with Donne, then what significance can we attach to this fact? Given the historical range and methodological diversity of the commentators I have cited, it will seem absurd to imply that a single explanation for this division of feeling is available. Certainly, it would be possible to write several books exploring the various shifts in aesthetic ideology and interpretive epistemology that have shaped the contexts within which Donne's merits have been debated. Nevertheless, I think that the extent and depth of the critical "love-hate" relationship that Donne continues to inspire reveals considerably more than just the historical contingency of aesthetic judgment. Therefore, at the risk of appearing to oversimplify, I will stick my neck out and assert that, at least since the publication of Donne's *Poems* in 1633, interpretive disagreements over Donne's work and worth have primarily turned on the evaluation of his own representations of desire. More specifically, critical divisions over Donne have tended to focus on the question of whether the multitude of desires expressed in his poetry, for sex, love, social mobility, or knowledge of God, can ultimately be characterized as either natural or unnatural, proper or improper, decorous or indecent, conservative or progressive, altruistic or self-interested, traditional or radical, patriarchal or protofeminist, and so on. The terms of the binary change according to the interpretive vicissitudes and intellectual prejudices of a particular critic or era, but the fundamental question has remained the same: do we explicate, echo, and admire Donnean desire (as liberatory, new, candid, healthy, other directed, and true to life), or do we diagnose, deny, and repudiate it (as repressive, depressingly familiar, insincere, pathological, self-serving, and perversely misrepresentative of experience)?

Most love-hate relationships are difficult either to terminate or to resolve, and the critical relationship with Donne has proved no exception. The interpretive work of reproducing Donnean desire as itself either desirable and productive or repugnant and harmful shows itself to be endless, so long as each of the alternative positions is presented as comprehensive. For as William Kerrigan has perspicaciously observed: "*Comprehension* is precisely what Donne studies have always been forced to defer. No one has fared very well with the riddle of how Dr. Donne emerged from Jack Donne, or with the rough draft of that transition implied by the simultaneous presence among the secular poems of energetic libertinism and celebrated mutual love. . . . Once one moves away from the unit of the particular lyric, Donne becomes notoriously difficult to talk about."[18] In other words, since Donne wrote both masculinist poems and poems of "mutual love," it is extremely hard to generalize in any satisfactory or conclusive way about the progressive or conservative nature of his gender politics. I would add that this observation holds equally well for those expressions of Donnean desire that extend beyond the realm of the sexual. Donne is not only a love poet who seems sometimes to loathe love and a celebrant of heterosexual desire who seems sometimes to prefer the company of men ("thou shalt see / Me fresher, and more fat, by being with men," he writes in "The Blossome"). Donne is also a religious poet who often flirts with blasphemy, a celebrant of the private and domestic who often flatters his social superiors in occasional and public writings palpably motivated by careerism, and a reader of the "new philosophy" who sometimes seems "in the depths of his soul . . . unmoved by Copernicus."[19] It is therefore no easier to generalize in any satisfactory or conclusive way about his intellectual skepticism, his personal ambitions, or his religious convictions than it is about his sexual attitudes (toward both women *and* men, as my second chapter demonstrates).

But, as Kerrigan knows, these awkward facts hardly prevent critics from offering their generalizations about the nature of Donnean desire as if they were indeed comprehensive. And in fairness, Donne himself seems to have understood the desire or, perhaps more precisely, the compulsive drive to comprehend the whole of a person's being: "Nor could incomprehensiblenesse deterre / Me, from thus trying to emprison her."[20] In fact, following Shoshana Felman's deservedly famous analysis of interpretive disputes over Henry James's *The Turn of the Screw,* it is tempting to read the compulsive, repetitious, and ultimately doomed critical attempts to comprehend Donnean desire as an unconscious replication of the similarly compulsive, repetitious, and ultimately doomed attempts to comprehend desire that are played out within Donne's poetry. Donne's corpus, divided by desire, divides desiring interpreters in turn, compelling them to reenact its own irresolvable internal conflicts. By these lights, the critical love-hate relationship with Donne that I have delineated only repeats "the primal scene of the text's meaning as division"; and in repeating the foundational divisions of the text, "the critics can by no means master the meaning of that division, but only act the division out, perform it, be part of it." Criticism begins with the intent to illuminate the text but ends always in its shadow, or rather *as* its shadow, imitating its movements with a greater or lesser degree of exaggeration and distortion. The desire of the critic is mimetic. Less kindly, critics are apes. This is one discouraging lesson regarding the operation of interpretive desire that, through Felman's lenses, we can read in the pages of Donne's reception history.

However, as Felman also notes, "to participate in a division is . . . at the same time, to fight *against* division: it is indeed to commit oneself to the elimination of the opponent, and through him, to the elimination of the heterogeneity of meaning, the very scandal of contradiction and ambiguity."[21] Felman's paradoxical insight at once confirms the status of criticism as an aggressively desire-driven activity; at the same time, it suggests why, if it is oriented toward the elimination of contradiction, the role of desire in its operation must be effaced; for if criticism were able to do away with the scandal of interpretive division that calls it into being, the achievement of its desire would make further criticism unnecessary. In other words, if literary critics were to think too much about what they want when they attempt to settle, say, the question of Donne's sexual politics, they would recognize that their reason for existing could last no longer than the attainment of their desire (as Donne himself puts it, "he that hath all can have no more"). Better, in such circumstances, not to think too much about what one wants! After all, even if, upon reflection, what one wants is neither possible nor even all that desirable, it may still be easier to pretend to want it and to proceed as if settling the question of Donne's sexual politics *were* possible and desirable, rather than think about what one *really* wants— or (potentially even more disconcerting) what one can actually achieve. Sometimes what the critic *really* wants is less than edifying (how many pages have been cranked out to meet the requirements of tenure or a promotion, out of intellectual vanity, or worst of all, out of the opportunity to grind axes and take revenge for real or imagined personal and professional slights?); and the question of what literary critics actually achieve through their work, even at their most successful, is difficult to answer in these days of posthumanist skepticism (having said this, I will try to address these questions in my conclusion).

But in the presence of Donne's texts, texts that represent desire in all its self-dividing contradiction, the aversion of the critic's gaze from the question of his or her own desire is more than a dubiously enabling evasion. Because desire is Donne's central theme, it is inevitably a focus of critical interpretations of his work, even as the critic's own presuppositions about what constitutes an appropriate representation of desire go unacknowledged. Thus, subjected to what we might think of as a basic Foucauldian reading (as opposed to a psychoanalytic analysis à la Felman), Donne's reception history dramatically displays the ways in which axiomatic yet mostly tacit assumptions about desire (which also vary considerably over time) effectively shape critical responses, modes of inquiry, and notions of the canonical. Ironically, although most critics assume the right to remain silent about their own desires, in the process of passing judgment on the character, direction, and moral rectitude of Donne's, they often end up revealing at least as much about their particular sexual, social, and religious values as they do about Donne himself. Changing perceptions of both the social consequences of unrestrained desire and the aesthetic value of its representation are consequently legible in the pages of Donne's critical history in ways that are unparalleled elsewhere in English literature, including Shakespeare criticism. We might even think of Donne's texts as literary litmus paper, exposing the levels of desire in the interpretive medium in which they are immersed.

The recent work of Michael Morgan Holmes corroborates and illustrates my point nicely. Expanding the category of "metaphysical poetry" to include Aemilia Lanyer alongside the usual suspects of Donne, Marvell, Vaughan, et al., Holmes argues that this entire body of seventeenth-century poetry, perhaps even more than the drama of the period, "prompts readers to discern the ideological work" performed by the category of the natural. Furthermore, Holmes contends, this "Metaphysical denaturalization occurs most provocatively in the context of mental perception, gender identification, sexual morality, and political organization." Thus, in a persuasive rereading of Samuel Johnson's well-known essay on the Metaphysicals (to which I have already briefly alluded), Holmes lingers over Johnson's characterization of Donne and his followers as engaged "in a wilful pursuit of things 'new and strange,' " without regard for the principle of "uniformity of sentiment" in their "violent" and "unnatural" imagery. For Holmes, Johnson's reading of Donne is hostile but perceptive nonetheless, because as a conservative Anglican who placed "enormous value on the . . . representation of an essential transhistorical order," Johnson clearly seems to have recognized something oppositional in the Donnean aesthetic. In Holmes's analysis, Johnson had no choice but to repudiate Donne, for he saw in Donne's work, accurately, in Holmes's opinion, a challenging reminder that "desire, perception, identity, and aesthetic taste are [not] always and everywhere the same."[22] In short, both Holmes and Johnson see Donnean desire as politically disruptive in character, but while Johnson repudiates Donne for this reason,

Holmes admires him. Having explicated Johnson's conservative value system through Johnson's reading of Donne, Holmes obviously realizes that his own value system will be apparent in his own reading of Donne, and is unembarrassed by the fact; indeed, he embraces the situation by letting us know on his very first page that he's all for political disruption in the sexual arena (where he jocularly declares that the quest for "same gender marriage rights entails an unnecessary endorsement of an unpleasant status quo").

Holmes's insight is obviously applicable to many more of Donne's hostile critics than Johnson. A glance through Larson's reception history will provide ample evidence that for hundreds of years "the interrogation and reformulation of cultural givens" implicit in Donne's representations of desire were simply too radical for the poet to receive the unequivocal blessing of the literary critical establishment, which, as an extension of the cultural establishment, generally reflects the dominant morality and political ideology of the era in which it is produced (a tendency that I think holds almost as strongly today in our age of ideological critique as it did in Johnson's era—but this is to run ahead). Holmes's further suggestion that Donne's work, and indeed metaphysical poetry in general, is ripe for reassessment by literary critics interested in the relationship between art and sexual dissidence strikes me as accurate and overdue. However, there is something about Holmes's unproblematic assumption that the disruptive force he ascribes to Donnean desire is entirely assimilable to his progressive political agenda that gives me pause. To see the problem clearly, it is necessary to consider the larger debate over Donne's "radicalism."

III

> [T]he western artistic canon . . . perverse and pornographic at its heart.
>
> —JONATHAN DOLLIMORE, *SEX, LITERATURE, AND CENSORSHIP*

Notions of what constitutes a radical representation of desire are obviously not static. In the present era, comparatively relaxed standards regarding acceptable levels of heterosexual display, combined with the social and intellectual paradigm shifts that have followed on the gains of feminism and the growing tolerance of alternative sexualities, obviously make for conditions of reception very different to those that Donne knew. At the same time, these changes have only increased the range of variation in individual attitudes on questions of sexual morality. Consequently, Donne's representations of desire will inevitably seem daring and moving to some, relatively tame to others, and depressingly retrograde to yet others. In my experience it is not uncommon to encounter all of these responses in a single classroom of students; indeed, this enormous diversity of responses, many of which are rooted in passionate personal conviction, is probably the greatest pedagogical challenge the modern teacher of Donne will face (once one overcomes the problems of initial comprehension).

However, as I have already suggested, in recent years and among professional readers, the dominant perception of Donne has been that of a morbid and misogynistic solipsist, a political opportunist, and a theological conservative. Although I am inclined to think this vision unfairly selective and even grossly exaggerated, it is not possible to dismiss it as an outright falsehood. Again, as I have already suggested, the simple fact is that Donne adopts contradictory positions on numerous issues throughout his long life as a writer of very different kinds of texts (poems, letters, prose exercises, political animadversions, sermons), and our sense of him as a "radical" or a "conservative" figure will vary not only according to our own understanding of these terms but also according to which textual events we choose to emphasize. By focusing on the interpretive desires that lie behind such choices, I hope to avoid being trapped by the terms of the opposition between "radical" and "conservative" or, at the very least, to provide some insight into the implications of emphasizing one vision of Donne over the other. I also hope that by considering both the virtues *and* the limitations of the most influential "radical" characterizations of Donne, I can gesture toward a type of critical practice that will be more productively nuanced with regard to the representation of desire in his poetry.

If I am right that Donne's texts provide ample material for both "conservative" and "radical" interpretations of his work, the question arises as to why so few readers seem to have recognized this radicalism in recent years. The reasons are complex and manifold. First, the fact that we tend to associate Donne's most influential twentieth-century admirers, the New Critics, with intellectual conservatism may have tarnished Donne with a kind of guilt by literary association. It seems to require a massive act of historical reconstruction for us to recall that the ideas of W. K. Wimsatt or Cleanth Brooks were once considered shockingly radical; and we have quite forgotten that T. S. Eliot himself could not retain an academic post in the Oxford of 1926—a point to which I will return. Second, we must take into account the enormous impact of the New Historicism, with its focus (or reverse-romantic fixation) on issues of "power" and, specifically, on the relationship between early modern courtly politics and poetics.[23] Again, Kerrigan has offered some of the sharpest dissenting commentary on this New Historicist Donne:

> When the magic word "power" appears in Donne studies, we almost always find a cruelly emptied out, vitiated Donne—the Donne of Carey, or the Donne of Marotti—who has nothing in him except simplistic ambitions and an immense appetite for exhibiting his wretched plight before a coterie of self-pitying no-accounts, now and then alleviating their misery by some manipulative appeal to their vicious and unimaginative fantasy lives, or the Donne of Goldberg, cringing self-interestedly before the absolutist pretensions of James.[24]

The third and perhaps most complicating factor in this construction of a conservative Donne is, of course, the transformation of the intellectual landscape wrought by feminism. Since I take up the question of Donne and gender politics in a subsequent chapter, I will for now only note the hostility of many early feminist responses to the poet, while emphasizing the ongoing and inconclusive character of this debate.

Nevertheless, there has also always been a radical strain in Donne criticism. Holmes's emphasis on "the denaturalizing cultural work performed by Metaphysical literature's marvelously strange visions" and particularly on "the operations of [Metaphysical] desire in bringing about surprising estrangements of thought and identity" is only the most recent attempt to produce, in the face of dominant trends, an intellectually and sexually radical Donne.[25] As Holmes himself acknowledges, perhaps the most important of these maverick interpreters, at least in terms of the last century of professional criticism, was William Empson.

Throughout his long career, from the 1930s to the 1970s, Empson ran what was almost a one-man critical campaign to wrest Donne away from readers he regarded as morally judgmental and intellectually conservative, publishing numerous articles excoriating Helen Gardner, Merritt Hughes, Clay Hunt, J. B. Leishman, Allen Tate, and Rosemond Tuve, among others. Empson argued his case with a passion that still throws sparks, even thirty years later, as can be seen in this brief example from the beginning of Empson's 1972 essay titled "Rescuing Donne":

> I am anxious not to give too feeble an impression of the loathing with which I regard the present image of [Donne]. The habitual mean-mindedness of modern academic criticism, its moral emptiness combined with its incessant moral nagging, its scrubbed prison-like isolation, are particularly misleading in the case of Donne; in fact, we are the ones who need rescuing, not the poet."[26]

Whoa! It cannot have been pleasant to be the target of Empson's intellectual scorn; his "take-no-prisoners" prose style spares no one's feelings. Still, I want to resist the urge to accuse him of indulging in some critical moralizing of his own here (of course, he is) *and* the temptation to read these remarks as a prescient admonition regarding the ideological critique of the present day (however worthy the worst examples might be of such damnation). Empson's practical humanism would never have led him to bemoan ideology critique *tout court,* and I suspect that he would have greatly admired the best contemporary political criticism, which always grounds its ethical claims in the act of close reading. Empson is instead identifying in his own era something that I have argued runs through the body of negative critical responses to Donne's work: a high-toned moral censoriousness that signals a deeper, politically inflected disagreement about the value of desire, both in literary representation and in the culture at large.

In stark contrast to the criticism he is concerned to displace, Empson offers the most sustained vision of Donne-as-progressive available to a modern student. His arguments are peppered with forthright declarations about Donne's "enlightened views" on religion, the state, scientific progress, and the relation of all these topics to human love. Empson's Donne fights "like a cat" to avoid dedicating himself to a "disgusting God"; he is "simply against burning people alive for their religious convictions"; and although, like all educated men of the seventeenth century, his "mind . . . was much cluttered with learned authorities who called women inferior to men," he did not hesitate "to say that [those authorities] were wrong" when it suited him. But Empson often goes further when describing what he takes to be Donne's heretical metaphysics of earthly love. For Empson, Donne's flirtations with blasphemy in his secular verse are more than isolated and hyperbolic compliments to his lady and more even than compelling revisions of the familiar trope of love as religion; they are in fact evidence of a larger project to elevate earthly love to the status of a *new* religion, one in which it is Donne's ambition to serve as a kind of proto-Lawrentian priest / martyr to the cause of Eros. In Empson's words: "Theologically the most reckless of Donne's poems are those in which he presents himself as a martyr to love and thereby the founder of a religion, the Christ of all future reckless lovers."[27] This strong assertion, itself "reckless" according to the mainstream of Donne criticism, comes from one of Empson's most imaginative and daring single essays, "John Donne the Spaceman," wherein he also claims that Donne's interest in post-Copernican astronomy led him to speculate about the theological and emotional ramifications of the possibility of extraterrestrial life. But despite his best efforts, for most of the twentieth century Empson's is a voice in the wilderness when it comes to proclamations of Donne's theological and sexual radicalism. Many of these claims were dismissed as "crack-brained" by no less an authority on Donne than John Carey.[28]

Though Empson failed to alter critical prejudices about Donne during his own lifetime, in the mid-1990s a major critic argued at length for the validity of Empson's approach. Richard Strier has explicitly described himself as "carrying on Empson's project of seeing Donne . . . as capable of genuinely radical thought" and has offered as part of that project an extraordinarily detailed reading of Donne's third "Satire," identifying within it several "radical" ideas about the relation of faith to individual conscience. Unlike earlier readers of this poem, including Carey, Strier regards "Satire III" as a protracted and intellectually scrupulous struggle through and against the aggressive sectarianism that characterized most post-Reformation politics. Like Empson, Strier sees himself as arguing against the grain of dominant critical perceptions, and his insistence on Donne's radicalism is self-consciously polemical in tone and style. One of the strongest insights of Strier's work is his recognition of the tendency of some historicist critics to ignore radical or oppositional ideas in literary works because such ideas are historically unthinkable. "The cry of anachronism almost always serves a conservative picture of the past," Strier forthrightly warns.[29]

For me, the "radical" Donne of Empson and Strier and the sexually "dissident" Donne of Holmes are desirable versions of the poet, refreshing alternatives to the conservative, ambitious, and cynical Donne of Carey, Goldberg, and Marotti or the Donne of masculinist self-assertion we find in many (though by no means all) feminist discussions. Nevertheless, I think it is important to qualify the notion of radicalism as it generally operates in this important strain of Donne criticism. As Terry Eagleton pointed out some years ago, Empson's philosophical baseline is that of "an old style Enlightenment rationalist whose trust in decency, reasonableness, common human sympathies and a general human nature is as winning as it is suspect";[30] and while Strier and Holmes might want to resist such a description of their own practice (indeed, Holmes's project is at some level a critique of Enlightenment rationalism), the emphasis of both critics on the politically progressive potential of Donne's texts aligns them spiritually with Empson's traditional humanism. To put the point a little more contentiously: while Donne's attitude toward freedom of conscience in matters of religion in "Satire III" may indeed be "radical" when compared to, say, that of most orthodox divines during the seventeenth century, and while his understanding of the relationship between nature and desire may also be more "dissident" than, say, that of Samuel Johnson, neither position seems particularly at odds with the (loosely) liberal-tolerationist political philosophy of the contemporary academy. Thus, when making their eloquent and refreshing arguments for Donne's "radicalism," Strier and Holmes sometimes seem to be trying to boost Donne's market value within contemporary literary scholarship by demonstrating that this "radicalism" makes him, well, rather like a politically sensitive contemporary professor of English. (In this respect, Strier's and Holmes's projects cannot really be equated with Empson's, who worked for most of his life within a more generally conservative intellectual paradigm and who could not rely on a possible identification between the values he imputes to his author and the critical institution at large.)

There are numerous reasons to be cautious about embarking on a critical recuperation of Donne's poetry that ultimately makes him appear no less (or more) radical than ourselves. Given the nature of power structures within the modern university system—where, among other things, the routine exploitation of graduate students in composition programs and the generally appalling treatment of most so-called adjunct faculty constitute some of the greatest hypocrisies of modern intellectual life—one might legitimately inquire as to whether English departments are really the radical spaces that both left- and right-wing commentators have claimed. Sympathetic and indebted as I am to readings that foreground Donne's "radical" or "dissident" potential, it seems to me problematic that Donne's radicalism, as conceived in these previous accounts, should only challenge ideas that nowadays the critical profession is comfortable seeing challenged.

But the problem is not just that our notions of "radical" may not be radical enough. The chief difficulty is with the unspoken presuppositions about the nature of literary value that drive both the attacks on Donne as a conservative and the defenses of Donne as (relatively) radical. Jonathan Dollimore's recent work is helpful in amplifying this point, concerned as it is to illuminate the blindspots of liberal/political as well as more conservative/traditional criticism. In *Sex, Literature, and Censorship,* Dollimore has argued that both the establishment and the enlightened political critic can "perform complimentary tasks in the medium run." Of course, by foregrounding the progressive political potential of a given literary text, the liberal critic can do important and necessary work; but, as Dollimore notes, he or she may risk making "the 'dangerous' book safe, if not for the whole culture, then for its liberal constituency." Elaborating on Dollimore's position, one might also note that when politically progressive critics argue either for the subversive potential of a text that has previously been subject to conservative readings *or* for the hegemonic and exclusionary tendencies of a supposedly "great" book or author, their arguments often remain curiously beholden to the idea that art is best evaluated in terms of its social and political efficacy. Thus, ironically, the old humanist faith in the redemptive power of letters returns to haunt the political critic, persisting in spite of and sometimes even alongside his or her overt repudiation of such traditional pieties.

According to Dollimore, then, while the (loosely speaking) liberal-tolerationist critical project is valuable as a riposte to conservative readers, these interpretive gains can come at the price of downplaying other significant dimensions of the literary experience. In Dollimore's words:

> Some artists, like certain intellectuals, seek out and embrace the dangerous knowledge which potentially conflicts not just with reactionary social agendas, but progressive, humane and responsible agendas as well . . . [Therefore,] if we approach literature insisting on an alignment of the ethical conscience and the creative imagination we blind ourselves to the fact that some of the most compelling writing is about the tension between, if not the incompatibility of, these two things.[31]

In my opinion, John Donne is one of those artists driven to "seek out and embrace the dangerous knowledge" that Dollimore describes (indeed, he provides Dollimore with several choice examples). For these reasons his art presents a particular challenge both to traditional (conservative) criticism and to its putatively radical counterparts—and he has often been poorly served by both.

Following Dollimore, then, I argue that a criticism ambitious enough to respond adequately to the challenge of Donne's art must recognize the tendency of traditional criticism to muffle, distort, or simply repudiate his most distinctive achievements; and at the same time it must try to avoid being caught in the interpretive logic that ultimately values artistic achievement only in terms of its relative political conservatism or radicality. It must avoid, in other words, what Eve Sedgwick and Adam Frank have wittily described as the "kinda subversive, kinda hegemonic" problem that is the current dead end of so much post-Foucauldian political and historicist criticism.[32] To do Donne interpretive justice, we need a criticism that can at least acknowledge (if never fully account for) the kinetic power of his texts to seduce, repulse, disturb, soothe, enlighten, mystify, bore, charm, amuse, and horrify (sometimes all at once).

In the course of the next three chapters, I will prove in a variety of ways that any first step toward this admittedly grand aim must begin with a greater self-consciousness on the part of the critic about the role of desire in his or her own interpretive practice. As L. O. Aranye Fradenburg has written, in the context of medieval studies: "The question for the moment is, How can we make these imbrications [of desire and interpretation, of knowledge and enjoyment] enabling, rather than disabling, for our work?"[33] This is indeed *the* question for the moment, and not simply for medievalists and early modernists but for anyone who believes in the value and production of literary criticism, broadly conceived: anyone, that is, who believes that critical activity is worth doing. To paraphrase a later portion of Fradenburg's discussion: If we cannot ask for value-free scholarship (and it seems that we cannot), we can at least ask the critic—whether he or she identifies as a historicist or a psychoanalyst, a poststructuralist or a Marxist, a feminist or a New Critic, a queer theorist or merely a slightly eccentric one—we can at least ask that critic to acknowledge and understand his or her own stakes in the practice, the purpose, the pleasure-pain of literary analysis, and perhaps to use this acknowledgment and understanding to reach a position of still greater insight.

To register the plurality of interpretive desires, and the related plurality of critical pleasures, and to consider when and how those desires and pleasures come into conflict, and when and how they may be conjoined—this, then, is the larger project toward which I hope this book will make some contribution. Such a project seems to me central to the articulation of the future aspirations of our profession, which, more and more, needs the broadest possible repertoire of powerful arguments to justify its continued existence in a world where most people read "literature" less and less.

IV

> Reason is and ought only to be the slave of the passions.
>
> —DAVID HUME, *A TREATISE OF HUMAN NATURE*

Some final possible objections must be proleptically addressed before I can bring this introduction to a close and invite you to explore the world of Donne's desire, and of critical desires for Donne, with me. The first concerns the possibility that in "unmasking" the structures of desire that lie behind the interpretations of previous readers I may appear to be suggesting that my own interpretations are not subject to similar shaping pressures: as if I could make the "real" John Donne, previously hidden behind the screens of critical fantasy, stand up and make himself known. This appearance may be compounded by the second potential objection. At appropriate moments in this introduction, and indeed throughout *Desiring Donne,* I have continued to speak of "Donne's" intentions, desires, and so on, as if I haven't also insisted upon the ultimate impossibility of distinguishing critical desires *for* the text from the desires *of* the text and its author. To phrase the objection in the form of a question: How can I expect anyone to be persuaded by my readings of Donne's verse when, if I am subjected to my own logic, I cannot even finally separate what I think Donne means from what I want him to mean? How can I claim to know "Donne" at all?

By way of addressing these points, I would first like to say a little more about this John Donne of mine. My Donne is not a self-serving careerist on the make, pragmatically turning his religious coat according to the current fashion. His circumstances were rather more perilous than those of a tenure-seeking academic, and I do not condemn him, as Carey seems to do, for not wanting to be a martyr. My Donne is certainly flawed: he is impetuous, self-absorbed, and as a young man, altogether too taken with his own cleverness. My Donne knew how to be charming, but as my former teacher, Professor David Aers, once said to me, in a tone of pointed disdain, "Charm is not a virtue." At the same time, my Donne, like William Empson's, is intellectually "brave" and profoundly engaged by the key theological and philosophical questions of his day (although, like many of us, his youthful radicalism increasingly gives way to conservatism in old age). He is capable of lifelong loyalty to friends like Sir Henry Goodyere; and despite the hardships that followed upon his marriage, my Donne did not stop loving his wife.

Most of all, my Donne is a masterful manipulator of language, a God-like ruler of his own world of words, wont to take delight in the material of his creations. My Donne was almost capable of falling for Anne More just because of the irresistible possibility of punning on her name alongside his (together they comprise their own version of supplemental logic: Donne and More). My Donne is therefore like Thomas Docherty's Donne to a degree, in that his performative performances appear to prefigure and illuminate many concepts of currency in contemporary critical theory, including the mediated nature of experience and the instability of the self. However, unlike Docherty's, my Donne is appealing, sometimes even admirable. In short, my Donne is not the "real" Donne—how could he be?—but the Donne of my desires, like James Kincaid's Dickens, "a fabricated bit of energy that seeks to find an audience and perform." And if you feel that my arguments are therefore circular and pointless, I will respond with Kincaid's answer to the same complaint: "so is a baseball, more or less."[34]

Should that answer seem too flippant, I will insist that no one else's Donne is ultimately any different from mine in this vital respect. To the extent that the "real" Donne is ultimately irrecoverable, every critic's Donne is inevitably over-Donne, an excess that emerges from an absence. You may eventually decide that someone else's Donne is "truer" than mine, but all that could ever really mean is that his or her fantasies—of knowledge, of history, of evidence, of the literary, of proper objects—are more in alignment with yours than mine. Fantasy itself remains inescapable, and truth is only the most seductive fantasy of all, as my Donne knew all too well.[35] To put the point slightly differently and, again, in what I hope does not seem too cavalier a fashion: my purpose is less to persuade others that I am right about Donne than it is to persuade others that Donne *and* his critics are worth reading, even in the twenty-first century, with care and attention.

I can best illuminate my own desires for this work by offering one final anecdote, about one of the master critics—perhaps *the* master critic—of the first half of the last century. Introducing the lectures that he hoped might eventually get him out of the bank and into the protective cloister of Cambridge University on a full-time basis, T. S. Eliot made the following anticipatory remarks: "It is necessary for me to point out, both in guidance towards the method to be adopted, and in common modesty, that these lectures will not continue or develop the use of scholarship. I shall make use, with due sense of obligation, of the work of scholars, such as Mr Grierson and Mr Saintsbury. . . . *But my point of view is not that of scholarship, but that of literary criticism.*"[36] I confess that when I came across these sentences for the first time, I laughed out loud. The distinction, offered "in common modesty," seemed incredibly cheeky, even courageous. *Not* "scholarship" *but* "literary criticism"? I wondered about the tone of this remark. Was the old possum being arch in insisting so pointedly on this, to a contemporary reader, somewhat odd-sounding opposition? Perhaps, slightly, but overall I have to say that I think not. Eliot surely didn't want to alienate the scholarly community at this delicate and troubled point in his life, as Ronald Schuchard's fine introduction to the text makes clear. He wanted the dons to embrace him, to rescue him from the drudgery of a job he hated, to grant him access to the professorial club, the space to write, teach, and make art: to give him, in short, whatever the 1926 equivalent of tenure was.

What, then, is Eliot talking about? I think that in contemporary critical historiography the distinction that Eliot here makes has most often been rewritten as an opposition between "historicism" and "formalism" (or between politics and aesthetics, or between context and close reading, or between Foucauldians and Derrideans, or any number of similar variations). And while this revision is no doubt accurate up to a point, it has also perhaps obscured or distorted something important that exists only in Eliot's original formulation. Reading on, we get a clearer sense that what has been obscured is *desire* in its most basic form: the impulse to create. For Eliot goes on pretty much immediately to collapse his interest in literary criticism (as opposed to scholarship) into his personal investment in poetic making: "My attitude is that of craftsman who has attempted for eighteen years to make English verses. . . . The interest of a craftsman is centered in the present and immediate future: he studies the literature of the past in order to learn how he should write in the present and in the immediate future."

It would be easy enough for a skeptic to say that Eliot mystifies "literary criticism" with this move, since we all have a rough idea what "scholarship" means here—editing, collating manuscripts written in difficult Elizabethan hands, identifying authors or biographical circumstances pertinent to the composition of poems, working in the archives of the Bodlean, the Cambridge University Library, and the British Library—while "literary criticism" remains by and large undefined except insofar as it is part of a necessarily obscure "creative process." But do we really have to be practicing poets to make a similar claim? What if one important job of the contemporary teacher-critic is indeed to give presentness to the past, to actualize and make relevant the texts that engage us "for the present and immediate future," *for no better reason than that we have loved and responded to those texts?* What if we claim this interpretive act as a creative act in its own right, distinct from scholarship not because it is frivolous, or easier, but precisely because it provides scope for creativity, leeway for present political and personal concerns, and finally, opportunities for the expression of *desire,* in ways that editing, attribution, literary biography, and other forms of archival work obviously cannot?[37] What, in other words, if literary criticism requires not simply or only or even primarily the disciplinary skills of the scholar but the exercise of creative imagination, acts of intellectual risk, and the will to make things up (or at least, to make unexpected connections), as well as to uncover forgotten facts? I hasten to add, I'm not advocating a simple return to criticism as Eliot practiced it, even if such a thing were possible (and, thankfully, the world has changed rather too much for that ever to happen). But it does seem to me that, reformulated with a broader sense of what might be said to constitute creative desire, T. S. Eliot's description of "literary criticism" is entirely compatible with the most radical developments of the last few years.

During those years, we have heard much talk about the "crisis" in English studies and complaints from the Right that the "relativism" of critical theory and the opening up of the canon to women and minorities have together contributed to a wholesale depreciation of the "Western cultural tradition" and, indeed, to a general devaluing of the humanities. I would suggest that such arguments are rooted in the fears and anxieties that attend upon the broad recognition of the impossibility of absolute objectivity when it comes to the most profound questions of culture, education, and aesthetic and moral value—anxieties that turn upon the uncertain but inescapable role played by desire within our intellectual lives. I have written this book exploring the role of desire in literary interpretation in part out of a wish to dispel some of that dangerous, reactionary, and ultimately anti-intellectual fear.[38] At the same time, however, it may be worth bringing this portion of my discussion to a close by reminding all critics, whether they see them-selves as conservative or radical in their methods or choices of primary texts, that the act of interpretive "creativity" that is literary criticism, committed for no higher or better reason than inspiring others to read, has *never* been an easy sell inside the academy, today or any day. Even T. S. Eliot, that bogeyman of political criticism, a man who has been saddled with the charge of almost single-handedly formulating the most oppressively monolithic and conservative conception of the literary canon, was *not* welcome in the university of 1926. After giving the Clark lectures from which I have been quoting, he was denied "elec-tion" to a prestigious research fellowship and booted out of Oxbridge for a time; the lectures themselves remained unpublished until the 1990s. And the thing that seems to have most upset the worthy old gentlemen on that fellowship committee? Like John Donne, it seems that Mr. Eliot had written some rather unsettling poems.

CHAPTER ONE

Donne's "Fore-Skinne"

Desire and the Seventeenth-Century Reader

In this chapter I think through some of the ways in which Donne was produced as an object of interpretive desire for seventeenth-century readers. My texts are the 1633 and 1635 editions of Donne's *Poems,* which I consider primarily from the perspective of their formal arrangement, and a single elegy written for Donne by one Thomas Browne, published for the first and only time in the 1633 volume, which I consider in close detail. The earliest recorded response we have to Donne's verse taken as a complete body of work, Browne's elegy describes the hermeneutic challenge presented by that body in terms of a governing opposition between the sacred and the sexual. Browne sees this opposition as central to the experience of reading Donne and as a problem that must be resolved before Donne can be constituted for seventeenth-century audiences as a good writer. Although "good" must be understood here in its most literal, ethical sense, rather than as an aesthetic quality, Browne is not what we would call a conventional Christian moralist, as I will show. Browne's main themes—religion, eroticism, and interpretation—therefore serve as my own keywords throughout.

I

> Arrangements at an unconscious level are alone intelligible.
>
> —PAUL RICOEUR, *THE CONFLICT OF INTERPRETATIONS*

The structural organization of John Donne's first printed book of poetry makes no sense.[1] Published posthumously in 1633, the collection eschews even the basic generic distinctions so familiar to Donne's modern audience: "Songs and Sonnets," "Satires," "Verse Letters," and "Divine Poems" (these groupings, which have persisted into the twenty-first century, emerge for the first time with the *second* printed edition of Donne's works from 1635). Several readers have commented on the disorderly configuration of Donne's 1633 text over the years; Leah Marcus, for example, has provided a detailed analysis of the collection in *Unediting the Renaissance,* itself an ambitious attempt to combine the traditional skills of textual bibliography with the insights of poststructuralist theory. Among other things, Marcus asserts that the very layout and internal composition of Donne's first collection constitute (ortho)graphic evidence for the ultimate impossibility of "fixing" him within any reductively binary scheme. Indeed, for Marcus, the version of Donne projected by the 1633 *Poems* confirms not only her deconstructivist principles but also her aesthetic taste more generally. In her words, the collection is "a striking mélange of sacred and secular that refuses to separate John Donne from Jack. Verse epistles ... jostle up against scurrilous amatory verses and evocations of human decay in a rough gallimaufry of mingled passions that projects a John Donne very like the Donne most of us value, a Donne for whom the sacred and secular are so closely entwined as to be inseparable."[2]

This reading would probably not be considered controversial in most quarters, and I, too, am in agreement with the main points of Marcus's argument, insofar as they go. However, I want to pause for a moment over one of the more undeveloped aspects of Marcus's interpretation, encoded in her use of the phrase "most of us." As the context makes clear, by "most of us" Marcus means a rather small band of atheist or liberal-religious, professionalized, contemporary readers. Of course, Marcus is perfectly justified in assuming that her audience will be drawn from exactly this narrow demographic (and I obviously include myself within its bounds), but at the same time it must also be admitted that "most of us" therefore only refers to the tiniest portion of Donne's actual historical readership. Given that Marcus is performing an analysis of Donne's 1633 *Poems,* then, one obvious question emerges from her account: How might readers in 1633 have responded to the collection's juxtaposition of the religious with "scurrilous amatory verses"? What might its disorganized layout have signified for them?

One possible answer to this question has been suggested by Arthur F. Marotti, perhaps the most influential of Donne's textualist critics. In *Manuscript, Print and the English Renaissance Lyric,* Marotti suggests, against Marcus, that Donne's first editors deliberately delay the readerly encounter with Donne's more earthly lyrics by burying them toward the back of the book. In other words, according to Marotti, the apparently random structure that Marcus values is actually an intentional blind—the result of a conscious attempt to "protect the reputation of Dean Donne from moral taint."[3]

Unfortunately, this ingenious theory is not without flaws. For example, we are required to accept Marotti's contention that "the first amorous lyric is the ninety-fourth in the book"; but this means discounting Donne's "Elegies," traditionally considered among his most explicit amorous writings, which appear much earlier in the collection. (The first elegy is the fifteenth or twenty-second poem in the book, depending on whether one counts "La Corona" as one or seven poems.) Naturally, Marotti is aware of the problem and explains that we should *not* count these poems because they would have been "taken as exercises in classical form" and therefore did not present any real threat to Dean Donne's name.[4] However, this suggestion is not entirely persuasive either: it is true that excuse of "classical precedent" was not uncommon in the period—in one now commonly adduced incident, Richard Barnfield responded to criticisms of his representation of same-sex desire in his sonnets by declaring that he was merely following Virgil—but the fact that Barnfield had to articulate this defense suggests that the aesthetic principle of *imitatio* would not have been sufficient to deflect controversy by itself.[5] Indeed, Donne himself does not seem to have imagined that he could rely on the mustiness of the classical library entirely to obscure the whiff of scandal when it came to these poems: "To my satyrs there belongs some feare," he wrote to a friend, "and to some elegies . . . perhaps, shame."[6] Still more troublingly, Marotti's thesis would seem to imply that Donne's 1633 editors were spectacularly naive. After all, the expedient of "hiding" material toward the back of a book ultimately achieves nothing. As long as Donne's morally "tainting" poems (to use Marotti's terms) are printed *somewhere*, the determined reader can be expected to find them sooner or later; and given that the structure of the lyric miscellany invites us to approach texts in a nonlinear fashion—browsing, dipping in here and there, paging forward and back—then sooner seems more likely.

But if the degree of editorial intent lying behind the disorderly layout of Donne's 1633 edition remains undecided, both Marcus and Marotti agree that seventeenth-century reactions to its strange brew of desire and divinity were uniformly negative. Indeed, both critics argue persuasively that the arrangement of Donne's *second* printed collection from 1635 works to "redeem the life of the poet from [the] . . . intermingling of sacred and secular" materials so scandalously on display in the earlier volume.[7] As I have already noted, this later volume divides Donne's poems into generic and thematic groupings, a fact that leads Marcus to postulate the hand of Izaak Walton, Donne's first and most influential biographer, holding the editorial reins. Notoriously, in his *Life of Donne,* Walton underplayed the significance of the erotic verses by dismissing them as the ephemeral productions of a misspent youth; and Marcus sees a similar "decorous separation" of the sacred from the profane in the rearranged order of the 1635 text—a reordering that also implicitly reinforces Walton's biographical chronology by placing the erotic verse at the beginning of the volume and the divine verse at the end.[8] As if to underscore the point, the 1635 text also advances a version of Walton's biographical claim on its very first page, in the form of an epigrammatic verse prominently displayed beneath Donne's authorial portrait:

> Most count [youth as] their Golden Age; but t'was not thine,
> Thine was thy later yeares, so much refind
> From youths Drosse, Mirth & wit.[9]

But does Walton's conservative, recuperative, and above all *orderly* editorial impulse represent the *only* kind of response that a seventeenth-century reader could have had to the generically confused and confusing text of 1633? Or might some seventeenth-century readers also have valued Donne's earlier collection precisely for the "mélange" factor now prized (according to Marcus) by "most of us"?

One possible alternative to Walton's "decorous separation" of the sacred from the secular within the Donnean corpus is provided by the 1633 text itself. I am referring to a short poem, "To the Deceased Author," attributed to one Thomas Browne, published for the first and only time among a group of twelve elegies for Donne appended to the main body of his book and almost entirely overlooked in previous analyses.[10] Perhaps picking up on a hint in the printer's prefatory epistle to the reader, which figures Donne's collection as "a scattered limbe of this author," Browne's poem turns on a striking image of textual embodiment.[11] Indeed, Browne ventures to name the authorial "limbe" in question rather more specifically:

> To the deceased Author,
> Upon the *Promiscuous* printing of his Poems,
> the Looser sort, with the Religious.
>
> When thy *Loose* raptures, *Donne*, shall meet with Those
> That do confine
> Tuning, unto the Duller line,
> And sing not, but in *Sanctified Prose;*
> How will they, with sharper eyes,
> The *Fore-skinne* of thy phansie circumcise?
> And feare, thy *wantonnesse* should now, begin
> *Example*, that hath ceased to be *Sin?*
>
> And that *Feare* fannes their *Heat;* whilst knowing eyes
> Will not admire
> At this Strange Fire,
> That here is mingled with thy Sacrifice:
> But dare reade even thy *Wanton Story,*
> As thy Confession, not thy Glory.
> And will so envie *Both* to future times
> That they would buy thy *Goodnesse*, with thy *Crimes.*[12]

Besides providing an unexpected (and yet somehow unsurprising) hint as to exactly which one of Donne's "scatter'd limbes" readers of the 1633 *Poems* found themselves holding, this curious tribute reveals just how "striking" Donne's "mélange of sacred and secular" was to at least one of his contemporaries. However, the poem is also somewhat obscure, and therefore, before embarking on a detailed explication, a paraphrase of its general argument may be helpful.[13]

Browne begins by speculating about the reaction of a certain group of readers to Donne's amorous writings. These readers, who prefer religious prose over all other genres, are imagined gazing censoriously upon the text ("with sharper eyes") and worrying that people may be tempted to imitate the negative example of Donne's "loose raptures" (lines 1–8). Nevertheless, another class of "knowing" reader—among whom we are presumably meant to count Browne himself—will "dare [to] reade" those same poems because they recognize them as acts of contrition (lines 9–16).

With this much established, it should be noted that Browne's response to Donne's book is unusual, at least in its immediate literary setting among the other elegies of the 1633 collection. It bears no formal resemblance to any of its companion pieces, which are composed almost entirely in conventional iambic pentameters. As if in deliberate contrast, Browne has woven an impossibly intricate metrical net, characterized by extreme syntactic compression and entangling a peculiarly anthropomorphic conceit in its various lengths of line. Browne's poem is therefore a tribute twice over: once in its theme, second in its form, which is a distinctive mimetic *homage* to what a later criticism would define as typically metaphysical mannerisms.

Perhaps more important for my purposes, "To the Deceased Author" is also distinctive in its direct focus on Donne's eroticism or, in Browne's phrasing, the "wantonness" of his "loose raptures."[14] But Browne's exact attitude toward that eroticism is difficult to discern. Does his poem positively embrace Donne's amorous verse, or does Browne only acknowledge Donne's erotic "crimes" in order to explain them away? What, shall we say, does Browne want from his explicitly phallicized fragment of "Donne"? To put the same question in more general and less contentiously personalizing terms: what model of reading does this poem assume, and what kind of interpretive desire does it express?

Ambiguities are encoded in the very title of the poem, thanks to Browne's choice phrase "*Promiscuous* printing," which itself means promiscuously, taking multiple referents. On the one hand, Browne may be appealing to what we would now consider the classist and misogynistic prejudices of the period by suggesting that the nominally female (and hence wanton) reproductive capacity of the printing press has made the once exclusive property of an elite coterie "promiscuously" available to all and sundry (in exchange for a small fee).[15] Such innuendo is perfectly possible during a period in which printers and publishers routinely represented texts as ravished and/or "loose" women. On the other hand, as the Oxford English Dictionary indicates, a nonpejorative application of the word *promiscuous* is also fully available; in fact, the phrase may not refer to the eroticized act of publication at all but to the haphazardly "promiscuous" organization of the volume itself—its provocative arrangement of Donne's "loose raptures" in the same textual bed with the divine verse.

The problem of promiscuous signification illustrated by the title also turns out to be one of the thematic concerns of the poem. While the first stanza depicts "sharper-eyed" readers worrying that others may be won to sin by Donne's wanton example, the second stanza wickedly imagines even that pious fear acting as a spur to still greater arousal ("And that *Feare* fannes their *Heat*"). Thus, according to Browne, those who would censor Donne's text because of its capacity to incite desire suddenly find themselves implicated in its "crimes" simply by virtue (if that is the correct term) of the interpretive stance that they have adopted. With this ingenious turn of the promiscuous screw, Browne displaces moral culpability for the titillating effects of Donne's "loose raptures" from the texts themselves to the minds of their readers; indeed, he makes the most puritanical prude seem prurient by implying that the sociopolitical consequences of Donne's sexual representations are entirely a function of readerly perspective and orientation.

This strategy not only has the effect of turning Donne's entire 1633 *Poems* into an Augustinian test of "right reading"; it also prepares the ground for Browne's clinching argument: that Donne's collection is morally unimpeachable because, seen from the correct ("knowing") perspective, it is only following another saintly Augustinian precedent ("whilst knowing eyes / . . . dare reade even thy *Wanton Story*, / As thy *Confession*, not thy *Glory*"). In this way Browne proleptically offsets the accusation that he himself might have a salacious interest in Donne's text by reminding his readers that even the most scandalous spectacle can serve a morally didactic purpose if it is interpreted "properly." To summarize, then, we might say that instead of dismissing Donne's "loose raptures" altogether, in Waltonesque fashion, Browne's poem directly confronts Donne's normatively subversive representations of desire and attempts to make sense of them, while also attempting to contain their disruptive erotic energies within the theological box of the confessional.

However, in the process, something of Donne's subversive desire appears to have communicated itself to Browne. Donne's "loose raptures" take on a new significance for Browne as the necessary acknowledgment of sin that begins every confessant's journey to salvation. Indeed, we might want to go further and say that Donne's passionate representations seem to have evoked an answering passion in Browne: a poetic, textualized, homoerotic passion to *have* Donne and to have *all* of Donne, a passion corporeally figured through the image of a complete, full-length, uncircumcised "phansie" that stands so prominently in the middle of the first stanza.

Turning now to this particular image, I am concerned that after a quarter century of feminist criticism the sheer masculinist arrogance of Browne's equation between phallic potency and literary prowess—between Donne's printed poetry and his penis—might appear almost too obvious to be worthy of comment. But in the context of Donne's "promiscuous" intermingling of the sacred and the sexual, Browne's invocation of circumcision as censorship demands fuller explication. To understand the nature of Browne's interpretive desire for Donne's 1633 *Poems,* we must pursue the problem of the "fore-skinne."

II

> The relations between bodily and cognitive systems of organization are in many ways most powerfully encoded in the symbolics of any given part.
>
> —DAVID HILLMAN AND CARLA MAZZIO, *THE BODY IN PARTS*

> They which are circumcised are not circumcised.
>
> —MARTIN LUTHER, *COMMENTARY ON GALATIANS*

It would be difficult to exaggerate the symbolic overdetermination of circumcision in early modern England. Nevertheless, Browne's metaphor is perhaps most immediately and easily interpretable as invoking the intertwined threats of castration and emasculation. Versions of this idea, familiar to twentieth-century readers in a Freudian incarnation, were also available in the seventeenth century; it accords with a whole set of medieval and early modern anti-Jewish stereotypes with emasculatory and/or effeminizing overtones, including the notions that Jewish men menstruated, were capable of breast feeding, and liked to dress up as women on feast days "against the law of God."[16] As James Shapiro dryly notes, most seventeenth-century gentiles "saw no contradiction between these effeminized portraits and those [equally common stereotypes] that depicted Jewish men as rapacious seducers."[17] That circumcision marked a sexual as well as a religious and ethnic boundary has obvious implications for our reading of "To the Deceased Author": Browne doesn't just want his Donne to be a good Christian; he wants him to be a manly and virile one as well.

However, during this period, circumcision derived most of its extraordinary significatory resonance—its too-apt capacity to mark and simultaneously divide multiple sites of distinction and difference—from Saint Paul and the aftershocks of Pauline commentary that followed the Protestant Reformation.[18] Paul's precise meaning and intentions are still a matter of debate among New Testament scholars, but the normative Christian understanding of his position is simply that the universal salvific effects of Christ's sacrifice rendered the Old Covenant with Abraham null and void (see Gal. 5:6).[19] The question of whether this understanding meant that observances of the Old Law, including circumcision, had been rendered sacramentally inefficacious or actually contrary to the declared will of God (whether circumcision constituted "a thing indifferent" or a sin, to put the question in post-Reformation terms) remained in dispute.

The extent to which early modern English Christians differed on the subject can be gathered from the violent state repression of so-called Judaizers such as John Traske. In the decades prior to the publication of Browne's poem, Traske preached circumcision, dietary restriction, and Saturday-Sabbatarianism, attracting sufficient public attention to prompt his eventual arrest, public branding, and imprisonment. Traske was not the last to express such opinions openly; less than a decade after the publication of Browne's poem, in the upheaval and aftermath of the civil war, religious radicals such as John Robins and Thomas Tany were equally capable of eroding the distinction between Christian and Jew in their belief that England was the new Israel of the last days (Robins, who was uneducated, claimed knowledge of Hebrew "by inspiration," while Tany declared "to have had it revealed to him that he was 'a Jew of the tribe of Reuben' " and was also reported to have circumcised himself).[20] At the other extreme, when writing on the "Strange inventive Contradictions against Nature practically maintained by divers Nations in the ordering of their Privy-parts," John Bulwer, a seventeenth-century doctor and antiquarian, argued that the "God that created these parts . . . intend[ed] their preservation in the state of Nature" (although elsewhere Bulwer seems to admit of occasional medical necessity because Nature is "so over-carefull sometimes . . . in providing for a decent covering of this shamefull part").[21] Meanwhile, at least since Aquinas, attempts had been made to steer some kind of middle course between these two positions (to follow the Law or not; to circumcise or not).[22] A succinct example is provided by John Milton in his early poem "Upon the Circumcision": "O more exceeding love or law more just? / Just law indeed, but more exceeding love!"[23] Here, the practice of the Law would not seem to constitute a sin (it is and remains "just . . . indeed") despite the fact that Christ's love "exceeds" or, in the precise Latinate sense, "goes from" it. Nevertheless, Milton's own audacious act of exegetical circumcision, slicing away seventeen hundred years of debate with two acutely balanced pentameter lines, clearly belies both the enormous range of possible opinions on the matter and the brutality to which those accused of observing the Old Law (including "Christians" like Traske) were subjected.[24]

As if these arguments over Paul's conception of "circumcision in the flesh" were not confusing enough, matters were further complicated by his simultaneous emphasis on what he called "circumcision of the spirit" (see, for example, Rom. 2:29) and by his own allegorization of the original covenant with Abraham (Gal. 4:22–31.).[25] These Pauline emphases placed circumcision at the center of highly abstract but no less bitterly fought debates, pitching post-Reformation Protestant advocates of the "plain sense" of Scripture against a traditional scholastic or Catholic "allegorical" hermeneutics. As a result, at the time of Browne's writing, circumcision was a major typological concept subtending basic theological and epistemological questions, including the distinction between literal and metaphorical levels of language.

Therefore, Browne's invocation of circumcision in the context of a poem that thematizes issues of good interpretive practice cannot be fully appreciated apart from a seventeenth-century high theological understanding of Paul and of his subsequent Patristic commentators. Browne's argument that the "sharp-eyed" censor conceals an impure mind-set behind his pious mask parallels Paul's own statement in Galatians 6:13 that the Judaizer's appeal to the moral authority of the Law conceals a deeper carnality: "[T]hey themselves which are circumcised keep not the Law, but desire to have you circumcised that they might glory in your flesh." Moreover, as Paul argues elsewhere, the Jew or Judaizer is actually incapable of interpreting the Law correctly— that is, "by the body of Christ" (Rom. 7:4)—because of this carnal orientation: "[T]he carnal mind is enmity against God: for it is not subject to the law of God, neither indeed can be" (Rom. 8:7). This interpretive incapacity is specifically figured by Saint Augustine both as the inability to read and as a failure of self-recognition: "The Jew carries a book, from which a Christian may believe . . . just as it is customary for servants to carry books behind their masters, so that those who carry faint and those who read profit. . . . The appearance of the Jews in the holy scripture which they carry is just like the face of the blind man in a mirror; he is seen by others, by himself not seen."[26] Thus, in depicting Donne's would-be censors as circumcisors, Browne is drawing on a well-established tradition of anti-Jewish rhetoric, apparently sanctioned by the New Testament and consolidated by its Patristic interpreters. Like the Jew who refuses to reinterpret the Covenant with Abraham in the light of Christ's Passion, Donne's "sharper"-eyed reader is also a bad reader; like the Jewish appeal to the Old Law, the "sharp-eyed" protestation of piety actually conceals a profanely carnal perspective; and, like good Christians, "knowing" readers may recognize the carnal origin of interpretive failure within the "sharp-eyed" critic, although the critic himself cannot even see to acknowledge the thing of darkness as his own. Browne's epithet of "sharp-eyed" is therefore more than a wince-inducing pun; in the context of interpretive blindness, it is bitterly ironic.

The implications of this anti-Jewish rhetoric are even more significant than its origins for our understanding of Browne's relationship to Donne's disorganized text of 1633. For it follows that if the bad reader is analogous to the recalcitrant Jew, then, by extension, Donne's collection occupies the position of the abused Christ. The identification of Donne's fleshly words with the Word made flesh is deepened by the common typological reading of Christ's own circumcision as a prefiguration of his later sufferings on Golgotha. Again, this idea is prominent in Milton's poem:

> [Christ] seals obedience with wounding smart
> This day, but O ere long
> Huge pangs and strong
> Will pierce more near his heart.[27]

The association between Donne's text and Christ's body adds resonance to Browne's application of the word *sacrifice* to Donne's divine verse in the final stanza of his elegy. Exploiting the tendency of typological exegesis to collapse every identity and chronology into one life and one story, Browne here momentarily renders Donne's poetic sacrifice and Christ's ultimate sacrifice equivalent; if only for a second we are allowed and even encouraged to see Donne circumcised as Christ crucified. The typological link between circumcision and crucifixion upon which this reading depends would have been reinforced by the popular belief (advanced in several scaremongering pamphlets during the two decades prior to the publication of Browne's poem) that Jews regularly kidnapped, circumcised, *and* crucified gentile boys.[28]

Of course, this is all to suggest that Browne deliberately dances to the edge of a blasphemous abyss in this poem. But even in so doing Browne is arguably still only paying a mimetic tribute to his subject by reproducing yet another aspect of the "loose raptures" he is ostensibly concerned to explain; for his heretical game is a characteristically Donnean one, of the type found in a poem such as "The Relique," in which Donne explicitly identifies his beloved with Mary Magdalene and thereby implicitly equates himself with Christ: "Thou shalt be a Mary Magdalen, and I / A something else thereby."[29] In fact, Donne had already imagined himself as Christ at the moment of his brutalization by the Jews in one of the many masochistic fantasies scattered throughout his "Holy Sonnets":

> Spit in my face yee Jewes, and pierce my side,
> Buffet, and scoffe, scourge, and crucifie mee,
> For I have sinn'd, and sinn'd, and onely hee,
> Who could do no iniquitie, hath dyed:
> But by my death can not be satisfied
> My sinnes, which passe the Jewes impiety:
> They kill'd once an inglorious man, but I
> Crucifie him daily, being now glorified.[30]

It is worth pausing here for a moment to note just how much power Donne is paradoxically able to wrest from the submissive posture. "Hurt me," he demands. "I deserve it; I've been bad. I deserve what Christ got, or worse. I'm worse than the worst; I'm even worse than a Jew." The libidinal investment of this doubled act of identification and repudiation is fairly obvious and no less obviously rooted in what may now seem almost banally familiar psychic economies of prohibition, transgression, abjection, and othering; but perhaps less immediately apparent is the fact that, in the wake of this sadomasochistic, orgiastic fantasy of abjection, Donne manages to claim more power for himself to harm Christ (even in His "glorified" state) than the "Jewes" had to harm Him when He was a mere mortal on earth. Indeed, although Donne begins by begging to be crucified, he ends the octave of this sonnet as the one doing the crucifying (it's apparently one of those "You do me, and then I'll do you" situations). I will address the "transgressive" eroticism of the "Holy Sonnets" at greater length in my next chapter, but for now my point is simply that we do not need to look very far to find precedents for either the anti-Jewish rhetoric or the sexually risqué and blasphemous associations I have found in Browne's poem: all Browne had to do was read his source carefully to find all sorts of inspiration.

However, Browne's association of the Donnean text with Christ's body may also work to give Donne's poetic masculinity a further boost, if we recall some of the popular cultural myths surrounding Christ's circumcision at this time. Despite the scorn of Protestant Reformers, it appears that at least seven different continental churches claimed to have Christ's foreskin among their holy relics during the sixteenth century; the one kept at Chartres in particular was claimed to have increased the fertility of the surrounding crops, cattle, and villagers.[31]

Browne's hint that Donne's text can be read as a kind of typographic *imitatio Christi* need not contradict his effort to project (and protect) a Donne of poetically priapic power.

It may be objected that Browne's borderline blasphemy is obviated by his simultaneous insistence that Donne's "loose raptures" are also "confession[s]." But Browne's particular notion of confession—one that could only have entered the culture after the Reformation—is also one that seems to confer a paradoxical value onto the sins confessed. For Browne, the significance of Donne's "confession" is *not* that it redeems Donne by purging him and hence absolving him of his "crimes." Instead, Browne's understanding of confessional practice is more Lutheran. As is well known, Luther warned worshippers to "beware of the great error . . . of leaning on that frail reed—that they have confessed . . . or that they have sent ahead of them their own prayers and preparations . . . for by these things they do not become worthy and pure, but rather they become *defiled through that trust in their purity.*"[32] In accordance with this warning, Donne's "confession" functions within the economy of Browne's poem as part of an anti-idolatrous strategy, confirming Donne's status as a man who could one day *hope* to be purified in Christ precisely because he knew himself to be irremediably sinful. In other words, Browne's blasphemous risk in representing Donne (or, more precisely, Donne's 1633 text) to the world as a type of Christ-like virtue is not simply offset by Donne's frank admissions of sin. Instead, in a perfect illustration of Protestant paradox, those same frank admissions actually make it possible for Browne to claim that Donne really is a model of Christian virtue after all. It is only because of Donne's evident imperfections that Browne can represent Donne as even potentially perfectible. In short, Donne might be a saint precisely and only because he makes no attempt to disguise his essentially sinful nature.

Another way of putting this would be to say that, according to Browne, Donne's "fore-skinne" is pinched in the logic of the supplement. At one level his "raptures," the "*Fore-skinne* of [his] phansie," are said to constitute the looser, lesser, inferior part of his work. Not touted as valuable in and of themselves, the erotic poems are tolerated and excused only because of the greater whole to which they are attached. Yet at the same time the poems are also an indispensable part of Donne's textual body. In fact, according to what we might call the inevitably supplementary logic of Protestantism, Donne's divine works are not simply rendered more admirable by contrast with the erotic "fore-skinne," because we can only even identify the divine *as* divine through the eye of the "fore-skinne," so to speak. It is the presence of this metaphorical prepuce that protects Browne's Donne from the prick of his own pride: the "fore-skinne" is the profane part that makes the holy whole.

III

> Now therein of all Sciences . . . is our Poet the Mon-
> arch. For hee doth not onely shew the way, but giveth
> so sweete a prospect into the way, as will entice anie
> man to enter into it.
>
> —SIR PHILIP SIDNEY, *A DEFENSE OF POETRY*

To insist that Browne's poem proclaims a certain positive contiguity between sexual and spiritual desire is to court the admonition of numerous experts. My invocation of Reformed theology to explain Browne's use of "confession" in the context of such an argument is perhaps most misinterpretable, given the many statements within that theology explicitly declaring that "all who endeavour to go to [Christ] must rid themselves of the earthly affections of the flesh."[33] Before I am accused of "evincing either historical ignorance or spiritual vulgarity,"[34] I should make absolutely clear what I am *not* claiming: that Browne's (or Donne's) sense of devotional erotics can be explained away as the product of a *sublimated* sexual desire. Such an argument not only assumes the priority of sexual over other experiences of desire, but also assumes that such desires are recognizable as entities in and of themselves, independent of their various cultural expressions. If Browne's poem demonstrates anything at all, it is that sexual desire cannot be conceived apart from the forms of its inscription.

But how, then, are we to read texts like Browne's—and indeed like so many of Donne's—that figure spirituality in terms that seem to us redolently sexual? As Debora Shuger has noted in a similar context, the question itself may be misconceived, "to the extent that medieval sexuality is shaped by the language of spiritual desires."[35] In other words, the terms of the question depend on thoroughly modern conceptions that reverse the ontological priorities of the earlier paradigm, making the sexual the shaping agent or "real" source of spiritual longing. In fact, it might be more productive to say that the question is itself evidence of the very transformation in relations between the sexual and the sacred that it seeks to address, because it would not even have occurred to a reader born before the modern era. Therefore, instead of asking *why* an author figures spiritual desire in sexual terms, we could simply begin by noting that once upon a time that's what a lot of authors seem to us to have done (perhaps because they generally saw the experience and vocabulary of sexual desire as ultimately derivative of and secondary to spiritual experiences and vocabularies), whereas nowadays they do not seem to do this quite so often.[36] Shuger is even brave enough to offer 1650 as an approximate cutoff date. In the modern era, she writes, "the link between religious subjectivity and erotic desire . . . snaps" or takes on a reverse priority. Shuger offers by way of example Pope's "Eloisa to Abelard," which she says is about "the *contamination* of religious devotion by erotic longing"; and it is the sense that the presence of eroticism *necessarily* contaminates the spiritual that is distinctly modern.[37]

Returning to Browne's poem, then: as I have argued, "To the Deceased Author" clearly does *not* view the presence of genital eroticism within spiritual desire as *necessarily* contaminating that spirituality. From this point of view, at least, it is clearly not a "modern" poem. However, neither does it seem to emerge from the inverse spiritual-sexual cultural matrix that Shuger identifies with the Middle Ages; instead, it renders genital eroticism (figured as a "fore-skinne") as essential to our appreciation of a spirituality (Donne's "goodnesse") that is also potentially eroticized (figured as the remainder of Donne's "phansie"). In short, Browne's poem can be distinguished from both an earlier discursive moment or theo-erotic paradigm that acknowledged the relation of sexual and spiritual desire (while viewing the former as an echo of the latter) and a modern discourse or theo-erotic paradigm that either gives priority to genital desire or else attempts to sever the link between the erotic and the spiritual altogether. As we might expect from a poem that was written on the historical cusp of a transformation from one paradigm to the other—like the Donne poems to which it is responding—"To the Deceased Author" represents a distinct version of devotional eroticism that is neither precisely "medieval" nor "modern" but that can be seen to contain elements of both, in uneasy relation.[38]

Of course, this uneasy coexistence of sacred and sexual elements must itself be understood as a consequence of larger epistemic shifts during the Renaissance that affected discourses other than the theological. Or perhaps it would be more accurate to say that the new relation of earthly and divine erotics found in the Renaissance, like all the significant cultural and intellectual transformations of the period, can be traced to the often painful and incomplete attempts of emergently "modern" discourses—such as the political, the erotic, the legal, or the medical—to *separate* themselves from the theological. For this reason, Renaissance discussions of the biological function of the "fore-skinne" (or "prepuce," as it is generally termed in medical contexts) make particularly interesting indices of such transformations in the early modern episteme, because they reveal the ways in which the developing discipline of natural science continued to be shaped by theological considerations.[39] The medical discourse of the prepuce, to the extent that it can be distinguished *as* a discourse, also suggests one additional way of interpreting Browne's desire for an uncircumcised Donne.

It is well established among contemporary historians of science and medicine that the early modern map of the body remained profoundly influenced by ancient Galenic models that only gradually came to be displaced by the "new anatomy"; and in many textbooks it is possible to discover both intellectual paradigms coexisting, side by side, sometimes in direct contradiction to one another.[40] Indeed, the conflicting visions of Galenic and early modern medicine seem to replicate the supplementary reading of the foreskin Browne offers in his poem. In Galen's account, the foreskin is described as having nothing more than a decorative function—it is "an ornament"[41]—and at the same time, many authors of the period also argue that the foreskin is an essential part of the penis because of the role it is thought to play in female pleasure during sexual intercourse.

Beyond this replication of Browne's representation of the "fore-skinne" as a supplement, it is the post-Galenic sense of the function of the foreskin during intercourse that has greatest potential significance for our understanding of Browne's poem and his readerly relation to Donne's text. For example, in one late seventeenth-century text by Sir Thomas Browne (perhaps the same Thomas Browne who composed "To the Deceased Author"), we discover references to the "fact" that Jewish women prefer non-Jewish lovers (they "affect Christian carnality above circumcised venery").[42] The origins of this notion have been traced to Latin medical treatises known to have been in Browne's library, such as Columbus's *De re Anatomica*, wherein it is claimed that "the rolling back and forth of the foreskin in sexual intercourse produces an infinite pleasure of which Jewish women are deprived under the Old Law."[43] Versions of this idea seem to have been relatively widespread. An early vernacular example appears in John Banister's popular lay textbook *The Historie of Man* as follows: "The extreme part of the yard [penis] is called *Praeputium:* beyng that skinne wherewith [the] *Glans* is couered, so, in the acte of venerie, now upward, now downe-ward, to the exceedyng delectation of the female, moued [*sic*]: this is that, whiche the Hebrues, in tyme of Circumcision, lose."[44]

This notion sounds very much like—and indeed probably is—an anti-Jewish claim of gentile genital superiority ("Christianity: Newer, Better, Longer-lasting, and Uncut!"); however, surprisingly, it turns out to have an analogue or perhaps even an origin within medieval Jewish thought. Isaac ben Yedaiah, described by literary historian Norman F. Cantor as a radical thirteenth-century follower of the great medieval Jewish scholar Maimonides, has a lengthy disquisition on the subject in which he asserts the spiritual superiority of circumcised penises, precisely by reason of their *inefficiency* as instruments of female sexual pleasure. In Cantor's translation:

> A man who is uncircumcised in the flesh . . . thrusts inside [the woman] a long time because of the foreskin, which is a barrier against ejaculation in intercourse. Thus she feels pleasure and reaches an orgasm first. When an uncircumcised man sleeps with her and then resolves to return to his home, she brazenly grasps him, holding on to his genitals and says to him "Come back, make love to me." This is because of the pleasure that she finds in intercourse with him. . . . They are united without separating and he makes love twice and three times in one night, yet the appetite is not filled. And so he acts with her night after night. The sexual activity emaciates him of his bodily fat and afflicts his flesh and he devotes his brain entirely to women, an evil thing. . . .
>
> But when a circumcised man desires the beauty of a woman, and cleaves to his wife, or to another woman comely in appearance, he will find himself performing his task quickly, emitting his seed as soon as he inserts the crown. . . . He has an orgasm first; he does not hold back his strength. . . . She has no pleasure from him . . . and it would be better for her if he had not known her. . . . Thus he who says "I am the Lord's" will not empty his brain because of his wife or the wife of his friend. He will find grace and good favor; his heart will be strong to seek out God.[45]

I will not attempt to map the historical ironies by which an apparently anti-Jewish claim of sexual inadequacy can also function as a pro-Jewish claim of spiritual superiority, all thanks to a still more pervasive theologically sanctioned misogyny. My purpose is simply to draw attention to another possible reading of Browne's equation between

Donne's poetry and his penis, which we can now see as considerably more than an anxiously insistent masculinization of the authorial subject (though it certainly is that). For in the light of this theomedical discourse, the consequence of circumcising the "fore-skinne" of Donne's "phansie" would be to remove the textual part directly responsible for the "exceedyng delectation" of the reader, to use Banister's phrase. Browne's vision of Donne's book is therefore one in which the text itself is designed to function as an instrument of sexual pleasure. However, if uncircumcised penises are more desirable than circumcised ones, Donne's uncircumcised "phansie"—his uncensored book—is still more desirable than either, because unlike a merely "real" penis, Donne's book can produce sexual pleasure *and* religious instruction *simultaneously*. It is nothing less than a divine dildo, elevating the spirit even as it excites the flesh.

Browne's poem therefore allows us to imagine Donne's 1633 collection as participating in what Andrew Taylor calls "a significant extension of the use of the technology of the book"—the possibility of what many would nowadays call "dirty reading" within sacred contexts. Indeed, Browne's poem, as I understand it, confirms Taylor's most interesting claim, that "owning a book one could read silently tended to promote an interior life which could be radically at odds with the reader's public persona; *the practise fostered religious individualism as well as erotic pleasure, and the two easily overlapped.*"[46] The full extent of this overlap is amply attested to by the fact that in 1623 (just ten years before the publication of Donne's text) the most notoriously "libertine" author of the previous century, Pietro Aretino, was being presented to potential reader-consumers not as a writer of deliberately titillating erotica but as a Christian moralist.[47] Against the background of what now seem laughably transparent and disingenuous claims, Browne's argument for the spiritually didactic potential of Donne's erotic verse might have appeared quite reasonable and perhaps not even particularly idiosyncratic.

Finally, it seems worth noting that this conception of the Donnean text as spiritual sex-aid (or sexual spirit-aid) does not necessarily produce a concomitant vision of the reader as passive or "feminized." In other words, Browne does not inscribe the pleasurable experience of reading Donne within a heterosexist paradigm, unlike many of Donne's subsequent critics. Similarly, unlike others of Donne's critics, from Dryden to the present, Browne does not distribute good and bad readers of Donne's poetry along the lines of sexual difference—both the "sharp-eyed" *and* "knowing" interpreters of the 1633 *Poems* are conspicuously ungendered. For Browne, Donne's sacred sex toy is potentially fit for all comers.

IV

> All those who . . . inhabit language are Jews—but in a tropic sense. What the trope comes to is locating the Jew not only as a poet but also in every man circumcised by language or led to circumcise a language.
>
> —JACQUES DERRIDA, *SHIBBOLETH*

In conclusion, I would like to draw some interpretive lessons from this analysis of Browne's poem, lessons that may perhaps help us to avoid some familiar critical pitfalls that have bedeviled Donne's readers during the intervening centuries.

First, Browne's argument that particular acts of interpretation can themselves be taken as guarantees of difference serves as a salutary reminder to those of us in the interpretive business that acts of ideological violence are often foundational to the establishment of interpretive communities. Browne implies that the contrasting reactions of the "sharp-eyed" and "knowing" readers to Donne's acts of sexual representation actually reveal their "real" religious and ethical natures. In Browne's hands, Donne's text becomes a test to help you tell difference—indeed, a better test than circumcision itself—because in Browne's world the way you read reveals who you are. It is a seductive move at one level, partly because it suggests that the greatest pleasure afforded by Donne's text to the knowing reader is the pleasure of knowing oneself to *be* a knowing reader. In other words, Browne offers up the pleasure of absolute security in interpretive practice. However, as the anti-Jewish origins of Browne's religiously derived rhetoric make apparent, absolute security comes at a social cost. What we today recognize as Browne's religious prejudice is also a reminder that anyone who claims the position of the "knowing" reader is always actually a "sharp-eyed" reader with delusions of grandeur; and his or her interpretive certainty is all too likely to be grounded in similar gestures of exclusion, repudiation, and othering. The free play of indeterminacy has had bad press of late, but to offer it as an alternative to this kind of certainty may be less a sign of decadence than it is of tolerance.

Second, and more positively, Browne's poem confirms my central thesis, laid out in my introduction, that the representation of desire constitutes *the* key interpretive difficulty in responses to Donne's work and, moreover, that this has been the case from the moment that this work was first instantiated as a corpus, embodied in a book. Browne anticipates, with remarkable prescience, that an oeuvre such as Donne's will inevitably inspire a value-laden and moralized response from the reader because of its inescapable investment in the language of sex; and as Browne also implies, arguments over the "proper" interpretation of Donne's poems will always stem from the fact that those poems cannot be interpreted apart from the reader's own ideas about what constitutes "proper" sociosexual relations. A better consciousness of the fact that when we discuss Donne's sexual values we are always and already saying something about our own sexual values, and those of our culture and community, may prove productive—as this chapter has suggested, productive not least in regard to questions concerning the relationship between sexuality and the sacred in his writing.

Third, and perhaps most important for future readers, Browne's poem implies that the relationship between sacred and sexual desire during the period in which Donne's poems were written was a relationship in flux. As I noted at the outset, just two years after the appearance of the 1633 *Poems,* the textual arrangement of Donne's works would be transformed by the edition of 1635 into a shape that has persisted without significant alteration to the present day: the poems separated into generic categories that assumed (or insisted on) a hierarchical and teleological distinction between sexual and spiritual desire, placing the "Songs and Sonnets" at one end of the volume and the "Divine Poems" at the other. Yet Browne's poem suggests that the hierarchical nature of this soon-to-be-made distinction—and ultimately the distinction itself—is rendered unclear by the experience of Donne's work when taken "as a whole." This fact may help to explain why "To the Deceased Author" was the only elegy from the 1633 edition to be withdrawn (one is tempted to say *circumcised*) from all subsequent seventeenth-century collections of Donne's work: it expressed ideas that were increasingly unintelligible, unpersuasive, and even disturbing, in the context of a newly emergent, "modern" theo-erotic paradigm.

Donne's "mélange of sacred and secular," so familiar to "most of us," is rendered less recognizable in this context of flux and transformation: less historically idiosyncratic and less precociously modern but also perhaps more daring—perhaps even *radically conservative,* to employ a deliberate oxymoron, in his medieval insistence on a contiguity between the sacred and the sexual that the culture at large was increasingly likely to understand as blasphemous. If, viewed through the lens of Thomas Browne's strange elegy, the Donne "most of us" thought we knew becomes a stranger once more, then one final pleasure that Browne affords us is the pleasure of getting to know Donne all over again. By forcing us to confront distant and distinctly different notions of devotional eroticism, and by forcing us to acknowledge the readerly capacity to take an eroticized devotional pleasure in the text, Browne also invites us to take a fresh delight in Donne's most familiar disorder.

CHAPTER TWO

Donne's "Frendship"

Desire, Convention, and Transgression

Here I develop questions of literary interpretation, devotional eroticism, and historical change opened by my previous chapter, focusing on the conflicting interpretive desires of twentieth-century readers and particularly on the desire to reproduce Donne as a "transgressive" figure. My point of departure: a recent critical conflict over Donne's so-called early verse letters and the homoerotic desires that those poems may or may not express. Locating the origins of this critical conflict in an insufficiently theorized notion of "conventional" language, I attempt to move beyond it by means of some recent scholarly analyses of the early modern slippage between the classically inspired discourse of male friendship and the theological/legal discourse of sodomy. Then, in a final section, I show how Donne's verse letters to his male friends can inform our understanding of some more canonically familiar and putatively "transgressive" works: the "Holy Sonnets" "Batter my heart" and "Show me deare Christ."

This chapter directly addresses an idea only implicit hitherto, the idea that sexuality *has* a history. As no one working in sexuality studies will be surprised to learn, my basic position is derived from the single most well-known proposition in the later writing of Michel Foucault: his claim that, as a category of sexual identity, homosexuality is an "invention" of the nineteenth century.[1] This claim has been accorded axiomatic status within the emergent scholarship of queer theory over the last twenty years.[2] The pages that follow were motivated in part by a desire to push Foucault's logic into the most notionally unreceptive of literary zones: to extend the insights of queer theory, which in Renaissance studies have been primarily confined to readings of the drama, not merely into the provinces of the lyric, but into the lyric corpus of Donne—ostensibly the paradigmatic English poet of heterosexual amour.[3]

To suggest that queer theory holds significant and largely unrealized implications for Donne studies is *not* to imply that Donne was "really" a homosexual (as if contemporary gay men and their allies would even have a particular investment in recuperating him). It is, rather, to insist that *all* representations of desire—*all* accounts of erotic practices and sentiments that we might now label homosexual, lesbian, bisexual, transgender, autoerotic, or indeed heterosexual—can be reconsidered in the light of Foucault's historicizing of the first of these categories. To this extent, queer theory is the opposite of a "minority" heuristic; properly understood, it has the potential to transform our understanding of all human sexuality.

I

> [H]ow can unreadable letters be read, even as they demand to be read as unreadable?
>
> —SHOSHANA FELMAN, *TURNING THE SCREW OF INTERPRETATION*

Donne's so-called early verse letters, a group of some fourteen short poems addressed to his male contemporaries, are generally passed over within the critical literature.[4] When these texts do receive professional scrutiny, they are often disparaged as aesthetically inferior productions or dismissed as thoroughly orthodox in sentiment. In fact, these two responses are generally run together: the poems are said to be artistically weak precisely *because* of their designation as transparently conventional.

Herbert Grierson initiates the dismissive tradition with his monumental edition of Donne's poetic works from 1912. Commenting on the poem addressed "To Mr. T.W." that begins "All haile sweet Poet," he quickly moves to inform the reader that the epithet "sweet" "must not be taken too seriously [because] Donne and his friends were . . . complimenting one another in the polite fashion of the day."[5] The same note is struck by R. C. Bald, who describes the poems as consisting "of little more than elaborate exchanges of compliment." This interpretation leads naturally to a negative assessment of the verse letters' aesthetic merit: "[The poems] are certainly the least mature of Donne's," Bald goes on, at once "unconvincing" and a "concession to the sonneteering vogue."[6] The few subsequent critics to consider the poems follow Grierson and Bald unquestioningly.[7] Even Arthur Marotti, who has done more than any other commentator in recent years to underline the significance of Donne's verse letters, gives these particular texts surprisingly short shrift; racing through eleven different poems in a page and a half of cursory discussion, Marotti concludes with an echo of Grierson, allowing that the poems express "affection" but only within "the formulas proper to . . . polite social relations."[8]

In 1994, however, George Klawitter challenged this critical consensus, insisting that, in the case of the poems addressed to Mr. T.W. at least, Donne expresses a level of affection that cannot be written off as merely conventional. For Klawitter, this sequence of four poems reveals Donne's passionate homoerotic desire for one Thomas Woodward, the younger brother of Donne's Lincoln's Inn friend Rowland Woodward (making Thomas sixteen years old, if we accept traditional compositional dates). Thus, for example, in their respective readings of "All haile sweet Poet," where Marotti discovers nothing more than a polite "acknowledg[ment of] the reception of some verse from his addressee," Klawitter finds a playfully risqué pun praising Woodward's penis ("no subject can be found / Worthy thy quill").[9] Klawitter sees other poems in the sequence as "fervent," reflecting "an obsession with the loved one" (11) and revealing Donne "trying to seduce the younger man" (12). As might be expected, Klawitter also suggests an alternative explanation for the critical neglect of these texts; for him, the interpretive lacuna does not reflect on the aesthetic quality of the poems (which he clearly admires) so much as on the prejudicially heteronormative ideology of prior readers. Clearly, a wide interpretive gulf separates Klawitter from the critics he is concerned to displace, raising an obvious question: Whom should we believe?

At one level, arguments concerning the formulaic or conventional quality of Donne's verse letters appear well founded. The poems belong to a historical milieu in which the category of humanist prose epistle known as the familiar letter stood chief among literary vehicles for the expression of "friendship," a public discourse of affection that regularly adopted the register of intense emotion. This larger tradition of friendship literature, in either its classical or early modern incarnations,

presents a fundamental challenge to Klawitter's reading: for who is to
say that the poems to T.W. are not simply versified examples of a con-
ventional epistolary idiom that almost everybody seems to have prac-
ticed at some time during the period, and that therefore tell us nothing
about Donne's sexual desires?

Klawitter does not address this objection. His argument merely re-
verses the reading strategies that he rejects: he declares present an erotic
cathexis that Grierson, Bald, Marotti, and others declare absent.
Without an alternative framework upon which to ground his interpre-
tation, Klawitter has no means to persuade his readers of the "intense
personalism" in these poems beyond his own conviction that the poems
are, indeed, intensely personal. As a result, he is forced to urge his case
in prose that is sometimes hyperbolic ("in no other group of verses by
Donne can we follow so meteoric a path from hot to cool, light to
dark, headiness to sobriety" [15]) and sometimes coercive ("there is an
anxiety in the first poem to T.W. that we best accept as genuine" [7]).
Ironically, in order to fortify his position, Klawitter closes down the
possibility of reading any other verse letter by Donne in homoerotic
terms, insisting that "none reaches the same intensity of love as those
to T.W." (18).

Nevertheless, Klawitter's argument has merit: boldly original, and
sensitive to the possibility of erotic nuance, it subjects the textual his-
tory of the T.W. poems to a previously unprecedented level of scrutiny,
paying particular attention to one of the most crucial manuscript col-
lections of Donne's verse, the Westmoreland manuscript. This collec-
tion, believed to be in Rowland Woodward's hand, contains several
poems unknown from any other source and more complete versions of
poems that do appear elsewhere; as a result, it is traditionally accorded
a higher degree of authority than many other manuscript collections of
Donne's verse that have survived from the period. Klawitter observes
that in three of the four poems to T.W in the Westmoreland manuscript
certain passages have been "crossed out," speculating that Rowland
himself censored any lines that seemed "too tawdry . . . to pass along
as any heritage of his brother" (12). He records the relevant lines in
his critical apparatus, along with his opinion that they "are among the
most compromising in the letters" (214). Of course, we do not have
to endorse Klawitter's notion that Rowland Woodward personally ex-
cised lines in the Westmoreland manuscript (surely they could have
been crossed out by someone else at a later date?); and his claim that
these acts of "excision" were inspired by "tawdry" or "compromising"

homoerotic content is no less problematic, since the question of what might be thought "tawdry" or "compromising" during this period is precisely the point at issue. But by giving these previously unremarked textual variants such prominence, Klawitter has raised questions that are not adequately explained by the traditional designation of these poems as merely "polite" and "conventional" complimentary exchanges.

Klawitter also draws attention to a verse epistle written in response to Donne by Mr. T.W., a poem reproduced (without comment) in the apparatus of both Grierson's and Milgate's editions. T.W.'s witty reply "To Mr J.D." supports Klawitter's general argument, unquestionably eroticizing the act of poetic exchange between men. Since the poem is relatively hard to find in modern editions, I will reproduce it in its entirety:

> *To Mr J.D.*
>
> Thou sendst me prose and rimes, I send for those
> Lynes, which, being neither, seem or verse or prose.
> They'are lame and harsh, and have no heat at all
> But what thy Liberall beams on them let fall.
> The nimble fyre which in they braynes doth dwell
> Is it the fyre of heaven or that of hell?
> It doth beget and comfort like Heavens eye,
> And like hells fyre it burns eternally.
> And those whom in thy fury and judgment
> Thy verse shall skourge like hell it will torment.
> Have mercy on me & my sinfull Muse
> W^c rub'd & tickled wth thyne could not chuse
> But spend some of her pithe & yeild to bee
> One in y^t chaste & mistique tribadree.
> Bassaes adultery no fruit did leave,
> Nor theirs w^c their swolne thighs did nimbly weave,
> And w^t new armes & mouthes embrace and kis
> Though they had issue was not like to this.
> Thy muse, Oh strange & holy Lecheree
> Beeing a Mayd still, gott this Song on mee.[10]

The first modern critic to comment that this poem "would leave a scandalmonger in no doubt that the two lads had been up to something together" was none other than William Empson, as Klawitter duly notes.[11] Empson, as always, is light-years ahead when it comes to addressing subjects that others miss or repress—but despite his typically bluff manner, his response perhaps betrays a desire to downplay the significance of the exchange. By emphasizing the youth of the participants, Empson seems to be drawing on the notion, familiar from both the Kinsey Report and the culture of the English private school, that sexual contact among young boys is quite common and "normal" (provided one outgrows the habit). But even if we insist on fixing the composition of this poem to the earliest probable date (that is, sometime shortly after Donne first met Roland Woodward upon entering Lincoln's Inn in 1592), then Donne was at least twenty years old and so not really a "lad" by early modern standards (although Thomas Woodward could perhaps still be considered in such terms).

Moreover, it hardly seems fair to imply that only a "scandalmonger" would read sex into this correspondence. T.W. is palpably flirtatious, coyly hesitating over whether the source of Donne's warm regard, his flaming(!) brain, is really divine or devilish ("Is it the fyre of heaven or that of hell?") and then self-consciously adopting a submissive posture before his poetic master ("Have mercy on me & my sinfull Muse"), while the central metaphor of the poem explicitly figures this male-male textual encounter as a female-female sexual encounter ("tribadree" being one early modern term for lesbian sex). Indeed, by the end of T.W.'s "To Mr J.D." the question is surely not whether the text is erotic as whether any contemporary categories of sexual identity adequately describe this eroticism. The poem starts out as a poetic conversation "between men" that it subsequently tropes as sexual intercourse between women, but it ends with the "strange & holy Lecheree" of a reverse-gendered literary version of the immaculate conception: the begetting of a poem-child by Donne's maidenly (that is, virginal) female muse, not upon T.W.'s own female muse but upon T.W. himself. Klawitter's analysis of this poem is not without problems—entirely eliding its potential significance as a representation of *female* same-sex relations, for example—but his assessment of it as "impishly sexual" is not so terribly scandalous.[12]

Framed as they are, then, we have two interpretive perspectives that appear irreconcilable: on the one hand, Donne's verse letters to T.W. are "formulaic" examples of the early modern literature of friendship that tell us little about Donne's actual emotional disposition, and nothing at all about his sexuality; and on the other hand, they are "intensely personal," revealing Donne's passionate homoerotic attachment to the younger brother of a friend, an attachment that appears to have been reciprocated. Dull and conventional, or queer and sincere? A commitment to one position would seem necessarily to constitute a rejection of the other; thus, the logic of noncontradiction forces us to choose between them, although neither reading seems entirely satisfactory.

II

> Everything is opened and read in order to divine, with the best intentions in the world, the name of a sender or of an addressee.
>
> —JACQUES DERRIDA, *THE POSTCARD*

It may be possible to locate the excluded middle, as it were, by turning to the texts themselves. I will begin with the poem Klawitter describes as the most "fervent" of the sequence:

To Mr. T.W.

Hast thee harsh verse, as fast as thy lame measure
Will give thee leave, to him, my pain and pleasure.
I'have given thee, and yet thou art too weake,
Feete, and a reasoning soule and tongue to speake.
Plead for me, 'and so by thine and my labour,
I'am thy Creator, thou my Saviour.
Tell him, all questions, which men have defended
Both of the place and paines of hell, are ended;
And 'tis decreed our hell is but privation
Of him, at least in this earths habitation:
And 'tis where I am, where in every street
Infections follow, overtake, and meete:
Live I or die, by you my love is sent,
And you'are my pawnes, or else my Testament.

(MILGATE, 60–61)

Perhaps the first thing that strikes me about this poem is not its extreme difference from Donne's other poems but, rather, the many elements that it has in common with them and particularly with other verse letters. For example, from his very first line, Donne makes a reflexive turn into the rhetoric of self-deprecation, addressing himself not to Mr. T.W. but to his own poem, which he then calls "lame" and "weake." In another verse letter, addressed to one "Mr. B.B." ("If thou unto thy Muse be married"), Donne takes up the same posture, dismissing his own "rhymes" as:

> . . . prophane, imperfect, oh, too bad
> To be counted Children of Poetry
> Except confirm'd and Bishoped by thee.
>
> (MILGATE, 68)

The same modest pose is again adopted in "All haile sweet poet" (the preceding poem in Donne's sequence addressed to T.W.):

> Now if this song be too harsh for rime, yet, as
> The Painters bad god made a good devill,
> 'Twill be good prose, although the verse be evill,
> If thou forget the rime as thou dost passe.
>
> (MILGATE, 60)

And the idea is expressed again, rather more succinctly, in "The Storme," when Donne tells Christopher Brook: "by thy judgement . . . [my lines are] . . . dignified" (Milgate, 55). Indeed, once we begin to look, we discover Donne deploying the topoi of humility repeatedly throughout this group of verse letters.[13] I will consider some consequences of this rhetorical posture later, but for now I only wish to note the sheer repetition of the device. Anyone familiar with a few of these works, and perhaps even somebody who had only received one, might be forgiven for thinking himself or herself in thoroughly familiar (that is, thoroughly conventional) territory on approaching "Hast thee harsh verse."

Nevertheless, if the first quatrain works to produce a sense of familiarity—as if to say, "This is just Donne doing as Donne does"—then that sensation evaporates with the second line of the second quatrain, when the language of self-deprecation is reversed. Where we might reasonably expect a further gesture toward the dignifying gaze of the reader (a compliment to Mr. T. W. and his taste, perhaps), Donne switches gears and offers instead a fairly outrageous compliment to *himself* and his creativity, explicitly identifying himself with God and his poem with the Son: "I'am thy Creator," he says, and "thou [my poem] my Saviour." This authorial appropriation of divine agency and power is striking enough to rattle even a twentieth-century editor like Milgate, who points out somewhat indignantly in his apparatus that "[t]he analogy . . . breaks down as soon as it has begun, since God's Son is not God's Saviour and does not plead for his Father with a third party."[14] But this literal-minded gloss, which seems intended to undercut Donne's self-aggrandizing project, only highlights the audacity of the image. Even the grammatical structure of the verse underscores

Donne's presumption, for the line functions syntactically as an aside or parenthesis, as if to suggest that his blasphemy were a casual matter.

Donne follows this reversal of conventional expectation with a similarly unconventional compliment to his putative addressee. Developing the religious conceit of the second quatrain into an oblique commentary on scholastic disputation ("questions . . . men have defended / Both of the place and paines of hell"), Donne suggests that such questions are now quite literally academic, because, separated from T.W., he already knows what hell is like: "hell is but privation / Of him." The extravagant force of this flattery will be heard only if we also recognize Donne's allusion to a specific doctrinal conception of hell, not as a burning sulfurous pit but as the *absence* of God, the total deprivation of His love. The idea is powerfully expressed by Donne himself in one of his most famous sermons:

> [W]hen all is done, the hell of hels, the torment of torments is the everlasting absence of God . . . to fall out of the hands of the living God, is a horror beyond our expression, beyond our imagination . . . what Tophet is not Paradise, what Brimstone is not Amber, what gnashing is not a comfort, what gnawing of the worme is not a tickling, what torment is not a marriage bed to this damnation, to be secluded eternally, eternally, eternally from the sight of God?[15]

The unmistakable implication of Donne's argument at this point in his poem, then, is that T.W. is *also* God; in other words, Donne bestows upon T.W. the name of Creator, which, moments earlier, he had applied to himself.

Klawitter notes some of these aspects of the poem in his own interpretation, but while he sees them as singular and unusual, and so as evidence of Donne's profound emotional involvement with his subject, it is hard for me to see them as anything other than what an older criticism called "typically Donnean." The contracted world of the octet in which Donne plays the King of Kings momentarily dilates in the sestet to include the object of address, in a rhetorical movement of expansion and contraction that is thoroughly recognizable from more famous hetero-amorous lyrics like "The Sunne Rising," "The Anniversarie," "The Canonization," or "The Good Morrow." As in those more familiar texts, a rhetoric that purports to be centripetal, spinning an outwardly directed message of affection to another, actually begins by turning centrifugally, becoming an inward-looking hymn to the independent and creative Donnean self, before it expands outward again to include the Other as part of a restructured universe that nevertheless continues to place Donne at its center. This entire process, which we might punningly call Donne's ego-centric spin on the Copernican Revolution, is enabled here by the insistently reflexive motion of a poem that actually *never* makes Mr. T.W. a direct object of address. The intimacy of the second-person pronoun is reserved throughout by the poet for the poem itself.

Moreover, coming as it does only after the position of the Godhead has already been ascribed to Donne and his works, T.W.'s deification seems more of a power-share scheme than a total abdication of omnipotence—as if Donne were suggesting that he and his beloved friend could run the entire universe together. Certainly, by the end of the poem, Donne cannot be said to have completely relinquished the position of the Almighty, for he concludes with another potentially blasphemous self-aggrandizing image. The application of the word "Testament" to his verse in the final line is glossed by most editors as a suggestion that the poem might function as Donne's legal will in the event of his death; but it is hard not to hear an echo of the biblical sense of "Testament" as well. In fact, in the context of his earlier blasphemies, Donne may be hinting that his verse could serve as a kind of "New (lover's) Testament" for future generations or, indeed, that his love for Mr. T.W. will inspire a new religion, as an earthly love that can adequately imitate or perhaps even substitute for divine love.

Once again, these suggestions are (by any orthodox standard) quite outrageous, but they could also be described as typically Donnean; similar arguments were traced long ago in "The Relique" and "A Valediction: Of the Booke."[16] Nor is Donne done with turning familiar poetic convention on its head, for in these final lines he takes the commonplace claim that love poetry confers immortality upon its subject— a claim perhaps most familiar to us today from Shakespeare's sonnets— and applies it to the poem itself: "Live I or die, by you [my poem] my love is sent." Stunningly, it seems that the only immortality conferred by Donne's poetic tribute will be his own; but once again, even this final solipsism could appear almost conventionally Donnean, at least to his more hostile critics.

To summarize: at least one of Donne's "conventionally affectionate" letters of friendship actually seems to employ extravagant conceits and rhetorical devices of a type associated with many of the "Songs and Sonnets"—poems traditionally identified as being among the most sincere, intimate, and loving in the canon of English literature.[17] However, by sketching these affinities, I do not mean to argue that the verse letters are therefore also sincerely erotic poems; nor do I intend to suggest a reverse, corollary argument, that the "Songs and Sonnets" are only conventionally affectionate. Instead, by demonstrating that Donne's ostensibly sincere heteroerotic love poems *and* the apparently conventional homoerotic letters of friendship both draw upon a remarkably similar image repertoire, and share numerous stylistic devices, I am attempting to offer an argument that cuts in both directions, as it were—placing a question mark over both the presumptive sincerity of the first category *and* the conventionality of the second.

We can draw out this argument by developing an apparent paradox that arises from the comparison between the Donne of the verse letters and the Donne of the amorous poems. For in declaring "Hast thee harsh verse" to be "conventionally Donnean," I am of course appealing to a long-standing critical commonplace that already defines "Donnean" as synonymous with extravagance, literal or figural conceit, and the disruption or reversal of convention. In other words, to say that "Hast thee harsh verse" is conventionally Donnean is also—or only— to say that it is conventionally unconventional, which ultimately suggests a distinction that cannot be maintained.

The paradox is only apparent, as I will show; but a version of it lurks behind the difference of opinion with which I began, between Klawitter and the traditional critics he repudiates. For the question of whether the verse letters are "formulaic" or "sincere" proceeds from the assumption that, in the final analysis, a distinction between the formulaic and the sincere can always be maintained. In other words, both sides of the interpretive dispute err in presuming the validity of an opposition between "conventional" meanings, on the one hand, and "sincere" meanings, on the other, and this error precipitates a further series of interpretive problems.

To elaborate: the hermeneutic stance adopted by those critics who dismiss the affective content of Donne's verse letters to T. W. (and others) as "merely conventional" provokes at least two theoretical objections. The first objection is to an initial presumption about the process through which literary conventions are identified. For example, Marotti's casual remarks about "proper social formulas" suggest that the conventional elements of the verse in question are available as self-declaring critical guidelines prior to any act of interpretation. But this cannot be the case, because to describe something as conventional is *already* to have interpreted it. This is not to say that Marotti, or anyone else, may not have very good reasons for declaring a passage formulaic.

It is simply a reminder that formulas and conventions do not float upon the surface of texts like so much social precipitate; they are not pre-established facts but are themselves the result of interpretive reconstruction, and as Klawitter's very different reading attests, their transparency cannot be assumed.

A second and more telling objection follows from the first; because even if conventional formulas were available as a priori interpretive guides, the question of exactly what they were formulas *for* would remain. After all, to say that these poems contain "conventional" or formulaic expressions of affection between men does not ultimately leave us any the wiser as to the order, intensity, social function, or limits of those expressions of affection.

However, similar objections can also be raised against Klawitter's argument. Klawitter's error is to believe that the sincerity of a text must be measured in terms of its distance from convention; that is, he seems to think that the less conventional something appears to be, the more genuine it must be. But as a rhetorician of Donne's stature would have known from any number of textbooks, sincerity itself is a rhetorical posture that comes armed with its own repertoire of conventions. To this extent, sincerity is always performed. To put the point in the now-familiar vocabulary of poststructuralism, *language is always already conventional*—which is simply to say that we can only convince one another of our sincerity, or indeed of anything at all, by deploying a sign system, the meanings of which have been previously (that is, conventionally) established.[18] Therefore, the most effective response to traditional critics who say, "Don't worry about the apparent homoeroticism of this language—it's thoroughly conventional" might not be to say in return, "No, in this particular case it's sincere" but, rather, to insist that the assertion of conventionality does not short-circuit further inquiry: "Yes, this homoerotic language *does* appear to be quite conventional. Now what does *that* mean?"[19]

In fact, by deconstructing the opposition between sincerity and convention, we can render the distance and the difference of history, the very pastness of the past, more apparent. Once we recognize that rhetorical conventions can be looked *at*, as well as looked *through*, then the rhetorical conventions of these verse letters by themselves constitute prima facie evidence that, whatever else might be the case, post-Enlightenment conceptions of sexuality are not operative. Thus, the question of whether these poems express sentiments that are "sincere" or "merely conventional" is rendered doubly meaningless, both to the extent that it is based on an unsustainable opposition and because in this case that opposition presupposes the universality of a distinctly modern attitude toward homoeroticism; it assumes that expressions of homoerotic desire are, always and at all times, *unconventional*.

In other words, the very interpretive system in which the false choice of "sincere" or "conventional" is framed rests on the assumption that homoerotic desire is only legible as a violation of convention, the transgression of a social taboo. Because all prior discussions of Donne's verse letters have taken place within this intellectual framework, those on the "merely conventional" side have been able to assume that since the writing, manuscript circulation, and eventual publication of Donne's verse letters to T.W. prompted no homophobic outcry, the poems could not have been intended as expressions of sincere desire; while Klawitter, on the "sincere" side, points to "evidence" that the verse letters did provoke some measure of homophobic anxiety after all. But if the vocabulary of intense affection between men is indeed thoroughly conventional during the early modern period (as we have for so many years been told), then there is no reason to think that these poems can't be both conventional *and* homoerotic at once. No evidence of transgression is required.

Indeed, in an interpretive universe where homoeroticism is at some level conventional, it becomes possible to imagine many activities, signs, gestures, and forms of social exchange that would be normatively received within our own culture as transgressive, but quite acceptable in an early modern setting. [20] By way of illustration, consider the following historical anecdote from the letters of a contemporary of Donne's, Dudley Carleton, as cited by Paul Hammond in his recent book, *Figuring Sex between Men from Shakespeare to Rochester*. The anecdote concerns a masque performed on New Year's Day in January 1604 in front of James I. Each gentleman participant presented James with a shield, decorated with an impresa, accompanied by explanatory verses. The participants

> delivered theyr scutchins with letters and there was no great stay at any of them save only at one who was putt to the interpretation of his devise. It was a faire horse colt in a faire greene field which he meant to be a colt of Busephelous race and had this virtu of his sire that none could mount him but one as great as Alexander. The King made himself merry with threatening to send this colt to the stable and he could not break lose till he promised to dance as well as Bankes his horse. [21]

As Hammond points out, "[T]he young colt who invited James to mount him" was Philip Herbert, younger brother of the earl of Pembroke and all of sixteen years old at this time. The king's response is no less aggressively flirtatious, hinting that he might take the young Herbert up on his offer and ride him like his own royal steed. This anecdote vividly reveals how a "merry" courtly encounter between an older, authoritative male and a younger man just beginning to take his place in the adult world could be structured around quite explicit expressions of homoerotic desire.

Donne, of course, is not James I. But is it *so* impossible to imagine the textual exchange between Donne and Mr. T.W. taking place in something like a similar spirit—that is, as participating in a socially sanctioned (and indeed, conventional) homoeroticism—without denying the frisson of that eroticism?

III

[A] letter always arrives at its destination.

—JACQUES LACAN, *SEMINAR ON "THE PURLOINED LETTER"*

It may be helpful at this juncture to make clear what I think can and cannot be gleaned from Donne's verse letters to T.W. and T.W.'s reply. It seems to me that one thing that remains beyond our reach is certain knowledge as to whether or not genital contact either occurred or was actively sought by either of the parties in this exchange. As Eve Kosofsky Sedgwick has observed with reference to Shakespeare's sonnets, "[T]he sexual context of the period is too far irrecoverable for us to be able to disentangle boasts, confessions, undertones, overtones, jokes, the unthinkable, the taken-for-granted, the unmentionable-but-often-done-anyway," and so on, with any degree of certainty.[22]

What *can* be said with certainty, however, is that while most manuscript versions of "Hast thee harsh verse" omit line 6 of the Westmoreland version, and while the first printed version of 1633 also omits line 5, and while in the Westmoreland text itself, as we know from Klawitter, these same lines, along with most of line 2 and lines 8–10 are crossed out—in short, while "Hast thee harsh verse" seems to have an unusually troubled textual history—poems like the following were generally reproduced entire:

To Mr. R.W.

If, as mine is, thy life a slumber be,
Seeme, when thou readst these lines, to dreame of me,
Never did Morpheus nor his brother weare
Shapes soe like those Shapes, whom they would appeare,

As this my letter is like me, for it
Hath my name, words, hand, feet, heart, minde and wit;
It is my deed of gift from mee to thee,
It is my Will, my selfe the Legacie.
So thy retyrings I love, yea envie,
Bred in thee by a wise melancholy,
That I rejoyce, that unto where thou art,
Though I stay here, I can thus send my heart,
As kindly'as any enamored Patient
His picture to his absent Love hath sent.

(MILGATE, 64–65)

This poem, presumed to be addressed to Thomas Woodward's elder brother Rowland, is the first sonnet in a verse letter made up of two sonnets and a four-line envoi, and even without taking the time for an exhaustive analysis, it is possible to identify numerous similarities between it and "Hast thee harsh verse." The witty equation of the poet's physical and spiritual essence with the material and formal properties of the poem is common to both, for example—right down to a repetition of the Sidney-esque pun on poetic "feet." The image of the text as a legal testament also reappears, and the general argument of both poems—that they figuratively, legally, and, in the case of the portrait, visually represent their author and his feelings—is the same. Even the grandiose analogy between Donne's creative powers and those of a God can be found in both poems, albeit translated here from a Christian to a pagan register.

By pointing out these more than superficial resemblances, I would not be misunderstood as saying that Donne felt the same passion for both brothers (although I don't think there is anything *inherently* unreasonable about such an idea; the theme of siblings as rivals in desire is common enough). My purpose is rather to foreground the bibliographical and historical questions that forcefully emerge from the juxtaposition of these two ostensibly similar poems: why does the first seem to have such a troubled textual history, while the second apparently does not? What is the content of this scribal and editorial anxiety, if it is indeed even anxiety we are seeing? Just what *is* the matter with Donne's "Hast thee harsh verse"?

At this point, Alan Bray's groundbreaking scholarship on the relation of "friendship" literature to questions of sexuality proves extremely helpful. In an influential essay on the "uncanny" symmetry between the image of the masculine friend and the image of the sodomite during the early modern period, Bray writes: "The distinction between the two kinds of intimacy was apparently sharp and clearly marked: the one was expressed in orderly 'civil' relations, the other in subversive. . . . But . . . on occasion one can also come across a document that appears . . . to be putting the two together and reading a sodomitical meaning . . . into just those conventions of friendship that elsewhere seemed protected from that interpretation."[23] Bray goes on to argue that the potential for some scenes or expressions of friendship to be read sodomitically depended on the absence or presence of additional social signs and conventions that "a contemporary would have seen far more readily than we do."[24] For example, "true" friendships, as distinguished from sodomitical relationships, were generally thought possible only between men of the same social status, because any suggestion that the affective bond in question was based on the desire for economic or social advantage rather than personal loyalty could mark a relationship as potentially sodomitical. At the same time, according to Bray, the category of sodomy was *never* exclusively linked to the incidence of sexual acts alone but always carried with it associations of political and/or theological transgression; thus, the "taint" of sodomy might cling to a friendship if one or the other parties were also to be suspected of condoning or practicing Catholicism, for example. In work building on Bray's initial foundations, Jeffrey Masten has suggested further that "what we normatively now call *homosexuality* is in English Renaissance culture dispersed into a number of discourses" besides that of sodomy, "each of which differently negotiates power relations." Thus, for example, "*pederasty* emphasized an age difference . . . [where] . . . *sodomy* . . . often suggested sexual relations between men of differing social class."[25]

Rereading Donne's verse letters with these ideas in mind, even ostensibly similar poems like "Hast thee harsh verse" and "If, as mine is" can start to look quite different. According to Bray's elaboration of the semiotics of sodomy, the first poem seems far more likely than the second to blur the line separating the literature of friendship from a representation of sodomitical desire. After all, "Hast thee harsh verse" is not only apparently addressed to a younger man but is also by far the more nakedly blasphemous of the two poems—indeed, as my earlier analysis implies, it stands among the more theologically daring poetical works of Donne's oeuvre. Further evidence of this interpretation may be seen in that fact that, as I have already noted, line 6 is the most regularly omitted part of the poem—that is, the line that specifically introduces the notion of Donne as a God-like creator ("I'am thy Creator, thou my Saviour"). It is therefore possible to accept Klawitter's suggestion that "Hast thee harsh verse" might have been thought "compromising," even in a Renaissance context—but only in a far more qualified sense than he intends, because this "compromising" content is almost certainly not reducible to the text's apparent articulation of homoerotic desire. Instead, that articulation seems to have provoked the hand of the censor only insofar as it occurs in conjunction with a display of blasphemous irreverence and/or a transgression of boundaries such as age and class.

Thus, while previous commentators have inevitably grounded their response to Donne's exchange of verse letters with Mr. T.W. in assumptions or speculations about the nature of Donne's sexuality, I would argue that, on the contrary, there is no sexual "truth" to be told by these poems—*not* because they are conventional but because they circulated within an interpretive economy formed prior to the modern disciplinary regimes of sexuality. At the same time, I think the poems *do* bespeak a special affect: the affect of "friendship." But friendship during the Renaissance is a less familiar concept than we have perhaps hitherto realized, with implications that reach beyond our own generally more limited sense of the term; it is an idealized bond of considerable social complexity, imbricated in the literary, educative, religious, and erotic discourses of the Renaissance, with potentially significant interpretive consequences for each of those discourses. This notion of friendship also relates to our modern categories of sexuality in ways that the academic disciplines of literary criticism and history are only now beginning to explicate.

But to say that we cannot discover the truth of Donne's sexuality in these poems of friendship is not to say that therefore they are not erotic or to deny that traditional criticism has determinedly ignored that eroticism. To presume a firm distinction between the language of friendship and the language of eroticism would simply be to reinscribe the binary between convention and sincerity within a new set of terms. Even Bray can be criticized on these grounds; Bray's argument, for all that it helps to explain the variant forms of a poem like "Hast thee harsh verse," defines "friendship" *in opposition* to the homoerotic, to the extent that it conflates homoeroticism with sodomy. For this reason, in a thoughtful engagement with Bray's work, Mario DiGangi has posited the necessity of a further distinction, between sodomy and what he calls "orderly homoeroticism," in order to avoid foreclosing consideration of the discourse of male friendship as itself potentially homoerotic. DiGangi warns us not to reduce homoeroticism to the performance of specific sexual acts, and reminds us that, in any case, "we cannot always be entirely confident we know which bodily acts count as 'sexual.' " For example:

> When is kissing an expression of sexual desire, of affection, or of a social bond? Under what circumstances might our ability even to distinguish these realms be frustrated? In a patriarchal culture, is intercourse always more "sexual" than kissing? Is it more *erotic*? Might nonpenetrative eroticism, such as kissing between women or "sport" between men, subvert patriarchal sexuality? These questions cannot be answered outside of particular contexts, and even then with reservations. In any case, the indeterminacy of the "sexual" should make us skeptical of approaches that deem homosexual "acts" more subjectively and socially meaningful than homoerotic desires or discourses, and that require "evidence" of sexual acts—what would this entail for nonprocreative sex?—before granting the possibility that erotic desire existed.[26]

The key point for my purposes is that homosexuality in the Renaissance cannot be reduced to the sodomitical; the homoerotic is discursively dispersed during this period and manifests in both perjorative and positive forms, including but not limited to the language of sodomy *and* the language of friendship. For these reasons, what H. L. Meakin misleadingly describes as "condemnatory references to homosexuality" in Donne's poetry are beside the point when it comes to the potential homoeroticism of his verse letters. Donne never condemns homosexuality. Instead, like almost everyone else in the period (with the possible exception of that bad boy, Christopher Marlowe), he condemns sodomy. But if he didn't himself think of his exchange with T.W. as sodomitical in character, and if "orderly homoeroticism" constituted an important thread of the social fabric during the period, Donne would have little reason to "veil" the sentiments that now strike some readers as "homosexual"—and indeed, he does not. We are the ones who are obsessed with the veiling and the unveiling, the presence and the absence, the coding and the decoding, and above all, the separation, categorization, and cordoning off of the sexual from other modes of relation; but in the exchange of verse letters between John Donne and Mr. T.W., while desire is certainly figured in an extraordinary variety of ways, combining erotic registers that we now separate into the categories of the homosexual, the heterosexual, and the lesbian, it is *not* cordoned off from other discourses (such as the spiritual or the literary), nor is it "veiled" or coded. John Donne's desire for T.W., however one may finally choose to characterize it, is on the surface of these poems, for all to see—and that, ironically, is precisely why it is so difficult for us to read.

IV

> Rare poems ask rare friends.
>
> —BEN JONSON, TO LUCY, COUNTESS OF BEDFORD, WITH MR. DONNE'S SATIRES

Thus far, I have tried to show why the "conventional" language of Donne's exchange with T.W. (and, by extension, why Donne's desire) is less immediately transparent than previous critics have tended to assume. Along the way, I hope I have also demonstrated that at least one of these "polite" and "formulaic" poems actually employs exactly the kind of hyperbolic and theologically daring conceit for which Donne is traditionally most admired—at least in heteroamorous contexts. Now I want to risk some speculations of a more radical kind by pressing a little harder on the conception of friendship that has emerged here, as both an affective bond and a hermeneutic principle; my ultimate purpose is to sketch some ways in which a deeper understanding of the relation between the social, the sexual, and the theological in Donne's verse letters can also inform a reading of some of the most notoriously powerful and challenging of Donne's "Holy Sonnets." In the final section of this chapter, then, I will build on and develop the following hypotheses:

1. For Donne, the complex literary and social hermeneutics of Renaissance friendship not only legitimated but actively fostered the exchange of erotically charged language between men.

2. Moreover, within the interpretive domain of friendship, these exchanges are (at least ostensibly) beyond aesthetic or moral criticism.

3. Finally, this same complex notion of friendship played a role in shaping Donne's literary imagination when it came to addressing not just his mortal equals and superiors but God himself.

As I have shown in my reading of "Hast thee harsh verse," the topoi of humility constitute a recurrent element throughout Donne's verse letters. One crucial consequence of Donne's humble (im)posture is to make the perspective of his addressee central to the aesthetic success of these poems. Indeed, Donne's self-deprecations are part of a rhetorical strategy that constructs or positions the "friend" as an ideal reader—someone who will always "impute excellence" or provide the confirmatory blessing that makes the poems worthy of the name. In a curious anticipation of reader-response theory, the production/recognition of a "good" poem—in this case, a verse letter—is repeatedly figured as a collaborative activity between author and reader: as we've seen, Donne repeatedly claims that he simply cannot produce good poems without good friends to read them. For Donne, then, one primary function of friendship is to cement the bonds within an interpretive community wherein "imperfect" and "prophane" verse will be "bishoped" (as he writes "To Mr. S.B."). In short, for Donne, there is no such thing as bad poetry between friends.

But Donne does not stop here. The power that Donne grants to friendship extends beyond the realm of literary production, into the domains of the ethical, the emotional, and the spiritual. Consider, for example, the following sonnet, also addressed to Rowland Woodward:

> Kindly I envy thy songs perfection
>   Built of all th'elements as our bodyes are:
>   That Litle of earth that is in it, is a faire
> Delicious garden where all sweetes are sowne.
> In it is cherishing fyer which dryes in mee
>   Griefe which did drowne me: and halfe quench'd by it
>   Are satirique fyres which urg'd me to have writt
> In skorne of all: for now I admyre thee.
>   And as Ayre doth fullfill the hollownes
>   Of rotten walls; so it myne emptines,
> Where tost and mov'd it did beget this sound
> Which as a lame Eccho of thyne doth rebound.
>   Oh, I was dead; but since thy song new Life did give,
>   I recreated, even by thy creature, live.

This critically neglected but quite moving poem is clearly a response to a prior verse letter Donne received from Woodward, now lost. Donne ascribes some remarkable effects to this lost verse letter; for instance, it has redirected Donne's own artistic impulses away from the writing of fiery satires (which are, of course, rooted in feelings of contempt for others) and toward the production of "better" poems (i.e., verse letters of friendship like this one, rooted in higher feelings). But Woodward's lost poem is also credited with restorative powers that go beyond these artistic and ethical realms. In terms that we would now consider classic indicators of clinical depression, Donne writes of his feelings of "emptines" (implicitly comparing himself to a hollow, "rotten" building) and of being "dead" to the world, before he received Woodward's "song." In fact, the depth of melancholia and self-loathing this poem indirectly exposes, even as it wittily expresses gratitude for the alleviation of those feelings, may be one of the most touching things about it. But the boldest aspect of "Kindly I envy" is probably its attribution, in the final couplet, of God-like agency to Woodward. In these last lines, Donne's Lincoln's Inn friend more closely resembles George Herbert's divine "friend" in the poems of The Temple than he does any ordinary mortal; his power is God's power, to create, and Christ's power, to restore life to the dead.

This idolatrous deification of the mortal "friend" is almost as common a device in Donne's verse letters to Thomas and Rowland Woodward as his posture of humble self-deprecation with regard to his own poetry. We've already seen both ideas at work in "Hast thee harsh verse" and "If, as mine is," and we can discover both of them again in the following short lyric, also addressed to Rowland Woodward:

> Zealously my Muse doth salute all thee,
> Enquiring of that mistique trinitee
> Whereof thou'and all to whom heavens do infuse
> Like fyer, are made; thy body, mind, and Muse.
> Dost thou recover sicknes, or prevent?
> Or is thy Mind travail'd with discontent?
> Or art thou parted from the world and mee,
> In a good skorn of the worlds vanitee?
> Or is thy devout Muse retyr'd to sing
> Upon her tender Elegiaque string?
> Our Minds part not, joyne then thy Muse with myne,
> For myne is barren thus devorc'd from thyne.

With the very first word of the poem, Donne characterizes his attitude toward his friend as a religious form of devotion, while the conceit developed over the next three lines transforms Woodward into a holy mystery: a new version of the Christian Trinity. Donne then proceeds to prod Woodward with a series of faintly desperate questions that, in tone at least, bear comparison with the kinds of inquiry that pepper his "Holy Sonnets." "Have you forsaken us all, Rowland?" he asks, even as he ruefully acknowledges that he can understand why he might be the object of Rowland's "good skorn." Adopting another metaphor that recurs in his religious writings, Donne also describes his separation from Rowland as a divorce in the final lines of the poem and expresses the hope that their two Muses (Rowland's being conspicuously genderless) will soon be joined together again, so that Donne's "barren" one can experience artistic insemination.

The small interpretive community of these particular verse letters, then, is made up of ideal readers in a most literal sense: they are men like Gods. If, for Donne, there is no such thing as bad poetry between friends, it appears that there is no such thing as blasphemy, either. But now comes a question. In an interpretive universe where friendship can guarantee both aesthetic and spiritual "perfection," where, between friends, there can be no such thing as bad poetry, and no such thing as blasphemy, is it not just a short step to imagine that for Donne, between friends, there can be no such thing as sodomy—*no matter what form that friendship takes?*[27]

For some, of course, this short step will feel like a giant leap. But don't most of us assume some version of this very same logic—don't we assume that, within the context of a divinized relationship, there can be no such thing as blasphemy and no such thing as sodomy— when we read a poem such as the following?

> Batter my heart, three person'd God; for, you
> As yet but knocke, breathe, shine, and seeke to mend;
> That I may rise, and stand, o'erthrow mee, 'and bend
> Your force, to breake, blowe, burn and make me new.
> I, like an usurpt towne, to'another due,
> Labour to'admit you, but Oh, to no end,
> Reason your viceroy in mee, mee should defend,
> But is captiv'd, and proves weake or untrue,
> Yet dearely'I love you, and would be lov'd faine,
> But am betroth'd unto your enemie,
> Divorce mee, 'untie, or breake that knot againe,
> Take mee to you, imprison mee, for I
> Except you'enthrall mee, never shall be free,
> Nor ever chast, except you ravish mee.[28]

And yet, despite many attempts at critical exorcism, the specters of blasphemy and sodomy continue to haunt interpreters of this text, perhaps Donne's single most famous "Holy Sonnet." As Richard Rambuss points out, "[S]cholars from an earlier generation, those writing in the

1950s and 1960s . . . candidly address and repeatedly fret over the moral and erotic implications of Donne's final metaphorical turn,"[29] if only to reassure us that nothing too unusual is going on here because, in the words of George Knox, "the traditions of Christian mysticism allow such symbolism."[30] In short, at one time criticism invoked prior literary and theological conventions to dispel the aura of transgression that clings to this text, in precisely the manner of traditional readings of the verse letters. A subsequent generation of scholars would prove more willing to register the frisson of Donne's language as a deliberately calculated effect in their interpretations of this poem; but, Rambuss also notes, many also preferred to heterosexualize the scenario that Donne evokes in his final line, describing Donne as "feminized" by the desire he expresses (witness, for example, Ann Baynes Coiro: "The most complete self-abnegation he [Donne] can imagine is, in 'Batter my heart,' to place himself before God as a woman, a woman begging to be raped").[31] As Rambuss cogently argues, such descriptions ultimately owe more to institutionalized heterosexism than to anything in the poem (unless one believes that men cannot be raped); and his own description of Donne's fantasy as that of becoming a "Christian Ganymede, carried off by God and ravished" rightly emphasizes the current of homoerotic violence that energizes this text.[32]

But if previous attempts either to conventionalize or heterosexualize "Batter my heart" are not entirely persuasive, the question remains as to how Donne himself conceived this exercise of rhetorical force. With its intense masochism, with its imagery of rising and standing (common euphemisms for erection in the period), with its extended metaphors of captivity and yearning, with its language of bad marriage and liberatory divorce, and with its final fantasy of divine rape, the poem obviously negotiates the territory of transgression, including the regions of the blasphemous and the sodomitical. But how, exactly, is this negotiation performed? For I suspect that no one would suggest that Donne is *endorsing* either blasphemy or sodomy in "Batter my heart," for all that the poem clearly partakes of those forbidden discourses in some fashion. We are reading Donne, not de Sade; and while it is interesting to realize that these two authors may be more closely aligned than traditional interpretations have ever allowed, they are clearly not engaged in identical literary projects. (I do not mean to imply that there is anything wrong with blasphemy or sodomy, or that all endorsements of either activity are necessarily de Sadean in character, but only to raise the question of Donne's relationship to the transgressive.)

Rambuss himself contends that when Donne begs to be figuratively sodomized by his male God, he is reaching after the sacred "through the violence of a broken taboo," like a seventeenth-century version of such great twentieth-century theorists of transgression as George Bataille.[33] This description certainly catches one effect of Donne's poem, but it does not address the question of how Donne might have arrived at or theorized his own literary practice. Moreover, while I think it quite correct to emphasize the self-conscious eroticism of Donne's language, his deliberately *transgressive* intent seems less obvious. Without entirely dismissing Rambuss's provocative argument, then, in a purely speculative spirit I want to suggest another way of thinking about the shadows of blasphemy and sodomy that fall across this poem. What interpretive spaces can we open up if we try to conceive of the "Holy Sonnets" as verse letters—verse letters written to a *very* special male friend?

After all, for Donne, the generic boundary that separates the religious lyric from the verse letter of friendship may be more indistinct than we have previously imagined. As I have shown, throughout the verse letters Donne's friends are accorded divine powers, becoming the objects of zealous devotion. At the same time, Donne often appears anxious that these friend-gods will turn away from him in his "vanitee," forsaking him as unworthy; and as we saw in "Hast thee harsh verse," the actual absence of the friend-god plunges Donne into hell. Similar expressions of self-doubt and anxiety, and similar fantasies of damnation, can of course be found throughout the divine poems. Besides these similarities, we can further note that the thing Donne seems to want most of all from his friend-gods is also the thing he wants most of all from his God-friend: love. Over and over, the divine poems and the verse letters proclaim love, and hope for its reciprocation, often in explicitly sexualized language. "Inseminate me!" Donne pleads in the conclusion of "Zealously my Muse"; "Ravish me!" he cries at the end of "Batter my heart." But it is also only within these two genres that Donne can express the desire for love in the plainest terms: "I love thee and would be loved," he writes in the conclusion of yet another poem to Rowland Woodward ("Like one who in her third widowhood"); "dearely'I love you, and would be lov'd faine," he writes in "Batter my heart." Interestingly, and I think tellingly, such poignantly simple statements—"I love you and want your love"—have no equivalent in the heteroamorous texts upon which Donne's reputation as a love poet is based.

It was, in fact, in a prose letter to his friend Sir Henry Wotten that

Donne referred to "friendship" as a "second religion."[34] But the generally unremarked resemblances that I have sketched here between his verse letters of friendship and the divine poems lead me to wonder whether this equation was also reversible: to what extent was religion conceivable as a "second" friendship, as it were? The implications for the "Holy Sonnets" are, to say the least, intriguing. For example, could the eroticism of those texts be rendered legible in terms other than the transgressively sodomitical?

I find some support for this suggestion in Arthur Marotti's insight that Donne assumes "a homologous relationship among the religious, political, and sexual orders" in prose tracts such as *Pseudo-Martyr;* Marotti also suggests that "being loved in the spiritual homoerotic context of 'Batter my heart' corresponded to being favored in the political order."[35] Similarly, in an important study of George Herbert, Michael Schoenfeldt has read that poet's religious lyrics with an eye to the dynamics of Jacobean courtly politics, noting the ways in which the language and concepts of earthly society inevitably shape notions of divine authority and heavenly society.[36] Building on the hints provided by this prior scholarship, I want to turn now to a poem that has recently begun to replace "Batter my heart" within literary critical accounts as the most "shocking" of all of Donne's "Holy Sonnets."

> Show me deare Christ, thy Spouse, so bright and clear.
> What! is it she, which on the other sure
> Goes richly painted? or which rob'd and tore
> Laments and mournes in Germany and here?
> Sleepes she a thousand, then peepes up one yeare?
> Is she self truth and errs? now new, now outwore?
> Doth she, and did she, and shall she evermore
> On one, on seaven or on no hill appeare?
> Dwells she with us, or like adventuring knights
> First travail we to seeke and then make Love?
> Betray kind husband thy spouse to our sights,
> And let myne amorous soule court thy mild Dove,
> Who is most trew, and pleasing to thee, then
> When she'is embrac'd and open to most men.[37]

A plea for guidance in matters of faith, playing throughout upon Saint Paul's figuration of the Christian Church as the bride of Christ, the poem's final four lines seem to figure theological certainty as a form of adultery, or perhaps even prostitution, with Christ cast in the role of smiling cuckold or pimp and the Church as willingly promiscuous whore. Numerous critics, in tones ranging from horrified disapproval to "wicked" delight, have now acknowledged this interpretive possibility, but fewer have addressed the obvious and difficult question it raises: what on earth (or in heaven) are we to make of Donne's apparent willingness to figure true knowledge of the Christian faith as a kind of spiritual swap session or metaphysical gang bang?

As it turns out, this poem has an unusually complicated editorial and critical history, making it even more difficult to fathom than "Batter my heart." "Show me deare Christ" is known to exist in only *one* early modern manuscript collection—the Westmoreland manuscript. Readers may recall that this manuscript collection, thought to have been written in Rowland Woodward's hand, is also the only collection to contain a complete version of "Hast thee harsh verse"; indeed, several other poems, including the verse letter to Rowland Woodward, "Kindly I envy," and Donne's "Holy Sonnet" on the death of his wife ("Since she whom I loved"), are also unique to this collection.[38] Thus, even in a culture where the modern distinction between public and private is only emergent, and where the notion of "private" writing is complicated by the fact of scribal publication, "Show me deare Christ" seems to have had a highly restricted audience. Of course, it may only be a coincidence that "Show me deare Christ" was uniquely preserved in a context that also uniquely preserves several of Donne's verse letters; but for my purposes, the fact that the "Holy Sonnets" and the verse letters are linked at what today constitutes their only surviving point of textual origin is resonant.

"Show me deare Christ" was consequently among the very last of Donne's poems to see print. Published for the first time in 1899 with several errors of transcription by Edmund Gosse (who printed it in the appendix of his biographical study of Donne), it would be another thirteen years before the poem finally appeared alongside the rest of Donne's verse, accurately transcribed, in Grierson's edition of 1912. Having emerged into the public domain, the final lines of the poem were passed over by commentators for the next forty years, in favor of attempts to read the poem in the larger context of Donne's theological politics. The first modern critic to acknowledge the "daring conceit of the close" was Helen Gardner in 1952; Gardner also speculated that Donne may have withheld the poem from publication (by which she must mean scribal publication) "because he thought it was too witty a poem for a man of his profession to write."[39] However, perhaps predictably, given the sexual politics of the era in which she wrote,

Gardner provided little indication as to *why* the conceit is "witty," and her actual paraphrase of the poem rather undercuts Donne's "daring." In Gardner's version, the speaker "prays that he may see the Spouse of Christ appear to men, as a wife who delights to welcome all her husband's friends, and whose husband, unlike earthly husbands, delights in her approachability."[40] Nowadays, this euphemism seems either unintentionally comic or unintentionally progressive—since it is normatively surely something of an understatement to gloss the act of taking multiple sexual partners in terms of "approachability." But these coy remarks constitute only the tiniest portion of Gardner's extensive discussion of the poem, the burden of which remains focused on questions of religious disputation and the degree of Donne's faith in Anglicanism.[41]

Where an earlier criticism preferred to puzzle over the problem of which church on what hill, several more recent responses to "Show me deare Christ" seem to imply that it is only the last four lines that are really worthy of attention. For example, Richard Rambuss is (once again) forthright in celebrating the "salvific transgressivity" of Donne's devotional eroticism but offers surprisingly little commentary on the poem beyond calling our attention to how kinky it is. Others tend to read this textual moment as "evidence" of whatever their larger thesis might be. Thus, for Arthur Marotti, the conclusion of "Show me deare Christ" only confirms his general claim that Donne wrote primarily for a restricted, "coterie" audience; while for Janel Mueller, Donne's depiction of "a spouse who fulfils her role by behaving like a whore" only betrays his inability to portray the divine-human relationship as appealing, and thereby confirms her central argument about the pathological relentlessness of Donne's heteromasculinity.[42] But this poem raises questions about the historical relationship between sexuality and religion that cry out for more sustained consideration. Scholars may have "agreed to be shocked by the concluding image," in F. L. Brownlow's words, but the more complex issue of whether and why Donne meant to shock us remains underexplored.[43]

In fairness, the matter is a very difficult one to address, and no simple answer is possible. As my previous chapter indicated, the question of how writers, readers, and auditors in the medieval and early modern periods experienced the deployment of sexual imagery in religious contexts is far from straightforward. Within the Judeo-Christian tradition the appropriation of an erotic vocabulary to represent theological yearning is as old as the Song of Solomon, and striking examples can be drawn from the writings of numerous central figures throughout the history of the Christian church. Moreover, the "shocking" conceit of "Show me deare Christ" emerges out of a thoroughly traditional trope, derived from no less a canonical authority than Saint Paul. Thus, it might be argued that this poem isn't really so outrageous when considered in a broader historical context and that Donne's final image participates in a thoroughly respectable rhetorical tradition that often conveyed the intensity of religious yearning by means of sexual analogy.

However, the secondary relation of sexual to spiritual desire that is always presumed in that respectable tradition seems less than self-evident in "Show me deare Christ." Instead, like Thomas Browne's elegy for Donne (discussed in detail in my previous chapter), this poem seems neither entirely traditional nor precisely modern in its expression of devotional eroticism. On the one hand, "Show me deare Christ" certainly proceeds *as if* the evocation of the spiritual in terms of the erotic should not in any way taint or compromise that spirituality—and to this extent the poem is obviously linked to earlier traditions. On the other hand, in the last four lines the sexual element seems to overwhelm rather than figure forth the divine. As Elizabeth Hodgson writes, "[I]t is the category of the bride, rather than the church itself, which seems in the end 'open to most men' "; the erotic thus takes on a priority over the spiritual in a manner that seems closer to a modern interpretive paradigm.[44]

For Hodgson, and for another perceptive reader of this text, William Kerrigan, this eruption of a contaminating and "whorish" female sexuality onto the scene of spiritual desire can only be understood as an artistic mistake. In Hodgson's words, the poem represents "Donne's *failed* attempt to remake marriage into a purely spiritual metaphor"; and in a similar vein, Kerrigan writes that "the last passage, beautiful as it is, nearly crumbles. Donne . . . *loses control* . . . leaving us aghast at the combination of great verbal power, unquestioned faith, neurosis, and stupidity."[45] As much as I have learned from these perceptive readers, I am less inclined to designate the poem a failure or even to attribute the interpretive problem it represents entirely to Donne's individual psychological temper. Again, as I argued in my previous chapter, at some level the coexistence of traditional and incipiently modern attitudes toward the sexual and the spiritual in this poem are a function of the fact that the relationship between those two terms is a relationship in flux during this period. More specifically, and as we can also see more clearly by reading the poem against the background of the verse letters, this poem belongs to an era when the erotic had barely begun to separate itself from other discursive modes (including the spiritual, the literary, the social, and the political).

But "Show me deare Christ" shows up the limitations of this historical explanation, too, to the extent that my explanatory appeal to cultural change risks transforming one of the most startling analogies in Donne's writing into a mere temporal accident—and, to my ear, nothing about the language of this poem seems accidental.[46] When Donne asks for permission to "court" Jesus' wife, he is also surely quite self-consciously courting the frisson of a near blasphemy (albeit within metaphorical terms that he could ultimately declare canonically sanctioned). Donne's calculated pursuit of a transgressive rhetorical thrill seems still more obvious if we register the pulse of scopophillic anticipation beating across the pentameters of a line like "Betray kind husband thy spouse to our sights," a pulse that is itself made all the more palpable by the hint of wrongdoing that clings semantically to a word like "betray." Add the unmistakably anatomical resonance of the word "open" as it appears in the final line—a pun that implicitly likens the doors of the church to the vaginal passage, and the scene of worship to acts of multiple penetration—and the suggestion that Donne is not fully conscious of the risqué effects of his text simply seems untenable.

In fact, Donne's sexualized allegory of spiritual desire may be even more risqué than has been previously recognized, potentially even more transgressive in an early modern context than "Batter my heart." For although post-Reformation clergymen seem not infrequently to figure themselves as brides of Christ, and even, like Donne in "Batter my heart," to beg for spiritual ravishment, Donne's attempt in "Show me deare Christ" to occupy Christ's position vis-à-vis spiritual marriage is unprecedented, as far as I am aware.[47] Even in a culture that posited the *imitatio Christi* as a means to salvation, this particular act of identification seems excessive. But more important, and as several accounts of Renaissance sexuality have emphasized in recent years, *any* sexual behavior perceived to violate either the "natural" or the social order during this period—including bestiality, interracial and interreligious sex, prostitution, and heterosexual adultery—could be categorized as sodomitical.[48] The adulterous act that Donne's speaker wants to perform with Christ's bride in the final lines of this poem is therefore, according to early modern standards, an act of sodomy.

In other words, with "Show me deare Christ," Donne seems to have pushed the representation of theological desire as far as he possibly can into the territory of the transgressive. But perhaps even more remarkably, he appears to have done so without ever undermining the impression that his poem is grounded in fundamentally genuine theological longing; for no reader of the poem has questioned the sincerity of Donne's desire for knowledge of the true church here, despite the form of its expression. To this extent, at least, "Show me deare Christ" strikes me less as a failure, marked by an unconsciously revealing loss of control, than as a quite brilliantly daring success: a little masterpiece, in fact.

But whether we see the balancing trick of erotic devotion in "Show me deare Christ" as successful or failed, I want to suggest that Donne's willingness to attempt it may owe less to the prior 1,500-year-long tradition of erotically charged theological rhetoric and more to the (no less traditional and erotically charged) rhetoric of patriarchal power relations—a rhetoric most obviously familiar during his own lifetime from the complex discursive and social formations of early modern friendship and that we have seen at work in his early verse letters. After all, by reminding Christ of His own capacity to take (voyeuristic?) pleasure in this erotically charged spiritual endeavor ("thy mild Dove / who is most trew, and pleasing to thee"), what is Donne doing, if not testing the strength of his bond with a powerful male figure—indeed, with *the* all-powerful male figure—through the proposed exchange of a woman (a woman whose own feelings about the deal are predictably left out of account, in classic patriarchal fashion)? If the poem was intended only for a highly select audience of upper-class male readers, as all the surviving evidence suggests, then Donne's attempt to appeal to Christ in such crassly masculinist terms might have been quite in keeping with their prejudices and values.

Further evidence for such an interpretation can be adduced from Donne's decision to make use of, or more accurately, to *return* to, the sonnet form in these addresses to the divine. It is now a commonplace within Renaissance studies that the conventions of the Petrarchan sonnet provided English courtier-poets with a literary vehicle for both hetero-amorous expression and self-promoting acts of male narcissistic display. It is also a commonplace within Donne studies that the poet eschewed the sonnet form in his more well known love poetry, perhaps out of a disdain for Petrarchist mannerisms and an ambition to appear original. But as the verse letters and the divine poems show, there is more than one kind of love; and although Donne may have avoided the sonnet form when writing to or about a *female* object of desire, he seems to have considered it the ideal poetic form when attempting to forge bonds of affection and trust with other men. In the context of the verse letters of male friendship, then, Donne's return to the sonnet as a vehicle for religious expression is more than a random decision and more even than a novel adoption of Petrarchan heteroamorous conventions for a divine love object. By addressing Christ in this particular poetic form, Donne is also approaching Him as if He were simply the most powerful and influential of possible male "friends."

Of course, if we choose to read the poem in this way, emphasizing its attempt to exploit traditional patriarchal bonds over what we might call its sodomitical heteroeroticism, then it may suddenly seem less radically transgressive, despite the fact that the desires it expresses are ostensibly nonnormative. Some kind of radicalism—perhaps a rhetorical or aesthetic radicalism, a self-conscious pursuit of new ways to say things—may be in evidence in "Show me deare Christ"; but if we regard Donne as making his proposition to Christ in all seriousness, then this radicalism ultimately only exposes, without actually critiquing, a deeper ideology of sexual traditionalism: the long and oppressive history of the traffic in women that lies just beneath the central Christian commonplace of church-as-bride.

In other words, the shadows of blasphemy and sodomy might indeed flicker across this poem, as they do across "Batter my heart" and as they do across some of the more theologically daring and intensely worded verse letters like "Hast thee harsh verse"; but in the context of a predominantly patriarchal power structure articulated primarily through the discourse of male friendship, and underwritten by the traffic in women, they are also *never more than shadows*. The relation between the two sets of writings, verse letters and divine poems, might even be described in terms of a deliberately oxymoronic or paradoxical chiasmus: with regard to blasphemy and sodomy, the verse letters are conventionally transgressive, while the "Holy Sonnets" are transgressively conventional. To offer a still more axiomatic formulation: in the world of the "Holy Sonnets," as in the world of the verse letters, trangression is, strictly speaking, impossible (although the interpretive consequences of that impossibility are obviously different in each case). Against this background, we might even feel entitled to risk a deliberate historical anachronism and claim that, in early modern terms, Donne's "shocking" proposition to Christ really represents nothing more outrageous than heterosexuality-as-usual.

Then again, perhaps it is not only eroticism to which we have become unaccustomed, either in conventional poetic exchanges between men or in religious lyric. Humor can also constitute an element of the unexpected in the rarified atmosphere of the literary, and particularly in sacred contexts. In fact, we seem so incapable of imagining a theologian cracking wise that no one who has written about this poem seems to have considered the possibility that Donne may to some degree be having us on here, and my own approach up to now has been guilty of the same literal-mindedness. But is it not possible that Donne might be trying to secure a comedic effect rather than the shocking intensity of transgression, or a traditional male-male bond, by means of his sexually suggestive conceit? Might he be trying to elicit the more complex and complicating shock of laughter? For Donne's attempt to reach the Son of God by means of his indecent proposal is not merely characteristically audacious: it is wildly, absurdly so. Donne's almost Pythonesque dialogue with Jesus in the final lines of this poem ("is she a goer, your wife—nudge, nudge, wink, wink, knowhatimean?") involves an act of anthropomorphism so spectacular and self-aggrandizing that to take it seriously is surely to be somewhat po-faced. (The recent critical tradition suggests that it is far easier for us to think of Donne always as a masculinist egotist than as a self-deprecating humorist, but the easier conclusion is not necessarily the right one.) Might we not therefore conclude that the last lines of this poem are so deliberately and self-proclaimingly audacious that they effectively undercut the anthropomorphosis upon which they depend? To put the question slightly differently: if I am right in suggesting that Donne's speaker in "Batter my heart" and "Show me deare Christ" attempts to close the gap between himself and his deity by appealing, at least in part, to a predominantly patriarchal power structure organized through male-male bonds, bonds that were themselves expressed, idealized, and often eroticized within the discourse of early modern friendship, then can we read that attempt in "Show me deare Christ" as *self-consciously* "failed"—that is, as an attempt that succeeds only in further drawing our attention to the very gap between Donne and deity that it would close and that thereby provides an ironic reminder of the gulf of understanding that divides every mortal from the divine?

If so, then the joke (for once) would not be on womankind but on the speaker and his inevitable postlapsarian condition of spiritual uncertainty, a condition that is reconfirmed by his inability to express the desire for higher spiritual truths except in terms of an all-too-earthly sexual politics. But the persuasiveness of this final reading depends on our willingness to accept some things that literary criticism does not generally seem inclined to believe: that sincere theological yearning is not incompatible with self-deprecating humor; that the narcissistic self-regard of heteromasculinity could sometimes be recognized and ironized by early modern poets, as well as by contemporary politically enlightened critics; and that structures of sexual, social, and political interaction such as the Renaissance discourse of friendship not only inform poetic attempts to address the divine during the period but are also sometimes exposed within those very same addresses as inadequate earthly tools for such a spiritually demanding task.

I do not mean to neutralize the intellectual, erotic, and political challenges of "Show me deare Christ" by arguing that Donne is merely joking—far from it. I have offered these alternative readings of this extraordinary poem in the spirit of speculation rather than certainty, and I know that quite differently nuanced accounts have been written and will continue to be written. But I am ultimately less concerned to convince you of the validity of the interpretations of the texts I have offered here than I am to emphasize the depth of the interpretive problem that Donne's articulations of desire present, both in (perhaps) deceptively "conventional" seeming poems like the verse letters and in (perhaps) deceptively "transgressive" seeming poems like "Batter my heart" and "Show me deare Christ." I have therefore tried to show that the critical debate around Donne's verse letters of friendship can be illuminated by broader issues, including, among other things: the legibility of desires that circulate in texts predating our modern tendency to separate the erotic from other discursive modes; and the degree to which the interpretive logic of a complex early modern discursive formation like "friendship" can cross the generic borders ostensibly dividing the verse letter from the amatory lyric or even from the poetry of prayer.

Finally, I should reiterate that my purpose in this chapter has not been to "out" Donne—an anachronistic project, as I have indicated—but rather to argue against the ongoing constitution of "the greatest love poet of them all" in relentlessly heteronormative terms that are demonstrably anachronistic and that circumscribe the meaning and application of the word "love" in ways that Donne himself does not.[49] If the interpretive histories of Donne's conventionally transgressive verse letters and his transgressively conventional "Holy Sonnets" teach us anything, they teach both the absolute necessity *and* the extraordinary difficulty of attending to the cultural contingency of eroticism.

CHAPTER THREE

Donne's "Irregularity"

Desire's Measure

My first chapter addressed historical transformations in the relationship between religion, eroticism, and the material conditions of literary representation, retheorizing seventeenth-century hermeneutics in order to make some proposals about Thomas Browne's interpretive desire for an "uncut" Donne. My second chapter addressed historical transformations in the relationship between sexuality and identity, retheorizing the conventions of friendship in order to make some proposals about the contemporary interpretive desire for a "transgressive" Donne. In this next chapter I address historical transformations in the literary-critical practice of prosodic evaluation, retheorizing the concept of meter in order to make some proposals about the long-standing interpretive desire for a "regular" Donne. Thus, where my first chapter attempted to imagine the interpretive conditions of the past, and the second emphasized the differences between the interpretive paradigms of the past and present, in this chapter I trace a more linear narrative, following the procession of answers to a single question—is Donne a metrically "regular" poet or not?—from the seventeenth century through to the twentieth.

A central claim of this study, that the representation of desire constitutes the fundamental locus of interpretive disagreement over Donne's work, is thus tested in the context of a discussion that ostensibly turns on the most purely formal of considerations. But I also hope that my argument demonstrates some of the wider implications of attending to the role of interpretive desire in our critical practice. My conclusions speak as much to our understanding of the concept of meter itself as to our understanding of Donne's texts.

I

> With poetic rhythm, we have come to a topic that is in some sense the very heart of the matter of poetry.
>
> —SHIRA WOLOSKY, *THE ART OF POETRY*

Can you hear what I hear? To ask such a question is to be reminded of the inevitably subjective nature of sensory data, even in the attempt to elicit some independent verification of our experience. But the question can also function as a test, intended to confirm not our own perceptions so much as the auditory competence of the person interrogated (as, for example, in musical examinations that require a person to sight-sing). In such cases, we do not judge our ears by the other but the other by our ears. The question of which question we hear—the request or the test—depends of course on where we hear the emphasis: "Can you hear what *I* hear?" or "Can *you* hear what I hear?" (or, perhaps, "Can you *hear* what I hear?"). The following argument turns on these basic issues of emphasis and cognition, although the particular emphases I have in mind are of a special, paradoxical kind; they are, first and foremost, unheard emphases, textual emphases, the emphases that we speak of "hearing" in the printed voices of English poetry. These silent stresses are traditionally the province of that increasingly rare bird, the prosodist, an academic species noted both for its rebarbative lexical plumage and for its peculiar habit of chopping poems into manageable bite-sized pieces and exhibiting them in taxonomic display, like frogs preserved in formaldehyde. In fact, since we are in prosodic territory, I should perhaps emend my opening question accordingly to, "Can you hear what I *see*?"—a synesthetic formulation that better reflects the difficulty of the prosodic task.

Prosodists have developed an impressive range of tools to describe the voices in their heads (or, to adopt a contemporary prosodic idiom, to describe what Garrett Stewart calls "the conjoint cerebral activity and suppressed muscular action of a simultaneously summoned and silenced enunciation").[1] According to historical context and theoretical bias, they speak variously of numbers, measures, and feet; of on- and off-beats and backwash rhythms; of stress, or accent, or pitch, or volume, and the differences between them; of metrical sets and grids; of the continuities between the rhythms of spoken English and the pulse of the blood, or the pounding of the heart, or the rise and fall of the breath; of amphibrachs and catalectics and the existence (or nonexistence) of spondees; of syncope and caesura; of morphophonemes and extrasegmental units; of tension and counterpoint; and, with ironic repetitiousness, of the importance of variation. But the sheer proliferation of these terms and vocabularies only serves to throw the failures of prosody into stark relief. As long ago as 1965 Seymour Chatman observed that "(1) Metrists do not agree upon the number of syllables in a given word or line; (2) Metrists do not agree upon whether a given syllable is prominent or not; (3) Metrists do not agree upon how the syllables are grouped";[2] more recently, the first sentence of a collection of essays titled *Meter in English* states, "An outsider would be startled at the lack of consensus among poets and metrists about the nature of metrical verse," indicating that little has changed since Chatman's time.[3] To make matters worse, prosodists are unusual even among literary scholars for heaping scorn upon their own enterprises and for the "savagely civil footnotes" with which they dispatch other members of their kind.[4] T. V. F. Brogan's comment that prosody has been subject "to more eccentricity and confusion, more nonthink and doubletalk, than probably any other discipline in the realm of letters" is no more than typical.[5]

But such self-flagellating rhetoric also tends to precede and perhaps even license a rather more grandiose claim; for despite the confusions and contradictions of the discipline, traditional prosodists can always contend that they alone attempt to describe the formal linguistic device most frequently proffered as the single essential characteristic of poetic language in general (or at the very least, of almost all English poetry written before this century and of much written since): that is, of course, meter. The notion that "meter is the first and only condition absolutely demanded by poetry"[6] (to quote Hegel in the place of numerous possible authorities) is a familiar critical commonplace; and even in the wake of the "free verse" modernist revolution, our understanding of nonmetrical rhythm has remained "theoretically dependent in significant ways upon metrical rhythm or versification," as Richard Cureton has recently noted.[7] This theoretical debt can be most clearly seen in the oft-cited remark of T. S. Eliot—a figure whose credentials as a practitioner of vers libre remain impeccable, whatever else may be said about him—that meter is an essential element "in even the 'freest' verse," lurking like "a ghost behind an arras . . . to advance menacingly as we doze, and withdraw as we rouse."[8]

Given the centrality of meter within almost all traditional prosodic theories, the diagnosis of metrical "irregularity" obviously constitutes a grave accusation, synonymous with the charge of being "unpoetic." Indeed, the seriousness of the accusation provides one explanation for the longevity of a critical argument over Donne and his own perceived metrical "irregularity"—a perception that has disconcerted some his most famous readers at various moments during the last 300 years.[9] It is to the argument over Donne's "irregularity" that I shall now turn, in the belief that its sheer persistence within Donne studies reveals not only something about his texts and the responses they encourage, but also something about the pleasurable excitations, the ideological functionalism, and finally, the explanatory limits of meter itself, as traditionally conceived.

II

> These lines can show you where the accent went,
> But with their content I'm not yet content.
>
> —JOHN HOLLANDER, *RHYME'S REASON*

Ben Jonson's remark to Drummond "that Donne, for not keeping of accent, deserved hanging"[10] constitutes the first recorded criticism of Donne's versification. Initially a lone voice of complaint, Jonson—always the most severely neoclassical of English Renaissance poets—anticipated what would eventually become an Augustan orthodoxy. Samuel Johnson's sardonic comment that the metaphysical poets wrote verses in "rugged" and "rough" meters that "stood the trial of the finger better than of the ear" is only the most familiar version of a position that we can find restated again and again throughout the eighteenth century.[11] Moreover, as Deborah Aldrich Larson has noted in her useful reception history, all the surviving "imitations of Donne's verse [dating from the period] 'regularize' his meter."[12]

These Augustan revisions of Donne's "numbers" often seem to displace anxieties about the content of the verse onto the form. Thus, for example, Pope's rewritten versions of Donne's second and fourth satires are praised by Joseph Warton specifically and only for the degree to which the meter has been enhanced: "Pope succeeded in giving harmony to a writer, more rough and rugged than even any of his age, and who profited so little by the example *Spencer* had set, of a most musical and mellifluous versification."[13] However, reading Pope's "improved" texts alongside Donne's, it is hard to believe that metrical regularity forms an exclusive or even primary concern; in his version of Donne's second satire, for example, references to dildos and sodomy are discretely cleaned up along with the scansion. In other words, Pope's prophylactic pentameters could be said to provide a barrier against the accusation of moral impropriety as well as that of technical imperfection.

To suggest that eighteenth-century complaints about Donne's metrical "irregularity" actually functioned as a euphemistic screen concealing larger anxieties about sexual "irregularity" is, of course, to expose a presumptively formal and aesthetic debate as simultaneously implicated in social and moral issues. But questions remain as to the precise nature of the role played by meter in the production of a readerly enjoyment that is itself conveyed in the redolently sensual terms of a vividly tactile opposition. Exactly what kind of pleasure does "smooth" meter make available to an eighteenth-century literary sensibility such as Warton's (or, indeed, to one such as Pope's), and exactly what kind of unpleasure does Donne's "rough uncouth measure" evoke?

The (to modern ears) somewhat hyperbolic language in which Donne's unmetrical verses are repudiated provides a clue. In most commentaries of the period, Donne's literary merit, if recognized at all, is characterized as a "disguised" or "buried" content that one must struggle to discern beneath a less worthy formal surface.[14] However, this formal surface is itself often described in strikingly visceral language. Returning to Warton, for example: in his edition of Pope's *Works* we find him complaining that "Donne . . . left his numbers so *much more rugged* and *disgusting,* than many of his contemporaries"; and elsewhere in the *Essay on Pope* that I have already cited he describes Donne as having "degraded and deformed" his "sterling wit" beneath his "harsh . . . diction."[15] Warton's language is echoed in a review of his *Essay* in an issue of *The Monthly Review* from 1776; the anonymous author actually criticizes Warton for being too soft on Donne (to use another tactile metaphor) before going on to ask, "[Has] any man with a poetical ear, ever yet read ten lines of Donne without disgust?"—a rhetorical question, of course, while the reference to "a poetical ear" confirms that it is once again Donne's irregular meter and not the content of his lines that inspires revulsion.[16] James Granger employs a similar vocabulary of abjection a few years later in his *Biographical History of England,* which describes Donne's thought as "debased by his versification"; and this phrase is also repeated verbatim in the *Encyclopaedia Britannica* entry on Donne from 1779.[17]

Disgusting, deformed, debasing, and degrading—these, then, are the adjectives with which Donne's meter is most frequently described during the period. But once the draperies of regular meter are overlaid upon his work by a "smooth" versifier such as Pope, something miraculous happens. According to one grateful reader, by making it possible for Augustan readers to appreciate his hitherto hidden qualities, Pope "preserved [Donne] . . . from perishing." As still another declares, Pope "shewed the world, that when translated into numbers . . . [Donne's satires] are not inferior to any thing in that kind of poetry."[18] Far from being "disgusting," then, Donne in metrical dress proves a considerable poetic talent after all. Regular meter curbs Donnean excess, becoming the means whereby readers may take pleasure in literary material that they would otherwise feel obliged to reject violently. Less prosaically, we might say that for these particular eighteenth-century readers regular meter provides a way to paddle in Donne's "disgusting" satirical sewer without becoming soiled themselves; or, to use a different but no less apt metaphor, they seem to have believed that a strict metrical diet would keep them "regular" in every other way, too.[19]

The anal origins of this impulse to regularize the positions of metrical stress are underscored if we recall Freud's remark in "Character and Anal Erotism," that "dirt is matter in the wrong place."[20] Indeed, the phrase "matter in the wrong place" not only provides a fairly precise definition of metrical irregularity in and of itself, but also suggests a psychoanalytic explanation for the strongly affective language of Donne's hostile eighteenth-century readers. The matter of Donne's lines does not coincide with the meter—it is in all the wrong places, so to speak—and consequently, the lines are "dirty": that is, disgusting, debased, and degraded. The rewriting of these lines as strict iambics can therefore be interpreted as a cleanup operation in several senses, as well as an example of the pleasurable imposition of orderliness that Freud also associated with anality.

In this context it is striking that Donne's second satire—the very poem that Pope first selected to "regularize"—should itself contains a passage that figures failed poetic creativity in unmistakably anal terms. After a wickedly funny series of lines condemning the bad poets of his generation as ineffectual and impoverished literary fashion victims, Donne pours his scorn upon the plagiarist, portrayed as the greatest poetic offender:

> But hee is worst, who (beggarly) doth chaw
> Other wits fruits and in his ravenous maw
> Rankly digested, doth those things out-spue
> As his own things; and they are his owne, 'tis true,
> For if one eate my meate, though it be knowne
> The meate was mine, th'excrement is his owne.[21]

Pope renders the same episode as follows:

> Wretched indeed! but far more wretched yet
> Is he who makes his meal on others' wit:
> 'Tis changed, no doubt, from what it was before;
> His rank digestion makes it wit no more:
> Sense, passed through him, no longer is the same;
> For food digested takes another name.[22]

It is hard to know where to begin anatomizing this episode of alimentary intertextuality, but we might start by observing that Donne's poetic plagiarist seems to be a lot hungrier than Pope's ("ravenous"). His adverb, "beggarly," transforms the poetic rival into a starving vagabond, gorging himself on Donne's wit and then, perhaps unaccustomed to such rich fare, vomiting it up again. Indeed, Donne's imagery here evinces an investment in orality at least equal to his investment in anality as a figure for the process of poetic production. The "maw" that "chaws" and "spues" is as significant as the digestive system that defecates. In this context, it is perhaps also worth noting that five of these six lines are enjambed, as if to suggest mimetically the breathlessness associated with rapid, gluttonous eating and also the uncontrolled "splurge" effect of a poetry that is spewed forth in an undifferentiated mass.

In contrast, Pope's lines are "end-stopped" (even the traditional prosodic terminology here suggesting constipation), while Donne's "ravenous maw" is quite literally "no more." At the same time, Pope's account arguably pays a more lingering attention to the passing of poetic passages through the plagiarist's metaphorical body, particular in that line, at once precise and evasive: "Sense, passed through him, no longer is the same." Interestingly, this line is one of only two in the excerpt to open with a trochaic rather than an iambic stress (a device that traditional prosodists call an "inverted first foot"—but perhaps we can do without adding further body parts to this particular scene). The initial stress/unstress pattern, combined with the difficulty of pronouncing aspirated, plosive, and dental consonants in swift succession, has the effect of slowing the line down considerably—almost as if Pope were trying to make the reader savor the metaphorical digestive process.

However, perhaps the most striking aspect of Pope's "regularization," when considered as a form of anal eroticism, is the unavoidable fact that Pope's relationship to Donne here is analogous to that of the plagiarist poet as described in Donne's text. This means that, in Donne's terms at least, Pope's poem is itself a piece of shit—the poetic "excrement" that results from a meal of Donnean wit. The traditional classical etymology that associates poetry with "making" takes on an unexpected resonance; but more important, an act that initially seemed to signify as aggressively revisionary or corrective reveals itself in its excre-mentality to be a primal form of homage, an offering of the most basic possible gift from a child to his poetic parent.

At the very least, these poetic excerpts suggest some interesting metaphors with which to redescribe the formal movement of the two authors' respective poetic rhythms—metaphors that may be no less useful than the descriptive terminology of conventional prosody. On the one hand, we can liken Donne's rhythm here to an emetic—spasmodic and convulsive, spilling over teeth, tongue and line-ending alike in a torrential slurry (and I am happy to see a partial confirmation of this idea in Stanley Fish's memorable characterization of Donne's rhetoric as "bulimic"); and on the other hand, we can describe Pope's rhythm, at least in this passage, as more laxative—indeed, Samuel Johnson's remark that Pope's style is "always smooth, uniform and gentle" seems almost too apt.[23]

III

[W]ho made you Inspector of Metres?

—OVID (TRANS. PETER GREEN), *THE AMORES, BOOK I*

If we turn to the nineteenth century for subsequent contributions to the discussion over Donne's prosody, the connection between anality and the desire to impose regular versification is once again discernible. The particular contributor I have in mind is Coleridge—a figure whose role in the rehabilitation of Donne's poetic reputation and whose troublesome bowels are equally well documented. Coleridge not only commented extensively and appreciatively upon Donne's verse, but he also adapted and revised Donne's lines on several occasions. In an effort to describe the principles upon which he based that revisionary practice, he records the following passage of typically ecstatic loopiness in one of his later notebooks:

> *The Filter*
>
> By successive chipping the rude block becomes an Apollo or a Venus. By leaving behind, I transmute a Turbid drench into a crystalline Draught, the Nectar of the Muses. The parts are another's: the Whole is mine. To eject is as much a living Power, as to assimilate: to excrete as to absorb. Give therefore honor due to the Filter-poet.[24]

In the current context, these lines serve as a useful gloss on Pope's activities, and even as a neat riposte to the Donnean charge of shitmaking, with the counterclaim that excretion is as much "a living Power" as absorption—all of which might lead one to suspect that Coleridge's reaction to Donne's versification was not all that different from that of his Augustan predecessor. However, Coleridge's response is actually very different from that of Pope, at once more complex and more confusing.

For example, some years earlier, Coleridge declared that Donne *was* actually a "strict" metrical poet after all, and that the appearance of "anti-metrical" lines, as he called them, were the result of the poems having been "grievously misprinted." Therefore, Coleridge argued, "we are entitled to alter the text, when it can be done by simple omission or addition of *that, which, and,* and such 'small deer'; or by meer new placing of the same words—I would venture nothing beyond."[25] This last deliberately modest locution, proffered with all the humble superiority of a Jeevsian butler gently correcting his master's poetic etiquette ("might I recommend the insertion of a conjunction at this point, sir?") is worlds away from the self-aggrandizingly transported "Filter-poet." But for my purposes it is significant that even in this less ecstatic mode Coleridge reserves for himself a small "regularizing" pleasure when reading Donne. However, in order to grant himself that pleasure, Coleridge must also perforce convince himself that the matter he rejects—or, perhaps, "ejects"—is not Donne's own "dirt" but rather an accretion that has built up upon the texts after years of careless treatment beneath rude, ink-stained hands.

At the same time, and somewhat contradictorily, elsewhere in his commentary Coleridge's descriptions of Donne's meter seem to acknowledge a lack of conventional Augustan "smoothness," as, for example, in the following: "Since Dryden, the meter of our poets leads to the sense; in our elder and more genuine bards, the sense, including the passion, leads to the metre. Read even Donne's satires as he meant them to be read, and as the sense and passion demand, and you will find in the lines a manly harmony."[26] Obviously, at one level, Coleridge's attempt to describe a formal aesthetic by recourse to some kind of normatively positive notion of the "manly" depends for its force upon a traditional sexist association of meaning with masculinity ("read Donne's lines as he meant...and you will find...a manly harmony"). But the more original and influential aspect of Coleridge's comment may be located in his suggestion that in Donne's poetry the relationship between the "sense" or meaning of the lines and the meter is of a special significance; according to Coleridge, we cannot hope to perceive the second unless we have arrived at an understanding of the first. The importance of this hierarchical connection of meaning to meter for Coleridge is attested to by the fact that he makes the same point again, still more emphatically, elsewhere in his comments on Donne: "in poems where the writer *thinks,* and expects the reader to do so, the sense must be understood in order to ascertain the meter."[27]

Of course, Coleridge hasn't solved the problem of Donne's perceived irregularity with this move so much as he has shifted the origin or location of that perception from the text itself to the interpretive activity of the reader. Thus, the immediate rhetorical implication of Coleridge's final position is that anyone who reads Donne as "antimetrical" has simply failed to understand him. At another level, Coleridge's contradictory postures suggest that he had not entirely surmounted the Augustan demand that any poetry worthy of the name must be "smooth" in its prosody. Even in this last cited argument, with its apparent emphasis on the "sense" of the lines, Coleridge can be read as underlining the priority of meaning over meter, on the one hand, while reinscribing the aesthetic centrality of metricality, on the other. Donne's "sense" is rendered significant precisely insofar as it reveals a "strict" metricality or "manly harmony"; which is to say that Donne's meaning matters only or primarily to the extent that it makes visible an essentially meaningless formal feature of the verse (a meaninglessness that is essential in at least two ways: first, to the degree that Coleridge's logic insists that we regard meaning and meter as related but separate entities; and second, since that same logic also seems to assume that, without the presence of meter, Donne could not be said to have been writing poetry at all, no matter how meaning-full his lines may otherwise seem).[28]

However, despite or perhaps because of the contradictory elements in Coleridge's various arguments, which are only partially obscured by his occasional recourse to an impressionistic and dubiously gendered vocabulary, his comments held great appeal for those twentieth-century critics drawn to wrestle with the question of Donne's "irregularity." Indeed, by claiming that a proper understanding of Donne's meaning necessarily entailed recognizing his metrical regularity, Coleridge initiated an argumentative strategy that persists to the present day.

IV

> Heard melodies are sweet, but those unheard
> Are sweeter . . .
>
> —JOHN KEATS, *ODE ON A GRECIAN URN*

Among Donne's twentieth-century readers who tackle the issue, Arnold Stein comes closest to critiquing some of the more limiting conceptions of traditional prosody. In the first and most important of several articles he devotes to the subject of Donne's meter, Stein moves to dismiss the absurd consequences of an overly narrow application of "foot-based" prosodic schemes—as if, in his words, "only the 'normal' foot is 'correct.' "[29] Stein's placement of scare quotes around "normal" and "correct" suggests a perceptive wariness on his part and perhaps even a sense of the disjunction involved in using a potentially morally loaded vocabulary in a putatively neutral taxonomic context. Stein is also clearly aware of the phantasmatic element of traditional prosodic discussions that claim to discover an underlying regularity in Donne's verse. Thus, he writes that those who "read Donne as if every foot were an ideal iambic" appeal to what he calls "esoteric methods [such] as reading with 'hovering accent,' 'level stress,' or 'veiled rhythm' "; these readerly strategies, according to Stein, ultimately "consist in refusing to commit oneself audibly, while enjoying infinitely delicate rhythms within the private recesses of one's own ear."[30] This striking image of the traditional prosodist "enjoying" private and quite literally unspeakable pleasures based upon acts of refusal or withholding would seem to bring us back to the little room of anal eroticism once again. But whatever the origins of the "infinitely delicate" enjoyment Stein describes might be, these "private" prosodic pleasures are for him acts of critical self-indulgence rather than objectively descriptive or didactically valuable pronouncements. While he accepts that some readers might not be able to help indulging themselves, he doesn't really seem to approve.

Nevertheless, Stein's article goes on to reinscribe many of the traditional prosodic formulas he initially repudiates. In fact, his conclusions are really little more than an elaboration of the second Coleridgean position outlined previously: that if we read Donne according to the "sense" of the line, we will also inevitably find him to be metrical. As Stein writes: "[W]henever [meter] comes into conflict with sense it is forced to submit, or what is more accurate, to compromise. The modification of meter to suit the sense actually improves the rhythmical beauty by furnishing variety and welcome modulations." We might begin by noting that Stein's preferred description of the relation of meter to sense here evokes (and then immediately shys away from) a vocabulary more sadistic than anal erotic in its associations—meter "is forced to submit" to sense. Still more important for my purposes, Stein, like Coleridge, leaves unexplained the process of how exactly metrical "modification" is supposed to occur. Although, again like Coleridge, Stein is determined that "poetry is not to be read as prose"—he criticizes Joan Bennett for reading Donne's verse as if it were—when it comes to indicating how stresses dictated by "sense" (or by a prose syntax) can take priority over stresses determined by "meter" (or a poetic syntax) in a linguistic idiom that is still somehow unmistakably metrical, we are only told that we are in the presence of an aesthetic "compromise," the details of which are left impressionistically vague.[31]

Stein then goes on to provide a series of descriptive readings that are often indistinguishable from the kind that he himself initially castigated for "refusing to commit." For example, without actually marking any positions of stress, Stein quotes the famous first line and a half of "The Goodmorrow": "I wonder by my troth, what thou, and I / Did, till we lov'd?"[32] Then he declares that the "line uses the iambic form only as a base for its own rhythms, the while making subtle variations, impossible to record exactly." At the same time, we are assured that "the iambic pattern which is implicit . . . gives . . . a beauty and a force beyond the reach of mere prose."[33]

One possible (traditional) response to this reading would be to say that it is not immediately clear that the first line, at least, is using "the iambic form *only* as a base for its own rhythms." Considering the meter of those first ten syllables—"I wonder by my troth, what thou, and I"—according to foot-based scansion, I am tempted to say that there is a fairly strong case for seeing it as a regularly iambic line (with the possible substitution of a spondee in the third foot), rather than as merely implicitly iambic. Indeed, even if you feel that you know what a phrase like "implicitly iambic" means (and I am increasingly uncertain that it has much substantive descriptive value at all), it still must be acknowledged that thousands of other similar lines in English poetry have never had their regularity called into doubt.

Alternatively, one might argue that the appearance of "irregularity" in this famous first line is actually a retroactive effect created by its sharp enjambment and the strong stress on the first syllable of the *second* line. This retroactive effect can be seen most clearly if we rewrite the entire line and a half so as to eliminate the enjambment, as: "I wonder by my troth, what thou, and I / Had done, until we lov'd . . ." To my eyes and ears, the first line suddenly appears far more "regular" once this change to the second line is made, even though it has not itself been altered in the slightest. To make such an argument not only exposes the way traditional foot-based scansion tends to hypostatize line endings over the syntactic significances that more than occasionally cross them, but also reveals the problematic consequences that result from our basing prosodic conclusions about the "regularity" or "irregularity" of a poet's meter on what are finally arbitrarily selected segmental units of verse.

However, in making this claim, I could still be accused of playing the game within traditional terms, because such a response continues to prioritize the issue of meter and the appearance of metrical "regularity" or "irregularity" as the prosodic matter of greatest moment. Indeed, I have come perilously close here to what Stein might have seen as typical prosodic self-indulgence, performing a Pope-like act of revision, ostensibly to score an interpretive point but actually in pursuit of, well, the pleasure of imposing regularity, if I am honest about it. Having admitted and even partially succumbed to this temptation, I shall therefore resist proceeding any further with this line of argument and instead refocus on the implications of Stein's apparently unconscious drift from initial skepticism into what I have suggested are all too commonplace prosodic platitudes about the persistence of an "iambic base" against or through which Donne's actual lines are said to produce "a beauty and a force beyond the reach of mere prose."

These implications are best unpacked by turning to another article, one of the last attempts to assert (yet once more) the "fact" of Donne's metrical "regularity"—Graham Bradshaw's "Donne's Challenge to the Prosodists," published in the Oxbridge-dominated journal *Essays in Criticism* in 1982. Perhaps predictably, Bradshaw begins by evoking and then rephrasing the Coleridgean dictum that priority must be given to "sense" in any proper reading of Donne's works: "prosody interacts with semantics," he declares, "and we cannot scan without understanding."[34] From these promising beginnings, Bradshaw goes on to repeat Coleridge's subsequent drift into the realm of contradictory double-assertion. Thus, quoting a line and a half from Donne's third satire—". . . but unmoved thou / Of force must one, and forc'd but one allow"[35]—Bradshaw freely admits that "any attempt to . . . make the verse sound . . . more conventional [that is, iambic]" would involve "turning Donne's passionate sense into nonsense." In short, Bradshaw concedes from the first that these lines cannot be articulated in such a way as to make them sound metrically regular without risking an obvious distortion of their meaning. But with his very next breath, Bradshaw makes a statement that flies in the face of this admission: "What, then, is the metre?" he asks. He answers, in firm italics, *"Regularly iambic, of course."*[36]

How is Bradshaw able to claim that, on the one hand, the line would become "nonsense" if spoken aloud in a manner that would sound the "conventional" iambic stresses and, on the other hand, that the meter is *"of course"* regularly iambic? As he will go on to say, he is basing this assertion on a distinction between what he calls "lexical stress" (that is, stress as it would occur in everyday speech or prose) and "metrical stress" (that is, stress as determined by an abstract metrical grid or set). Therefore, according to Bradshaw, those critics who would describe the above lines as metrically "irregular" simply because they cannot be pronounced as strict iambs are guilty of a "failure to distinguish between metrical *ictus* or stress, which is a metrical phenomenon, and the lexical stress or accent, which is not."[37]

But what has Bradshaw achieved by insisting on this distinction between metrical and lexical stress? What, finally, can he claim to have proved about Donne's metrical "regularity"? In fairness, it should be acknowledged that the conception Bradshaw elaborates here is common to many traditional foot-based prosodies, and, as may already be apparent, it is basically a Platonic conception, in which we are supposed to experience two lines within any given single line of verse. The first of these is "the line as it sounds when read in accordance with normative pronunciation," while the second is an "ideal line, hovering above the first one, and consisting, for any given meter, of the pre-scribed number of perfect feet, each syllable and stress in place."[38] Only the first of these lines is heard by the ear, while the second resounds in the mind. Thus, according to this traditional logic, while lexical and metrical stress may sometimes coincide in the line-as-spoken, metrical stresses persist in the inner experience of the sensitive reader, unspoken and unspeakable. Indeed, for Bradshaw, these inner, inaudible, and in-articulable "sounds" are the very essence of meter—actual articulation being subject to all kinds of less-than-ideal syntactic and lexical factors. It may come as something of a surprise to discover that metricality is essentially an inaudible and unperformable phenomenon, but that is precisely the conclusion that Bradshaw's argument entails.[39]

In other words, in order to assert the "regularity" of Donne's meter, Bradshaw has committed himself to a version of what poststructuralist thought would identify as a metaphysics of presence; in this case, a kind of hyperphonocentrism that prioritizes not just speech before writing but a still more idealized inner "speech" before physical speech—speech before it is spoken, the voice before it is voiced. The ideal line sounding inside the sensitive reader's mind is imagined by Bradshaw as resonating with the full range of interactive possibilities suggested by the combination of lexical and metrical stresses, all of which are conceived as *simultaneously present,* so long as the words remain unspoken; but in actual articulation, the reader must perforce choose to emphasize either lexical or metrical stress, and so the line-as-spoken is characterized by a profound absence or lack.

By pointing out that such Platonic notions of metrical appreciation rest upon a metaphysics of presence, I am in some ways only reframing in the language of poststructuralist theory a point that nontraditional prosodists have made slightly differently and, in some cases, long ago.[40] But, as the mere existence of Bradshaw's article attests, the idea that "real" poetic appreciation depends on the readerly ability to recognize idealized or abstract metrical forms, to hold them in one's head, and then to respond to an infinitely complex interplay between those met-rical ideals and textual or lexical actuality, has proved remarkably per-sistent, despite its demonstrable theoretical untenability. In fact, tradi-tional conceptions of meter continue to dominate the (admittedly increasingly rare) prosodic discussions that occur in our textbooks and criticism; and this sheer persistence is in some ways precisely the point, for it suggests that meter has a phantasmatic function within the literary critical imaginary that goes far beyond the merely explicatory or descriptive.[41]

Another way of putting this would be to say that the ideological power of traditional metrics has always been as important—perhaps more important—than its descriptive power. This fact explains the persistence of its basic tenets, even in a period where actual prosodic criticism of almost any kind is almost never performed. Moreover, the ideological power of meter is often that of mystification and exclusion. For when Bradshaw declares that Donne's meter is *"regularly iambic, of course"* he is not simply giving priority to his own inner experience of the Donnean line, a line that cannot ever be spoken. He is also insisting that anyone who really understands how meter (and hence poetry) works will also be able to "hear" that same metaphysical line in his or her head. Indeed, Bradshaw articulates explicitly what Coleridge and Stein only imply: that those who read Donne as a metrically "irregular" author display a deficient understanding or impoverished sensibility. In short, they are simply "bad" readers. Furthermore, since the ideal experience of a poetic line is necessarily internal, that experience is not susceptible to demonstration or verification. Therefore, the only way to prove that you are having the proper poetic experience is to agree with Bradshaw's conclusions or be excluded de facto from the "good" readers club.

However, for me, Bradshaw's inexorable slide into the language of mystification and cliché remains important because it reveals the extraordinary persistence of an aesthetic investment in some notion of the "regular" as an unexamined a priori condition of poetic excellence, a persistence than we can see extending through and even uniting the various Augustan, Romantic, modern, and contemporary responses that I have considered. Despite their otherwise quite divergent reactions to Donne's verse, after all, every commentator that I have so far discussed, from Ben Jonson to the present, makes some version of this aesthetic investment. The only real difference between them consists in the extent to which they are actively prepared to interfere with the Donnean corpus in order to produce the "regularity" that they feel must be there. Thus, in the eighteenth century, Pope and others rewrite Donne's texts with impunity in order to make them "regular"; while in the nineteenth century, Coleridge argues that Donne is already "regular" if read in the right way, while also endorsing the practice of actual textual revision to a lesser degree; and in the twentieth century, Stein and Bradshaw seize upon those aspects of Coleridge's interpretation that argue for Donne's "regularity," while judiciously repressing his suggestion that substantive acts of rewriting are occasionally necessary to discern its presence.

To summarize, then: one important lesson that we can draw from the argument over Donne's "irregularity" is that the notion of meter, at least as it is constituted here, functions less as a definitive and descriptive aspect of poetic language than as a kind of aesthetic ideology—one that we might call "metricentrism." Moreover, in the case of Donne, the ideological pressure of metricentrism proves so great as to produce what I do not think it is too extreme to call a series of almost pathological reactions. In the eighteenth century this pathology manifests itself in the peculiar displacement of anxieties about content onto form; while in the case of Coleridge, Stein, and Bradshaw we can observe as symptomatic their sacrifice of logic, internal consistency, and descriptive precision in the effort to assert the presence of a metricality that is also always already there, if only one could read the poems as they were "meant" to be read. Indeed, the symptomatic aspect of these later arguments is itself implicit in the very superfluousness of this double claim; for if matters were really so simple—if we really only needed to read Donne's lines as he "meant them to be read" to discern their "strict" and "manly" meter, in Coleridge's terms, or if Donne's regularity were "implicit" in Stein's terms, or if he were *of course* iambic, in Bradshaw's terms—then why would anyone need to argue for it?

However, in demonstrating the negative ideological consequences of metricentrism, I may also have raised some disturbing questions about the nature of my own project—questions for which I set myself up when I admitted a moment ago that the kind of traditional prosody that Bradshaw's article represents is not much practiced these days, at least among elite members of the literary critical profession (even if the prosodic principles upon which such work is based have persisted in more general contexts). After all, it might be said, we hardly need to be told that traditional prosody is ideologically and theoretically suspect, since nowadays it is the methodological exception rather than the rule. Therefore, the skeptic might ask, haven't I gone the long way around the house merely to demonstrate a conclusion that most members of the critical discipline already seem to have acknowledged by their actual practice—that conclusion being that any methodology, including traditional prosody, that prioritizes "purely" formal questions runs the risk of artificially dehistoricizing or depoliticizing the aesthetic by abstracting literary objects from social reality? Couldn't I be accused of trying to persuade people not to do something that, in general, they are already not doing?

Of course, the observation that nowadays people don't—or can't—publish articles like "Donne's Challenge to The Prosodists" very often is valid; but just because the notion of a "pure" formalism has been so thoroughly discredited, it does not seem to me to follow that all prosodic questions must also therefore be dismissed as dull at best, dangerous at worst. First, to dismiss prosody as a "purely" formal matter, and to cheer its disappearance from literary analysis, is to ignore its persistence in the discipline of creative writing (where many of its myths and confusions continue to thrive) and to display a peculiar but all-too-familiar critical contempt for the actual stated practice of quite a few poets. Moreover, to insist on the "purely" formal nature of prosodic questions is also to risk reinscribing an idea that so much critical writing of the last thirty years—poststructuralist, feminist, historicist, queer—has challenged: the idea that it is indeed possible to describe the interpretive workings of a text in a "purely" formal way. To make what is really a version of the same point from the other side, but also in a way that some practitioners of the critical methodologies I have just named seem occasionally inclined to forget: just as there is no such thing as a "purely" aesthetic or formal question, so there is no such thing as textual analysis without a measure of close reading. To speak aphoristically: within textual analysis, "pure" formalism may be impossible, but "impure" formalism is inescapable.[42]

Therefore, to the extent that the battle against traditional prosody seems to have been won, at least insofar as critical practice (if not critical theory) is concerned, I would not be seen as arguing against it. Instead, my primary motivation has been my desire to add my voice to that small but growing band of critics in favor of what might be called a New Prosody. My foregoing discussion of Donne's "irregularity" should therefore be understood as emerging from what I consider to be the most basic and important premise of that New Prosody: that is, that the study of versification cannot afford to be less sensitive than any other branch of contemporary literary criticism to the ideological effects and historical contingencies of even the most apparently formal linguistic properties.[43]

How does all this change the way we read and analyze Donne's prosody in particular? A full answer to this question would require a separate analysis, but one might begin by suggesting that a radically historicized reading of Donnean "metrics" should take the bold step of refusing to apply a traditional foot-based schematic to his verse. As

Charles L. Stevenson once wrote in a more general context: "If the concept of the foot poorly illuminates [a poet's] work, there is a reason for suspecting that [the poet in question] did not think in terms of it."[44] But, of course, to accept that Donne did not think in terms of "feet" only raises the further question of how he *did* conceive of versification; and there are several avenues that might be explored in the attempt to provide an answer. For example, O. B. Hardison Jr. has shown that a "syllabic" prosody, derived from French rather than Middle English or Latin traditions, was perfectly available in the English Renaissance (though less frequently theorized than the more well known accentual foot-based systems).[45] Perhaps Donne's work represents an important "Englishing" of this romance tradition? To make such an argument would cast a new light on the old question of Donne's "originality"— once almost as popular a bone of critical contention as his "irregularity" and something that Donne himself quite self-consciously insisted on (as is evident in the passage from the second satire that I have quoted above). Perhaps Donne's "irregular" prosody is actually the result of a deliberate desire to distinguish his verse from a popular near contemporary like Gascoigne, and not so much an aesthetic failure as the productive result of the anxiety of influence? Still another type of inquiry would question the relation of prosodic principle to poetic genre, asking whether Donne adopts distinct principles of versification according to his poetic mode. Perhaps Donne had more than one prosodic mode in mind when he composed, and a set of (no less historicizable) notions of genre to guide his compositional choices? These and other possibilities emerge from my discussion; but I have been less concerned to resolve the debate with which I began—to finally settle the question of whether Donne is or is not "regular"—so much as to show what the debate itself reveals about the implication of the aesthetic in the psychosexual and moralistic spheres.

V

A little formalism turns one away from History but
. . . a lot brings one back to it.

—ROLAND BARTHES, *MYTHOLOGIES*

In conclusion, I should like to sketch just a few of the wider implications of the debate over Donne's "irregularity" for the business of prosody in general. At one level, the history of the strange, obsessive, idiosyncratic, and even slightly pathological arguments that I have traced here supports Richard Cureton's contention that meter be dethroned as the exclusive object of prosodic study, if not reconsidered entirely.[46] However, while I applaud the attempt by Cureton and others to escape the ideology of metricentrism as it is manifested in traditional prosody, I also think that a differently inflected study of meter still has a great deal to teach us. For if the history of the argument over Donne's "irregularity" reveals anything, it is that the ability to recognize metrical regularity in a piece of poetic language has constituted one of the more abiding and even downright weird cultural fantasies of the literary profession. This is not to say, absurdly, that readers who think that they know what an iambic pentameter is when they see it are in the grip of a terrible delusion that must at all costs be dispelled; but it is to say that when we "identify" the meter of a line we are clearly doing far more than simply counting the number and position of accented syllables.[47] Indeed, from the example of the argument over Donne, it is tempting to conclude that the iambic pentameter is not something that exists in the world at all, like a species of frog or item of clothing. Instead, it may be thought of as having what Terry Eagleton would call a functional rather than an ontological status; which is to say that as an ideal notion it has been collectively and institutionally established, and, like all such abstract ideals—"freedom," "democracy," and even "literature" itself—different people often turn out to have quite different notions about its form, when they actually get down to specific cases. Again, just because this is so doesn't mean we should conclude that there is therefore no need to teach students about it, anymore than we would consider banning the discussion of "democracy" from political science classes simply because it is also at some level a cultural fantasy and an abstract ideal. What we might consider, however, is a shift of stress—to employ an irresistible pun for the final time—a shift of stress with considerable pedagogic potential.

For example, a reflexive and historicized notion of prosody can be employed to encourage students to rethink the very nature of interpretation itself; to see it not as the pursuit of a final and transparent reading but as a form of dialectical engagement between observer and object. The practice of a New Prosody can therefore help students to see, as Fredric Jameson has written, that

[i]n matters of art, and particularly of artistic perception . . . it is wrong to want to *decide,* to want to *resolve* a difficulty: what is wanted is a kind of mental procedure which suddenly shifts gears, which throws everything in a tangle one floor higher, and turns the very problem [in this case,

"What is Donne's meter?"] into its own solution [in this case, "What are the varieties of meter"] by widening its frame in such a way that it now takes in its own mental processes as well as the object of those processes. In the earlier, naive state, we struggle with the object in question; in this heightened and self-conscious one we observe our own struggles and patiently set about characterizing them.[48]

To put the point slightly differently: once we have accepted that the ability to "recognize" an iambic pentameter is not a neutrally descriptive act, but a productive, creative, interpretive one, more closely resembling an act of conjuration than an act of discovery; and once we have accepted further that in some cases—such as that of Donne—the critical conjurer is so determined to evoke the metrical spectre that he or she is often driven to the rhetorical equivalent of smoke and mirrors; then we are still left with the task of explaining the bizarre spectacle of metrical conjurers tricking themselves into believing their own illusions, and leveling the terrible curse of "bad reader" upon those who dare to dismiss their magic. In carrying out this task, we cannot only "direct the attention [of students] back to history itself, and to the historical situation of the commentator as well as of the work"; we can also perhaps, ideally, transform their understanding of the hermeneutic process.[49]

As anyone who has taught poetry knows, the ghost of meter continues to haunt the classroom in the inquiries of students—those who would know what makes poetry "different" from other literary genres, for example. When that ghost appears, we are expected to address it ("Thou art a scholar—speak to it, Horatio!"); we would perhaps do well to remember that, even "after theory," we can be surprised and enlightened by what it has to say. Finally, the persistence of the metrical fantasy suggests that whatever work the concept of meter may once have done, and whatever work it may be marshaled to do in the future, it has always borne witness to a profound psychological need within literary culture—the depths of which we have only begun to plumb, the causes of which we have not begun to diagnose, and that no amount of antiformalist argumentation seems quite able to dispel.

CHAPTER FOUR

Difference and Indifference

Fantasies of Gender

My previous chapters focused primarily on the interpretive conse-
quences of *readerly* desire: that is, on the unacknowledged or unex-
amined desires that produce and reify different versions of "Donne"
(as uncut, "conventionally" heterosexual, "transgressively" homo-
sexual, metrically regular, and so on) and on the hermeneutic distor-
tions that attend such critical productions. In my subsequent chapters
I focus to a greater extent on the often conflicting desires articulated
within Donne's texts, while continuing to assume the centrality and
importance of desire for all acts of interpretation (including my own)
and engaging the critical tradition at large.

Here I consider Donne's response to the "facts" of sexual difference,
exploring his variously inflected expressions of both female desire and
desire for the female. I begin with a brief and relatively abstract dis-
cussion of the ontological and rhetorical status of sexual difference
within contemporary feminist theory, wherein I suggest that both "es-
sentialist" and radical "constructivist" understandings of sexual differ-
ence are necessarily and differently productive fictions: *fantasies,* in the
strict psychoanalytic sense. I then render the implications of this the-
oretical discussion for Donne studies in more concrete terms by re-
hearsing and critiquing some recent interpretations of Donne's own
constructions of sexual difference; I show that what must be grasped
in addressing "women and Donne" is the double problem of the pro-
duction of woman as a category *and* the production of Donne's poetry
as a signifying system.[1] In the third and longest section of the chapter,

I reread several Donne poems, arguing (against the grain of much recent criticism) that Donne collapses distinctions based on sexual difference at least as often as he reinscribes those distinctions; finally, I offer some speculative conclusions, both historical and psychological in character, as to why this might be so.

I

> [T]he only guarantee any theory can give about itself
> is to expose itself as a passionate fiction.
>
> —TERESA DE LAURETIS, *THE PRACTICE OF LOVE*

It is an awkward fact of Donne studies that while his representations of women have often been regarded as sexist, they have equally been praised as "extraordinarily self-reflexive in relation to gender,"[2] as protofeminist, and even as positively erotic: in short, not sexist, but sexy.

Of course, at one level, it is hardly surprising that the distinction between the sexist and the sexy proves problematic. Legislators, lawyers, and literary critics have often had trouble demarcating such boundaries. The problem in a theoretical nutshell is that the social and political signification of a potentially erotic image, text, or practice is not necessarily an inherent feature of that particular image, text, or practice. Instead, for any given individual, the social signification of an erotic image, text, or practice is inseparable from that same individual's prior conceptions of, among other things, sexual difference and relative power relations. For the same reasons, our sense of the meaning of a text or image will often change according to our perception of whether the author or speaker of a text is male or female and according to our own presumptions about the difference sexual difference makes. Thus, as feminist Renaissance scholar Elizabeth Harvey has put it, signification "depends upon the imputation of gender."[3]

The history of critical responses to Donne's work often seems to confirm the validity of this interpretive principle. However, that same history also reveals some potentially negative hermeneutic consequences of this principle, when too rigidly applied. For while meaning may indeed depend on the imputation of gender, the meanings of "gender" itself—including the biological categories of "male" and "female"—are themselves historically contingent and unstable. Nevertheless, criticism tends to proceed as if this were not the case, through a reification of those categories. In making this observation, my purpose is not simply to restate the now well-worn critical cliché that gender is "constructed." Instead, I will show how "naturalized" concepts of sexual difference return as the repressed but determinative ground of interpretation, even in recent work on Donne that putatively takes the cultural contingency and constructedness of gender as a guiding presumption. This return of essentialized notions of sexual difference as the repressed content of arguments ostensibly demonstrating the constructedness of gender suggests the presence of a still unresolved conflict at the root of such critical inquiries, and it is this unresolved conflict that I really want to explore.

I would go so far as to diagnose this unresolved conflict as the product of two incompatible and yet compelling intellectual fantasies about sexual difference: competing fantasies that we have called "essentialism" and "constructivism." These fantasies simultaneously emerge from and give shape to the same progressive desire, to end inequality and exclusion on the basis of gender discrimination. I should quickly add that by describing these divergent positions as fantasies I do not mean to denigrate them, as if I could oppose them to some readily available notion of the way things "really" are. Instead, I am using the term "fantasy" in a specifically psychoanalytic sense, not to name dreams or delusions that can be simply opposed to "reality" but, rather, to denote a structuring principle that shapes the ways in which individuals order their experience of the world.[4] I believe that, as far as theories of sexual difference go, fantasies of this specific kind are all we ever have.

The first of these fantasies originates in the traditional and explicitly political feminist project of organizing individuals around the signifier of "woman" in order to fight gender oppression. Proceeding from the (thoroughly reasonable) premise that any identity politics requires relatively stable conceptions of identity to be effective, traditional feminism tends to posit the notion of *fundamental* divisions between male and female experience. In some more theoretically inflected accounts, this concept of fundamental division is self-consciously acknowledged as a fiction, to the degree that no basis for making absolute distinctions between genders at the level of experience can be imagined working in all places at all times; but the fiction of fundamental difference is nevertheless understood as a *necessary* or enabling fantasy, an intellectual foul that must be allowed for the sake of rhetorical and political pragmatism. Hence the name commonly given to the strategy: "tactical essentialism."[5]

The radical constructivist fantasy emerges out of some powerful critiques of this essentialist position. For example, Judith Butler has famously and influentially argued that even the most strategically "constructivist" of traditional feminist accounts tend to ground their concept of gender-as-constructed in an essentialized notion of biological sex (the familiar sex/gender distinction of traditional feminist theory). Butler responds by asking: "[W]hat is 'sex' anyway? Natural, anatomical, chromosomal, hormonal?" "If the immutable character of sex is contested," she goes on, then "perhaps . . . [it] . . . is as culturally constructed as gender; indeed, perhaps it was always already gender." In other words, the distinction "sex/gender" is not parallel to "nature/ culture": instead, "gender is also the discursive/cultural means by which 'sexed nature' or 'a natural sex' is produced and established as 'prediscursive,' prior to culture, a politically neutral surface *on which* culture acts" (emphasis in original). Thus, the sex/gender distinction "turns out to be no distinction at all." For Butler, the (sexed) body is *not* simply written *on* by culture because it can't even be thought of as a surface to be written on without already having been picked out, demarcated, inscribed, written precisely as "the body."[6]

If the body must be inscribed *as such* within a cultural system of meaning before we can even call it "the body"—if it is always already written, always already represented—then this has profound implications for the traditional questions of feminism. Instead of asking whether there are fundamental differences between male and female experiences, for example, or even insisting on the rhetorical necessity of such concepts, Butler suggests that we should be asking how the discursive system we call "gender" brings apparently fundamental differences (such as the notion of the sexed body) into being as *apparently* fundamental. Indeed, for Butler, the traditional understanding of the sexed body as an unconstructed phenomenon passively awaiting cultural inscription is highly problematic, because it obscures the primacy of systems of inscription and representation—and for Butler it is those very systems that enable oppression on the basis of gender difference in the first place.

Thus, proceeding from the (again quite reasonable) notion that sexual difference cannot be imagined outside of representational and social practices, practices that are themselves historically and culturally contingent, Butler implies that, in a profound sense, sexual difference has no "real" existence at all: that is, no basis outside of the contingencies of representation. For Butler, gender is always already discursively produced or, in her much-cited phrase, "performatively enacted."[7] Indeed, as Joan Copjec has written, in a respectful critique of Butler's work, Butler at times appears to argue that "the deconstruction of the fiction of innate or essential sex is also, or must lead to, a rejection of the notion that there is anything constant or invariable about sexual difference, that sex is anything but a construct of historically variable discursive practices into which we may intervene to sow 'subversive confusion.' "[8]

My purpose here is not to critique Butler's constructivism so much as to underline the extent to which the radical constructivist argument that sexual difference is ultimately a product of discursivity is the logical inverse of the essentialist argument that sexual difference is fundamental and prior to discursivity. This reverse symmetry suggests that, like essentialism, radical constructivism may also be most valuable as an enabling fiction, and no less amenable to strategic deployment, even if inadequate or overstated as a description of "reality" (the political promise of constructivism obviously being that if something is demonstrably a product of culture rather than nature, then it can be changed). Indeed, it is possible that the day may come when we speak of "tactical constructivism" as much as "tactical essentialism." The point to be grasped is that the notion of a fundamental difference between the sexes *and* the notion of a fundamental indifference are themselves differently productive *and* differently frustrating critical fantasies, each of which will create and shape the conditions of rhetorical possibility in different ways.

As structuring principles, these critical fantasies often dictate our interpretive responses, sometimes in ways that we recognize, but more frequently in ways that we do not recognize, for the simple reason that these structuring principles are generally the ground of literary analysis, not its object (a fact that also explains the necessity of this preliminary theoretical discussion). For the remainder of this chapter, I propose to read Donne's interpreters, and thence to reread Donne, with an eye for those moments when these two fundamental and opposed structuring fantasies—of sexual difference and sexual indifference—make themselves felt. Attending not just to the problem of difference but to the problem of attending to the problem of difference, it may be possible to see something more than the usual screens of critical fantasy allow. Indeed, it may be possible to weave a new fantasy from the cloth of the old.

II

> [I]t is not sexual difference as such that must be challenged—if this is understood as the different relations to lack and to the phallus taken up by men and women—for this does not secure the identity men/masculine and women/feminine. Instead it is the fantasies (of women as well as men) that arise from the difficulty of assuming a sexually differentiated position that must be addressed.
>
> —ELIZABETH COWIE, *THE WOMAN IN QUESTION*

The implications of the foregoing may become clearer if rendered less abstractly. Turning to some specific responses to Donne's "treatment" of women, then, let us consider the diametrically opposed reactions of Arthur Symons and Evelyn Simpson. In 1899, Symons wrote: "If women most conscious of their sex were ever to read Donne, they would say, He was a great lover; he understood."[9] Symons's flair for critical melodrama is somewhat undercut by the directness of Evelyn Simpson's comment, a quarter century later, that, quite to the contrary, "few great writers have shown so little insight into the secrets of a woman's heart."[10] That criticism has not been able to find a way to resolve or even adequately explain these utterly polarized readings of Donne is confirmed by the fact that positions almost identical to those of Symons and Simpson are still articulated in contemporary exchanges, transformations in critical vocabulary notwithstanding. Thus, on the one hand, Ilona Bell speaks of Donne's "Songs and Sonnets" as "the first Renaissance love poems written for adults, loving and empathetic enough to grant the man's and the woman's point of view equal credence."[11] Thomas Docherty, on the other hand, argues that Donne's poetic rhetoric "always" characterizes the female as "the Other." This rhetorical strategy, says Docherty, "works to suggest that the human self is primarily male, and that anything which does not cohere with this male-oriented notion of selfhood is a 'deviation.' "[12]

To the extent that Docherty and Bell (or Simpson and Symons) describe the value and effects of Donne's poetry in utterly opposed *moral* registers, their positions may well be irreconcilable. Nevertheless, from the perspective of poststructuralist gender theory, these contrasting interpretations proceed from a common basis: both finally presume and uphold a traditional binary model of sexual difference. In other words, Docherty's accusation of chauvinism and Bell's accolade of empathy ultimately rely on the same conceptual system. One praises Donne for being able to cross the readily discernible boundary of sexual difference, while the other damns him for continually reinscribing that boundary; but both finally assume that such a boundary can indeed be unproblematically located. Whether we think Donne constantly creates woman as Other, or whether we think Donne really "knows" woman, and can speak for "her," the term "woman" is always already defined in complementary opposition to the term "man."

At this point, one may be tempted to ask, "What's wrong with that?" Or perhaps even to say, "Yes, it is disturbing to discover the final interdependence of apparently oppositional terms such as 'male' and 'female,' but isn't it absurd to reject the binary model of sexual difference because of it?" As Butler has remarked, part of the difficulty lies in persuading readers to see that there *is* a difficulty here. However, Eve Sedgwick provides some cogent suggestions on this score in a methodological essay that builds upon Butler's prior work:

> It may be . . . that a damaging bias towards heterosocial or heterosexist assumptions inheres unavoidably in the very concept of gender. This bias would be built into any gender-based analytic perspective to the extent that gender definition and gender identity are necessarily relational between genders—to the extent, that is, that in any gender system, female identity or definition is constructed by analogy, supplementarity, or contrast to male, or vice versa. . . . [T]he ultimate definitional appeal in any gender based analysis must be to the diacritical front between different genders. This necessity gives heterosocial and heterosexual relations a conceptual privilege of incalculable consequence.[13]

In short, a criticism that posits the terms "man" and "woman" as limit sites for readerly identification, or as the ontologically given bases for interpretive conclusions, will almost always rest on unexamined presumptions of normative heterosexuality. I would go further: the problem is not only that readings based on such presumptions slide into heterosexism, though this is indeed the case (witness Bell's definition of "adult" sexuality as a necessarily equal marriage of male and female perspectives). Just as frequently, such readings also serve to hypostatize notions of "proper" heterosexual desire within narrow, conventional, and atemporal boundaries, valorizing, for example, monogamy and long-term partnership over polygamy, polyandry, and promiscuity, love over "mere" lust, and married love over any other kind, maturity over youth, the (so-called) reality principle over the pleasure principle, and so on.

In relation to Donne's interpretive history, we can immediately see one result of this false hypostatization in the long-standing critical tendency, stretching from the seventeenth century to the present, to subdivide Donne's hetero-amorous lyrics into poems addressed to his wife and poems written for "other" women. Almost invariably, the poems claimed for Anne are picked out for special praise, while those it is claimed Donne could not have written for her are less highly regarded—as if the only woman literary criticism can allow to have inspired Donne's most moving amatory rhetoric must also be the one he happened to marry.[14] Such arguments continue to be made despite the fact that, when it comes to positing biographical "settings" for these poems, we generally have no external evidence upon which to base our conclusions; such interpretations derive less from our historical knowledge of the relationship between John Donne and Anne More than they do from what Michel Foucault would describe as the "interpenetration of the deployment of alliance and that of sexuality"[15] around the marriage bond.

However, even among critics who write with an apparent awareness of the "damaging bias" of narrowly heteronormative, conventionally moralized, or transhistorical notions of gender and sexuality, the concepts of "male" and "female" have a tendency to return in reified forms and to restrict interpretive possibility in unnecessary ways, at least when Donne is the object of investigation. This limitation is particularly apparent in an essay on Donne by Bruce Woodcock, published in a collection of "state-of-the-art" New Historicist articles in 1996.[16] After quoting Foucault, Sedgwick, and others, with approval, and after reminding us that "our notions of . . . sexual identities are . . . post-nineteenth century phenomena" (54) and therefore culturally contingent, Woodcock offers a surprisingly essentialist interpretation of the "lesbian" ventriloquism of "Sapho to Philaenis," stating in no uncertain terms that "under the veil of female homoeroticism, this Donne text is in fact an invitation to male narcissism or homoeroticism" (64).

Now, while I would not dispute the suggestion that "Sapho to Philaenis" at least potentially represents female-female sexual relations as a titillating spectacle, Woodcock's implicit conclusion that *only* male readers are able to take voyeuristic pleasure in such a spectacle seems particularly odd in context; and while one might want to be skeptical of an anachronistically utopian reading that transforms the poem into a politically progressive "brief for lesbianism,"[17] Woodcock's no less reductive "unveiling" of the text seems entirely predicated on his prior knowledge that the poem was "in fact" written by a man. Lifting

"Sappho's" poetic skirt and finding himself confronted by Donne's erect penis, Woodcock recoils from the sight as necessarily incompatible with any progressive sexual politics. This of course begs the question of whether the sight of an erect penis is indeed incompatible with a progressive sexual politics—a question that in a roundabout way I'm attempting to address.

Woodcock then goes on to make some alarming generalities about the reaction of "women readers" to "male texts." Constructing a heroic critical narrative of personal enlightenment in which he "discovers" that Donne's poems are "male texts which speak of men, for men, through men and about men," Woodcock concludes: "I myself have come to recognize more clearly how irritating or even irrelevant these texts can be to women readers" (65). The possibility that a woman could identify with a Donnean speaker is not one that Woodcock entertains, perhaps because it would complicate his own disavowal of desires he designates as "male." Indeed, his essay ends with a call for "male critics" to stop "masquerading [Donne's] poems as somehow complimentary to women" when they are really "masculine fantasies" (66). This is tantamount to saying that a female critic capable of finding a compliment in Donne must be too "male identified"; that "masculine fantasies" about women can be easily measured against some essential and readily available notion of "real" women; and that those same "masculine fantasies" will always and inevitably be retrograde or negative (who could imagine a pleasant *masculine* fantasy, after all?). At the same time, Woodcock has gone from (quite correctly) stressing the radical difference of Renaissance notions of sexuality to presuming an entirely heterosexual interpretive community in the present (composed, in an unfortunate rhetorical misfire of "female *readers*" and "male *critics*"). The enlightened ones among this community—and Woodcock offers no positive examples of "male critics" besides himself—are not merely heterosexual, but modern liberal heterosexuals who generally know better than to approve of suspiciously "masculine fantasies" and desires. In short, they are heterosexuals who don't like "masculine" men and who presumably cannot even feel anything other than pity for the men and women who do.

Woodcock's incoherence at this point is primarily a consequence of hermeneutic distortions attendant on a (residual) absolutist fantasy of sexual difference—a fantasy that persists or returns *despite* his laudable attempt to acknowledge the contingencies of history and the pluralities of sexuality. A version of the same problem also undermines Elizabeth

Harvey's important study of what she calls "ventriloquized voices"—that is, male-authored texts ostensibly spoken by women. Though her reading of "Sapho to Philaenis" is more nuanced than Woodcock's, Harvey finally interprets the appropriation of Sappho's voice by Donne and Ovid as a kind of intertextual sexual assault, neutralizing the threatening notion of a distinctly "female" form of authorship through a double strategy of mastery and erasure; by severing the female voice from the female body, Harvey argues, Donne's act of poetic ventriloquism works to efface female authorship altogether.

In raising questions about the dynamics of "appropriation," and in underlining the potential violence of intertextuality, Harvey's argument is both provocative and valuable; however, it is also problematic to the extent that it seems to imagine both Ovid and Donne as necessarily engaged in roughly identical (masculinist) projects simply because—although they may hide behind a nominally "female" text—they are both "really" men. As Janel Mueller has commented, Harvey's argument would seem to imply that "a male poet cannot do other than assimilate, dominate and silence the self-expression of a female predecessor . . . whom he incorporates in his work."[18] Still more problematically, the question of gendered *authorship*—of what, precisely, it might mean to write "as a woman" or write "as a man"—goes begging. Instead, biological sex works almost in the manner of an "author function," determining and limiting interpretive possibility.[19]

In yet another essay on "Sapho to Philaenis," Barbara Correll has expressed dissatisfaction with this type of approach to Donne, which, in her terms, "project[s] a conspiratorial masculinist intentionality and neglect[s] questions of representation such as the notion of masculinity itself as ventriloquized."[20] By this remark, I understand Correll to be claiming (like Butler) that questions of gender and sexuality cannot be thought apart from one another or from questions of representation. This position is one that I would also endorse, but it perhaps requires some further elaboration, if only to prevent possible misunderstandings.

First, by insisting with Correll and Butler on a shift of interpretive ground, from gender to representation, I do not mean to dismiss the value of Harvey's demonstration that male authors frequently write as women during this period, and that, equally frequently, these acts of ventriloquism emerge from and sustain an epistemological and social structure in which male identity is marked as originary and female identity as secondary or belated. Obviously this hierarchical gendered perspective is integral to the dominant belief systems and public discourses of the period; we need only recall Milton's aphoristic line from *Paradise Lost* on the relation of Eve to Adam, and of both to their Creator ("He for God only, she for God in him" [4:298]) as perhaps the most succinct and rhetorically powerful formulation of the position. Harvey's interpretation of male acts of poetic "ventriloquism" as revealing symptoms of patriarchal and misogynistic ideology, sanctioned by medical, legal, and theological vocabularies, is not unpersuasive— but to the degree that her interpretations sometimes appear to derive their necessity from authorial biology, I would sound a note of caution.

Second, and perhaps of greater critical significance: by insisting that gender and sexuality must be considered in relation to representation— or, to put the point in its strongest Butlerian form, by insisting that any notion of gender is itself always already a representation—there is a danger that I may be seen as eliding or erasing the significance of sexual difference, not simply as an interpretive category within literary analysis but as a brute (and often brutal) fact of lived experience. Harvey makes this point herself in a proleptic attempt to offset the charge of essentialism that Mueller, Correll, and I have leveled at her (it's not as if she did not anticipate the challenge). In Harvey's words, the question does not concern "whether male poets *can* adequately represent the female voice, but the ethics and politics of doing so" (12). Thus distinguishing the ethical and political spheres from what she refers to as the "epistemological," Harvey endorses a "tactical essentialism" in "the belief that even while we recognize the constructed nature of gender, we can still adhere to a conviction that women and men (and their respective voices) are not politically interchangeable" (12–13).

My response to Harvey's explicitly politically motivated self-justification is, again, twofold: first, without wanting to foreclose the positive value of "tactical" essentialism (I have already acknowledged its potential as an enabling fiction), the specific kinds of ethical and political consequences Harvey fears may not *necessarily* follow from a more rigorous emphasis on gender as always already a matter of representation. Second, and again more important, the particular form of Harvey's "tactical" commitment to gender as an interpretive ontology can itself result in acts of elision that actually *undermine* her feminist project of recovering female voices. The difficulty manifests itself quite clearly in Harvey's articulation of her proleptic defense; for when she announces her "conviction that women and men (and their respective voices) are not politically interchangeable," her parenthetical aside links the terms "women and men" to "their respective voices" in an entirely unproblematic way—as if the concept of what may be said to constitute the gender of a textual "voice" were not precisely the issue under interrogation.

If at this point in her argument Harvey seems to have committed herself to a fantasy of fundamental difference, elsewhere in her text she seems equally attracted to the second fantasy I have described—that of a subject position that transcends or escapes gender altogether. Consider, for example, her valorization of anonymous texts, such as the seventeenth-century dialogue between a "feminine man" and a "masculine woman" known as *Haec-Vir*. "It is crucial that we read *Haec-Vir* as anonymous," Harvey claims, because "in its refusal to present itself as the property of a (proper) name . . . [it] forces us to recognize the role custom plays in fashioning gender" (49). Here Harvey's "tactical" essentialism leads her to assume that arguments about the social construction of gender are best made from a position nominally outside of its limits—that is, once the name (and hence the gender) of the author is placed under erasure. This valorization of gender-less anonymity is somewhat ironic in the context of a study designed to expose the historical tendency to efface female authorship. But more troublingly, Harvey's reading provokes an obvious question: would a text like *Haec-Vir* cease to have the positive function that she assigns to it if we were to discover, at some future date, strong archival evidence for attributing it to a man?

But such awkward inquiries can be avoided altogether if we simply insist on locating the capacity of any text to challenge negative and essentialist conceptions of gender *not* in the fact of authorial anonymity, nor in facts of authorial gender, but in the status of the text as, precisely, a form of representation and hence, always already, open to interpretation. Which brings me to a key concept: the (potential) capacity of any representation to problematize hierarchized and essentialist notions of sexual difference does *not* simply emerge from accidental lacunae within our available historical knowledge, *but from the very conditions of representation;* and, concomitantly, the (potential) erasure of sexual difference that Harvey fears is not necessarily or only the result of deliberate masculinist strategies of intertextual appropriation but is in fact *a consequence of textuality itself.*

I realize that such observations can try the patience of readers, for a variety of reasons; some may consider them overfamiliar, while others may find them overly generalized or abstract. Nevertheless, I consider it important to return to these theoretical principles in any discussion of Donne's representations of women because I believe the relationship between textuality and the "facts" of sexual difference also interested

Donne a great deal; moreover, I believe that on occasion Donne delib-
erately exploited the conditions of textuality in order to escape from
some of the more misogynistic conceptions of gender that predomi-
nated during his own era—to create what Teresa De Lauretis has
termed (borrowing from the idiom of the cinema) a "space-off."[21]

In making this last claim, I am flying in the face of much recent and
important criticism. Of course, I am not attempting to get all of
Donne's works off the misogynistic hook, as it were; nor am I unaware
of the tendency within critical and philosophical thought for masculine
perspectives to reproduce themselves as "neutral" or "ungendered" (to
extend Lauretis's metaphor, I realize that the projected "space-off" fre-
quently turns out to be already colonized by the very forces one hoped
to escape). Nor, finally, am I trying to transform Donne into a
seventeenth-century version of Judith Butler. Clearly Donne's interest
in the relationship between sexual difference, sexuality, and represen-
tation emerges from an entirely different intellectual milieu and is not
reducible to a single, coherent epistemological and political program.
However, I make no apology for suggesting that Donne's texts and
contemporary feminist theory can be thought of as mutually illumi-
nating; and the idea that Donne is at least *interested* in the represen-
tation, performance, and interpretive effects of sexual difference should
not be revelatory to anyone familiar with his work and the literature
that surrounds it. Therefore, although my subsequent claims are
against the grain of most recent thinking on the subject, I should em-
phasize that by assuming Donne's interest in questions of gendered
difference I am at least beginning with an observation that has also
been made, with a variety of emphases, by several authoritative readers,
including Barbara Correll, Ronald Corthell, Thomas Docherty, Stanley
Fish, Achsah Guibbory, Richard Halpern, and Janel Mueller, among
others.

III

> If our two loves be one, or, thou and I
> Love so alike, that none do slacken, none can die.
>
> —JOHN DONNE, *THE GOOD MORROW*

In fact, according to the aforementioned critics, to describe Donne as
"interested" in questions of gendered difference is to court understate-
ment. The Donne of their analyses obsessively returns to and worries

the issue in ways that are often diagnosed as rooted in psychological ill health—that is, driven by profound anxieties that border on the pathological. Of course, within this diverse body of critical literature the etiology of Donne's pathological anxiety receives a variety of explanations; but it is possible to identify a common focus on the idea that "women are threatening to Donne insofar as they represent a possible blurring of the lines of difference."[22] The evidence for this conclusion is almost always located in the "Elegies," where, in its most extreme form, anxiety over the feminine manifests itself in the repudiation of women as "abject" (in the Kristevan sense). The textual example most frequently proffered as a central exhibit in this case is "The Comparison," a paradoxical tour de force in which readerly pleasure seems at least in part predicated on the capacity to enjoy disgust, and disgust at a woman's expense; the poem describes in lingering detail the fluids that leak from a repudiated mistress's body: "Ranke sweaty froth thy Mistresse's brow defiles, / Like spematique issue of ripe menstruous boiles."[23] But even when Donne stops short of such visceral abjecting strategies, the argument goes, he nevertheless continually attempts to reproduce his own (masculine) poetic identity as fixed, constant, and unchanging by representing women as fluid, inconstant, and endlessly fungible.[24]

In sum: According to most recent critics who have considered the matter, whenever Donne's imagination leads him to reflect on questions of sexual difference, he exhibits a form of repetition compulsion, desperately asserting that difference as essential and hierarchized; these compulsive acts of assertion are interpreted as originating in Donne's repressed terror at the possibility that sexual difference cannot finally be maintained—that he, Donne, might actually occupy the abject feminine position he is so concerned to repudiate—and this repressed notion, like all repressed notions, is then seen as returning to haunt his poetic rhetoric in ways that the critic/analyst expertly diagnoses and explicates. The evidence for this reading of Donne is often persuasively marshaled, particularly in Stanley Fish's essay, which may constitute the most powerful negative response to the poet since C. S. Lewis described Donne as a "hot-eyed" bore; Fish frankly presents his analysis as a diagnostic intervention addressing Donne's "sickness."

Such interpretations were without question necessary correctives to those offered by some among the previous generation of professional readers who, in emphasizing the less vitriolic amatory verse, presented a sentimentalized distortion of the poet to their readers. However, the suggestion that Donne's *only* posture in the face of sexual difference is one of furious masculinist assertion risks a distortion of its own. For at least as often as he writes poetic "tests designed to confirm distinctions based on gender,"[25] Donne also attempts to evaporate those distinctions.

In the poems of "mutuality," as they are sometimes called—that is, the great love lyrics upon which Donne criticism once tended to focus—this evaporation is most frequently affected by the introduction of a third term, itself imagined as transcending the binary opposition of lover and beloved. This rhetorical device has a low, comic form and a high, tragic, or profound one: the third term of choice can be a bloodsucking mite, as in "The Flea" ("This flea is you and I"); a scratched pane of glass, as in "A Valediction of my name in the window" ("here you see me and I am you"), or the mysterious phoenix of myth, as in "The Canonization" ("The Phoenix riddle hath more wit / By us. We two being one are it."). However, I do not think it has been previously observed that this elision of distinctions based on gender occurs not only within Donne's more "mutual" poems of amatory persuasion, but also in the kinds of text that have been considered irredeemably masculinist. Consider, for example, a poem like "The Indifferent," which begins:

> I can love both faire and browne,
> Her whom abundance melts, and her whom want
> > betraies,
> Her whom loves lonenesse best, and her who maskes
> > and plaies,
> Her whom the country formed, and whom the town,
> Her who beleeves, and her who tries,
> Her who still weepes with spungie eyes,
> And her who is dry corke, and never cries;
> I can love her, and her, and you and you
> I can love any, so she not be true.[26]

In recent accounts, this poem has often been named (if not actually interrogated) as a chief witness for the prosecution in the case for Donne's "sexism." Commonly, this charge is made as part of a double move repudiating earlier critical accounts that dismissed or excused any putatively sexist content in Donne's verse as no more than the unpleasant residue of Donne's Ovidian source material or as a consequence of Donne's "original" desire to "invert" overfamiliar idealizations of the beloved in Petrarchist rhetoric—thus allowing questions of sexism to be bracketed as matters of mere literary convention rather than as expressions of Donne's own sentiments or "sincere" feelings. However, if we refuse to exculpate this poem on the grounds of Ovidian influence or anti-Petrarchism, does it follow that we must then read it, with Janel Mueller, as an "unwittingly negative" act of "self-disclosure"? Or might the poem be more than simple sexist "attitudinizing," whatever its possible literary provenance?[27]

In an extended reading of the poem, Arthur Marotti emphasizes the potentially self-canceling aspects of Donne's argument, foregrounding the internal conflict and complexity within this seemingly straightforward display of the "rambunctiously libertine." But even Marotti seems to assume that this first stanza can only be read as crudely masculinist posturing; for him it clearly addresses "an audience of sympathetic males ... celebrating the brash erotic adventurism of the young male lover."[28]

One immediate problem with this interpretation is the fact that, as so often in his work, Marotti imagines an all-male coterie of readers to be the only "real" audience for this kind of poem (a speculation that is hardly subject to demonstration for all its vaunted "historicism"). The poet, however, speaks clearly and directly to an audience of *female* listeners in his eighth line. Of course, Marotti is too attentive a reader not to notice this fact; but he would have us see it as an abrupt switch of address, occurring not only in midstanza but in midsentence. Giving Donne a little more credit as craftsman, we can see that, whatever the gender composition of Marotti's "real" interpretive community in which this poem circulated, the "imaginary" audience projected by the speaker of the poem also includes women. Indeed, the form of address suggests that Donne's projected or imagined audience may be *exclusively* female from the second stanza; and, reading retroactively, there is no reason to imagine that the speaker of this poem imagines himself addressing any men at all.

By framing the issue in terms of the "imagined" audience, I am of course suggesting that both putative interpretive communities—Marotti's all-male coterie, and Donne's mixed or possibly all-female audience of direct addressees—are something less than "real." If we accept that at some basic level *both* audiences are fantasy constructions, then the question of interest becomes *why* Marotti imagines an all-male crowd listening in, while Donne's own speaker appears to have eyes only for the women. Once again, we might suspect that gender is being utilized as a ground of interpretation, a way of fixing meaning, at least in Marotti's analysis. After all, his projected all-male community of readers produces an account of the poem as self-evidently masculinist discourse, at least in this opening stanza. This is not to say that Donne's own differently gendered "imaginary" audience may not ultimately work to enable a discursive performance that is equally masculinist; but unless we really think that difference makes no difference, the tone of that performance may be something quite other than a libertine *sexism* and closer to a libertine *sexiness*—if I may return to a distinction that I have already admitted can be difficult to maintain.

Looking again at these opening lines with an alternative "imaginary" audience in mind, then, we might notice that the scenario the poem presents is also "imaginary"—a fantasy—rather than an account of personal history. The speaker is declaring his sense of his own impossibly voracious and inexhaustible sexual appetite, not publicizing a series of actual conquests: he says to an (imaginary) audience of women that he "can" make love to all types of women (if they will only let him), not that he has. The poem is therefore less a bragging confession of "adventurism" than an obviously exaggerated form of self-advertisement, a piece of sexual self-promotion perhaps more familiar to us today from recordings and performances within the blues and rock traditions. It might even be helpful to liken Donne's pose here to that of a "hootchie-cootchie man" who ain't talking about being true when he talks about love. Indeed, the last lines of the stanza ring with an uncanny resemblance to the repeated refrain of a classic Muddy Waters lyric: "I don't want you to be true / I just want to make love to you."

Admittedly, such a reading risks anachronism, and in offering it I do not mean to pretend that there are no important distinctions to be made between performances of heteromasculinity in the seventeenth and twentieth centuries. Instead, what I mean to emphasize by making such a comparison is the simultaneous investment of this poetic speaker both in the performance of sexual fantasy *and* in sharing a fantasy of sexual performance. On the one hand, he articulates a fantasy in which sexual activity is valorized independently of matters of propriety (be they moral, social, legal, or even aesthetic) and, on the other hand, he presents a fantasy of himself as the best of sexual performers in the most literal sense—untiring, undiscriminating, and "all flavors guaranteed to satisfy." Contra Marotti, then, the "her and her and you and you" does not signal an abrupt shift from male to female addressees but is more like a familiar stage gesture, a kind of finger-pointing from the spotlight—as if Donne were picking women out of the crowd and inviting them to join him, not so much back stage as in the public space that he has made of his fantasy. Thus, despite the misleading title (which is almost certainly not Donne's invention and which does not appear anywhere in the text itself), the point of this poem is not to collapse all women into an "indifferent" mass (the descriptions actually emphasize difference, after all; the women are rendered equivalent only to the extent that Donne's speaker claims to find them all equally attractive). Instead, the point may be to present a fantasy of indiscriminate multiple sexual couplings, without emotional commitments—a fantasy that the poem seems to want to offer as *equally available to the women* who are themselves the fantasized audience of the poem.

This last point is worth emphasizing, for it foregrounds the way in which the evocation of a fantasy scenario can complicate questions of identification and so render interpretations based on the gender of the reader problematic. As I have already noted, psychoanalysis emphasizes the nature of fantasy as a structure or scenario, "a matter of staging, of *mise-en-scène*" in which individuals may play more than one part and indeed may identify with sexual subject positions other than their own.[29] This thesis, that the fantasized scene as a whole rather than any one specifically gendered subject position can be the focus of identification, is actually one that Donne himself seems to rely on in order to achieve his most persuasive effects. He imagines his (imaginary) female audience identifying with this fantasy scenario *in the same way that he identifies with it.* Thus, the identification with the role of tireless sexual performer is imagined as equally possible for Donne's female addressees as it is for him. The speaker wonders aloud whether women restrain their own desires out of a mistaken sense that men do the same: "Or doth a feare that men are true torment you?" The rhetorical question works to imply that the appearance of sexual difference at the level of desire is a product of a misrecognition of the other, a misrecognition whose origin is itself located in intersubjective relations rather than "natural" libido; the verse goes on to suggest that if that act of misrecognition can be exposed as such, sexual difference at the level of desire will disappear: "Oh, we are not, be not you so / Let me, and do you, twenty know." In other words, this poem depends on a remarkably complex understanding of the ways in which identifications within fantasy scenarios take place. We might say that the "real" fantasy of this poem is one in which the capacity of both sexes to identify with the same fantasy scenario eliminates sexual difference at a basic level: "if you (mis)recognize my fantasy as a reality," the poet seems to say, "then you will recognize that my fantasy is also your fantasy, and yours mine; you will recognize that in our desire we are the same." (Or, as another poet once put it, in another fantasy of shared fantasies, "I'll let you be in my dream if I can be in yours.") Thus, insofar as identification at the level of sexual fantasy is concerned, for the purposes of this poem the difference between men and women is imagined as no difference at all. All of which leads me to the point that I first set out to make: that if a form of distinction *is* collapsed into indifference by "The Indifferent," it is a form of distinction *between* the sexes; for it is the notion that men and women can and should be set apart on the basis of their respective sexual appetites that Donne specifically challenges here, through the fantasy of a sexual fantasy that both men and women can share or enter into equally.

The final stanza adds a further wrinkle. Donne's speaker fantasizes that his fantasy has the endorsement of the Big Other, a God, or in this case, a Goddess, Venus; in short, the final fantasy of the "The Indifferent" is a fantasy in which the sexual utopianism of the speaker actually describes social "reality." But, with what I think is a deliberate and painful irony, the result is distopian. Practitioners of the normatively dominant (Christian) sexual ideology of monogamy are branded as dangerous "Heritiques" (a potentially lethal accusation, as we should remember, in the early modern period). It is perhaps a sign of just how invested he is in his dream of sexual "freedom" that Donne has to push it until *someone's* happiness is threatened; the poem subsequently and abruptly ends, as if the exuberant boisterous fantasy of shared libertine pleasure runs aground at the point of recognizing the pain that may attend upon loving someone who refuses to be "true."

"The Indifferent" is not the only poem in which Donne attempts to render an equivalence out of sexual difference, through the concept of matched or mutually powerful and compelling fantasies of desire. The "everybody fuck" antimonogamy logic of this text reappears in several other Donne poems, some of which are traditionally assigned to "female" speakers. Donne's use of such speakers in these contexts raises the possibility that separate poems within the Donne canon exist in a kind of mutually canceling opposition; to put it bluntly, Donne may occasionally present himself as a rapacious horn-dog, but he also presents women as similarly rapacious desiring subjects, and the one kind of representation (presumably) complicates our response to the other.

The possibility that Donne deliberately and self-consciously intended to complicate our response to the "masculinism" of some of his libertine Ovidian verse by juxtaposing poems that articulate or ventriloquize female desire in similarly "masculinist" terms—thereby raising questions about just how uniquely "masculine" that desire is—must surely complicate any simple assertion of his misogyny. Of course, it is impossible to prove that Donne ever set out to organize his poetry with such intentions in mind, but the fact that this interpretive possibility was recognized by Donne's contemporary readers is quite tenable; it has been effectively demonstrated by Marotti that the placement of poems in mutually complicating or canceling relation was an activity fostered and encouraged by the interpretive dynamics of the manuscript culture in which Donne's poems first circulated.[30]

A comparison of the order or sequence of Donne's poems in all of the manuscript collections featuring selections of his verse is beyond the scope of this chapter or indeed, of any individual commentator—Peter Beal has noted that, "probably more transcripts of Donne's poems were made than of the verse of any other British poet of the sixteenth and seventeenth centuries"[31]—but to take the single example of the Dalhousie manuscript collections, it is noteworthy that in both miscellanies, although other poems common to both collections are rearranged in relation to one another, Donne's "Communitie" is twice paired with another poem, "Womans constancy."[32] The first of these poems caused embarrassment among Donne's admirers even before the advent of feminist criticism, and nowadays the poem is often passed over as one of Donne's "simpler libertine lyrics."[33] Certainly, it seems beyond dispute that on what we once called the literal level "Communitie" is an argument for male promiscuity (rather than the more general promiscuity urged by "The Indifferent"). Furthermore, this masculinism takes on a particularly misogynistic quality in the final lines; the sexually utopian dream of multiple partners with "no strings" that we find in "The Indifferent" gives way to a darker fantasy in which, after the act, the sexual partner is reduced to a waste product to be discarded:

> Chang'd loves are but chang'd sorts of meat,
> And when he hath the kernall eate,
>   Who doth not fling away the shell?

(DONNE, 30)

Or, as Mick Jagger expressed the same idea: "who wants yesterday's papers? / who wants yesterday's girl?" However, in pairing "Communitie" with "Womans constancy," Donne, or at least a few of Donne's contemporary readers, may have seen an opportunity to carve out a space of discursive possibility for "yesterday's girl" that the Rolling Stones have never been capable of creating. The poem has not attracted much commentary and is short enough to quote in full:

> Now thou has lov'd me one whole day
> To morrow when thou leav'st, what will though say?
> Wilt thou then Antedate some new made vow?
>   Or say that now
> We are not just those persons, which we were?
> Or, that oathes made in reverentiall feare
> Of Love, and his wrath, any may forsweare?
> Or, as true deaths, true maryages untie,
> So lovers contracts, images of those,
> Binde but till sleep, death's image, them unloose?
>   Or, your own end to Justifie
> For having purpos'd change, and falsehood; you
> Can have no way but falsehood to be true?
> Vaine lunatique, against these scapes I could
>   Dispute, and conquer, if I would
>   Which I abstain to doe,
> For by to morrow, I may thinke so too.

(DONNE, 5)

Here the question, "What difference does difference make?" cannot be distinguished from an equally familiar and resonant inquiry: "What does it matter who is speaking?" As it turns out, criticism is at once not sure who is speaking here and absolutely certain that it matters. To be less cryptic: some have "heard" a man's voice speaking in "Womans constancy," and some a woman's, and the interpretations that either kind of "auditory" experience produces are, of course, grounded in and limited by that initial act of gendered "hearing."

In general, those critics who have heard a man speaking these lines dismiss the poem as a "mere celebration of sexual infidelity"[34]—that is, they offer an implicitly moralized response in the guise of a purely aesthetic reaction. More substantively, in the first half of the century, some readers saw (and "excused") the poem as a "sincere" lashing out from the wounded Donnean psyche, directed at a "real" unfaithful female lover.[35] Later critics question the "sincerity" of the verse, foregrounding its rhetorical cleverness, before finally (again) dismissing it as a pose that nevertheless "shows no complex consciousness behind it."[36] In both cases, aesthetic and moral responses are clearly mutually implicated without being examined. Thomas Docherty, who also hears a male speaker, and who self-consciously acknowledges the mutual implication of the moral and the aesthetic, is even more damning. Indeed, Docherty goes so far as to offer the first five lines of this poem as a central exhibit in his version of the argument to which I have already alluded: the argument that Donne constructs the feminine as fungible in order to facilitate his construction of the masculine (and hence of himself) as consistent, unchanging, and even immortal. In Docherty's words:

> These lines . . . indicate Donne's alignment of . . . changeability or promiscuity with what is characterized as the female Other. . . . The Other, woman, becomes the condition of Donne's literary self. . . . Alongside the ideological contempt for the female there runs what is perhaps the real rationale for such a suppression of this Other; not only a fear of historical death, but a fear of woman, and a tacit acknowledgment that the female is the source of whatever authority Donne appropriates in his poetic attempts at self construction. (61)

But what if the poem does not represent one of those "typical" Donnean speakers castigating a woman for her inconstancy, cruelty, and sophistry? Indeed, what if the very notion of that speaker as "typical" of Donne is one that this poem problematizes? Those critics who have heard a woman's voice speaking "Womans constancy" raise and answer this question in ways that, predictably enough, turn Docherty's interpretation on its head. Thus, in James S. Baumlin's reading, "Womans Constancy" is a metapoetic critique, "a poem about libertine poetry, about the folly and triteness of its reasoning."[37] Marotti, in *John Donne, Coterie Poet*, agrees and goes further. For him

> the pointed conclusion [of the poem] suggests not only that the woman could hold her own with counterarguments . . . but, as she indicates, she probably shares her lover's libertinism. In the internal rhetorical space of the lyric, then, the speaker . . . serves as a useful means of displacing male libertinism from its privileged position by co-opting its arguments and attitudes. The emotional advantage is the woman's because she dramatically disappoints her lover's expectations that she will be hurt by abandonment. (74)

To summarize: It appears that if the poem is heard in a male voice, it is understood as either aesthetically slight—as simply not a very good poem—or, more complexly but no less damningly, as part of a politically retrograde masculinist project of self-substantiation that strategically denigrates "woman," rendering her as "Other" or as abject; however, if the poem is heard in a female voice, it is transformed into a clever metapoetic commentary on masculinist discourse, a discourse it may even neutralize through subversive appropriation. Furthermore, once juxtaposed with more conventional texts, the arguments of "Womans constancy" spread corrosively, like acid leaking from a battery, gradually destroying (or at least significantly undermining) the masculinist apparatus that surrounds but cannot contain it.

Can the poem be both of these things? What kind of evidence would settle the question? The title doesn't help—it has clearly been read by some as indicating a male speaker and by others as indicating a female speaker, and in any case, as I have already noted with reference to "The Indifferent," it is almost certainly not Donne's (in the two Dalhousie manuscripts the poem is untitled). What other clues are available, then? Those critics persuaded that they hear a male speaker can of course simply point to the preponderance of "masculinist" lyrics in the Donnean canon and argue that there's no strong reason to "give" the poem to a woman. But this argument can just as easily be reversed: as long as *some* poems are admitted as being "ventriloquized" performances, then why not more? Indeed, perhaps we should not be insisting on the preponderance of male and masculinist speakers in Donne's work but asking just how many of the texts can be convincingly (re)assigned to women; again, as I have already noted, certain of Donne's manuscript readers seem to have placed this particular poem in canceling relation to the overtly masculinist "Communitie," suggesting that it *was* read by some readers in a female voice during the early seventeenth century.

However, such acts of historical contextualization provide no further interpretive guarantees, since other equally "historical" contexts can be offered that will complicate our response yet again. To gesture toward another possible turn in this seemingly endless masculinist/feminist dance of hegemony and subversion, it might be pointed out, contra Baumlin and Marotti, that a poem can of course be written in a female "voice" and nevertheless speak in the service of an ideology that is ultimately patriarchal and misogynistic. As several recent studies have observed, "one of the most striking characteristics of early modern pornography is the preponderance of female narrators," among whom Aretino's Nana is only the most famous.[38] On these grounds, Ronald Corthell interprets Donne's acts of heterofemale ventriloquism with their "sexually free and active" female speakers as a less than progressive embodiment of "male fantasy." For Corthell, while such poems may "critique gender stereotypes" (or, in the terms I have used, while these poems may indeed refuse to distinguish between men and women at the level of desire), they also "release the sorts of fantasies that help to produce those stereotypes."[39]

It is tempting to conclude from all of this that (once again) the only real lesson that the tradition of Donnean criticism teaches is one regarding the nature of interpretation itself, rather than one regarding the objects ostensibly under investigation; and (once again), in this case that lesson turns out to be a feminist principle: meaning depends on the imputation of gender. However, as I have unfolded the story, I hope that perhaps a further element has become apparent: the complex role played by fantasy in this process. As Corthell's particular evocation of the "pornographic" demonstrates, when dealing with Donne's fantasies of gender we are also often dealing with critical fantasies about the gendered nature of fantasy itself. Thus, for Corthell, the evocation of a "pornographic" analogue is quite enough to render Donne's female speaker suspiciously masculinist (even though he also admits that many of the poems actually offer "little in the way of prurient interest"). Corthell's argument at this point depends on a particular (and admittedly widely held) fantasy about the nature of "pornographic" fantasies, one that sees such fantasies as *necessarily* in the service of a negative masculinist politics. But, of course, Corthell's sense of the term represents only one possible understanding of the political dimensions of the discourse we call "pornographic," as is readily apparent from the bewildering variety of stances that feminist and other thinkers have taken on the question in recent years.[40] Something similar might be said of Marotti's fantasy of an all-male audience for "The Indifferent" (and so many other Donne poems) or, indeed, his fantasy of a "liberated" female speaker in "Womans constancy"; these are interpretive fantasies that see fantasy itself as gendered in readily interpretable ways.

The interpretations that I have considered in the foregoing pages thus might all be said to rely on a false dichotomy between the psychic (Donne's sexual fantasies and their possible meanings) and the material (sexed bodies). What these analyses of Donne's sexual politics forget, in other words, is that for any account of the relations between desire and power, of a politics of sexuality, a theory of fantasy as a production of meanings and identities is essential.[41] Again, this is not to suggest that "fantasy" must or even can be thought of in some space "outside" of gender; it is only to point out that *gender is itself a fantasy*. Grounding our interpretations of sexual fantasies in notions of gender is not something we can choose *not* to do—but it might be likened to attempting to hang a picture while standing on a rocking chair.

Having considered the role of critical fantasies of gender in the production of "Donne's" meanings, my own critical fantasy regarding Donne's fantasies of gender, at least as they operate in a poem like "Womans constancy," is slightly different. For me, the astonishing thing about the poem is not that it can be read as masculinist or feminist according to the presumed gender of its "speaker" but, rather, that it has been so insistently read as *either* one thing *or* the other. Perhaps unsurprisingly, given my argument regarding Donne's attempts to elide as well as reinscribe gendered difference, when I attempt to see the poem without imposing reified fantasies of gender, I notice that its final lines actually function in such as way as to make distinctions based on gender *irrelevant*. In other words, *whatever* the gender of the speaker or the addressee of the poem, and *whatever* power relationship may be implied by that gendered dynamic, the last lines work to reverse that relation: "To morrow I may think so too." In sum, the poem's final lines feature a speaker of uncertain gender talking to another speaker of uncertain gender and saying: "Your perspective and mine on questions of sexual relationships are interchangeable; at the level of desire there is no difference between us." It is the institution of criticism that has continually insisted upon reinscribing gendered difference as essential to the signification of this poem; but the logic of the poem itself—if I may be forgiven an old-fashioned locution that depends, of course, on the most fundamental critical fantasy of all—the logic of the poem itself works precisely to escape or elide that difference.

Having finally revealed my own fantasy of "Womans constancy," I will now cast aside my interpretive inhibitions altogether and suggest further that this poem has been consistently (mis)interpreted in the ways that it has precisely because it asks us to take the somewhat counterintuitive step that I have been urging throughout this entire chapter (with the support of Butler, Correll, and others): it problematizes the function of sexual difference as a ground of meaning and thereby demands that we reconsider the relation of representation to sex and gender. Indeed, the poem demonstrates that the gender of a representation is no more "inherent" or self-declaring than any other aspect of its meaning; and concomitantly, it shows that gender is itself always already a form of representation and therefore something that is recognized and produced in the interactive process of interpretation, rather than something "given."

In the wake of such arguments, even certain Donne poems that ap-

pear overtly to reinscribe sexual difference can be shown simultane-
ously to partake of fantasies that collapse that difference, at the level
of desire. To return for a moment to "Sapho to Philaenis," it certainly
seems true that passages such as the following, wherein Donne's
Sappho urges her female lover (who has left her for a man) to come
back, are dependent for their rhetorical effect on a fundamental notion
of sexual difference:

> Plaies some softe Boy with thee, oh there wants yett
> A mutuall feeling, which should sweeten itt,
> His chin a thorny-hairye unevaneness
> Doth threaten; and some daly change possess . . .
> Menn leave behinde them that which their sin showes
> And are as theefes tract, which rob when it snowes
> But of our dalliance, no more signes there are,
> Than fishes leave in streames, or birds in aire . . . [42]

Sexual difference manifests itself as unmistakable in these competing
depictions of the sex act—although, at the same time, it is obviously
not being asserted in the manner that recent criticism has taught us to
expect (that is, to bolster the speaker's masculine anxiety at the thought
of becoming a woman).[43] But even leaving that fact to one side, some
little-remarked details of the poem complicate the picture. Just a few
lines after this description, "Sapho's" pleas take an autoerotic turn.
Standing before a mirror, "she" tells us that "Likeness begetts such
strange selfe flatterie, / That touchinge my selfe all seemes *done* to
thee."[44] I do not propose to consider this moment in relation to the
now much discussed question of whether Donne here figures same-sex
desire as narcissistic and hence as "failed." Such banal Freudianisms
obscure the question of what normative patriarchal culture gains by
insistently positing the narcissism-of-the-other (a disavowal of its own
narcissism perhaps?) and also project a conservative psychoanalytic
heteronormativity on the text that seems to me to be quite at odds with
its emotional tone.[45] Instead, I simply want to raise the possibility (rel-
atively neglected despite the burgeoning critical bibliography) that
Donne is punning on his own name with the phrase "all seemes *done*
to thee," as he does in numerous other works (perhaps most famously
in the repeated refrain from the "Hymn to God the Father": "when
thou has done, thou hast not *done*"). What are the possible effects of
this half-hidden authorial signature (if that is what we are glimpsing)?
Is it simply a sign that Donne could not bear to speak a whole poem
in Sappho's voice and so momentarily doffed his poetic mask to remind

us whose masculine creative force is really at work here? In other words, does this potential "slippage" between Sappho's ventriloquized voice and the authorial voice simply confirm that Donne's strategy is finally one of appropriation (as Elizabeth Harvey's reading suggests)?[46] Or could this be a "witty" and self-consciously titillating attempt to link Sappho's autoeroticism with his own activity in writing the poem? (Donne would hardly be the only male author to associate writing with masturbation, if so, although the cross-gendered form the association takes here is surely unusual.)

Having raised these questions, I will hesitate before attempting to answer them, since any answer would surely be complicated by another possible pun, just a few lines later still: "O cure this lovinge madnes and restore/Mee to mee, thee my halfe, my all my *more*." Anne Donne's maiden name, as I noted in my introduction, was More; and while Donne's tendency to pun on his wife's name is less well known than his tendency to pun on his own, some critics have suggested that he enjoyed playing this game, too (as, for example, in the second stanza of "A Valediction of my name, in the window": " 'Tis *more,* that it shewes thee to thee").[47] I am unaware of any analysis of "Sapho to Philaenis" that attempts to link both puns in a single reading.[48] But if Donne has inserted not only himself into the poem, but himself *and* his wife, then this would perhaps open up the possibility of a more radical reading than those that insist on condemning Donne for his masculinist "appropriation" of the female poetic voice (whatever that might mean in an early modern context) or lesbian desire (whatever *that* might mean in an early modern context). For in "Sapho to Philaenis," Donne does not seem to imagine and inscribe female-female desire in terms of his own marriage so much as he attempts to reimagine and reinscribe his marriage in terms of female-female desire. "Strange selfe flatterie," indeed? Yes, perhaps even strange enough to expose the imaginative limits of a criticism whose primary concern always seems to be whether this seventeenth-century text represents the female poet, or female-female desire, in a manner compatible with contemporary politics.

I'm not suggesting that one should never consider the issue of whether canonical authors of the past express attitudes and values that we would now want to question or challenge (of course one should).[49] But such projects must also consider whether and how authors question and challenge attitudes and values in their own present (although the kinds of interpretive reconstruction involved in such considerations must inevitably be speculative, not to say highly demanding of the interpreter). And while I'm not sure that I would go quite as far as H. L. Meakin, for whom " 'Sapho to Philaenis' demands that we question the fundamentals of human relationship in ways unlike any other poem of its time," I do think that if Donne is even potentially aligning one of the most significant cross-gender relationships of his life with one of the few cultural models of female-female desire and agency available to him, then it may be reductive, not to say unjust, to accuse him of antifeminist appropriation, with Holstun and Harvey, or to dismiss him as a male narcissist writing for other male narcissists, as Woodcock does, or to insist that he sees female-female desire as paralyzed by failure, as Correll claims, or to read his depiction of female-female desire exclusively in the context of the "lesbian" scenes in contemporary male-oriented pornography, as Corthell does.[50] After all, when the structure of human relations we now call "heterosexuality" is indistinguishable from a value system we now identify as misogynistic, can we blame a man who loves women for being interested in alternative models and configurations of desire? At the very least, the critical readings that I have surveyed are blind to the possibility that even in "Sapho to Philaenis," as elsewhere in his work, Donne is drawn to the fantasy that, at the level of desire, the difference between men and women may be no difference at all.[51]

IV

> What happens to souls once they are separated from their bodies? Do they or don't they lose their identities?
>
> —PIERRE KLOSSOWSKI, *THE BAPHOMET*

In arguing for the presence within Donne's work of a tendency to collapse as well as reinscribe notions of sexual difference, it may be thought that, despite my judicious use of poststructuralist theories of gender and sexuality, I am finally allying myself with that strain of Donnean interpretation that emphasizes the "mutuality" or "protofeminism" of his verse—a strain of interpretation that, as I have already observed, has always run counter to that which emphasizes his acts of masculinist assertion and sexist attitudinizing. However, this would be a misunderstanding of my position. While I hope that I have complicated the picture of Donne's attitude toward sexual difference as it is presented in the work of those critics who focus exclusively on Donne's masculinism and misogyny, the fact that I am *not* trying to argue that Donne is not "really" a misogynist after all bears repeating. Instead, I am interested in the simultaneous co-presence *and* mutual exclusivity of two postures toward sexual difference—the posture of reinscription *and* the posture of collapse—in Donne's work; and I have been diagnosing not Donne but rather the critical tendency to focus always and only upon *one* of these two postures at the expense of the other. Part of the purpose of this chapter has been to locate one explanation for this critical tendency in the fact that our own fantasies of sexual difference, and, indeed, our fantasies about sexual fantasies, are often reified as forms of interpretive ontology; and I have attempted to counter the powerfully influential accounts that portray Donne as constantly in the grip of an anxiously masculinist pathology by drawing on the principle (cogently summarized by Valerie Traub) that "desire and anxiety . . . involve fantasies of the other, fantasies that transform and recombine elements of the existing social formation."[52] But an obvious question—indeed, perhaps the harder question—remains: what impulses might finally be pushing Donne to repeatedly engage in such seemingly opposed acts of representation? In short (and if we assume for the moment that I am correct to see Donne as reinscribing sexual difference in some places *and* blurring that difference in others), then why does he do as he does?

The question is perhaps a little misleading, in that it is unlikely that a single explanation could be found, or even should be sought—each individual representational act would have to be considered on its own terms. Nevertheless, I would like to conclude by offering some speculations that address this issue, speculations of perhaps a more traditional literary-historical kind that I have heretofore provided.

It is a familiar commonplace of Donne criticism that many of his poems are "anti-Petrarchan."[53] By this, it is generally meant that Donne is hostile to the long-standing tradition of Neo-platonic spiritualizing associated with Petrarch and many other Italian humanists—a tradition best represented by Castiglione's heterosexual revision of Plato's *Symposium* in the final *Book of the Courtier,* wherein physical love is denigrated as the lowest rung on a philosophical ladder that ascends toward a disembodied ideal. In poems that thematize what we might call "simple anti-Petrarchism," this Neoplatonic ladder is inverted so that physical love, often metaphorized as "the body," comes to represent the apogee of emotional experience. I think the best illustrations of this kind of "simple anti-Petrarchism" are not found in Donne's work but in that of his massively influential English poetic predecessor, Sir Philip Sidney. Consider, for example, the fifty-second sonnet of *Astrophil and Stella*:

> A strife is grown between Virtue and Love
> While each pretends that Stella must be his:
> Her eyes, her lips, her all, saith Love, do this
> (Since they do wear his badge) most firmly prove.
> But Virtue thus that title doth disprove:
> That Stella (O dear name) that Stella is
> That virtuous soul, sure heir of heavenly bliss,
> Not this fair outside, which our hearts doth move;
> And therefore though her beauty and her grace
> Be Love's indeed, in Stella's self he may
> By no pretence claim any manner place.
> Well, Love, since this demur our suit doth stay,
> Let Virtue have that Stella's self; yet thus,
> That Virtue but that body grant to us.[54]

Here, the personifications of "Virtue" and "Love" represent opposite ends of the traditional Neoplatonic ladder. For the first twelve lines the poem appears to grant the traditional Neoplatonic view—that Stella's true "self" is not her "fair outside" (that is, her body) but rather "That virtuous soul, sure heir of heavenly bliss." The logic of this commonplace argument leads us to expect a commonplace conclusion; that, as a good Christian Neoplatonist, "Astrophil" should learn to love Stella for her soul, not her body—and if this poem had been written by Petrarch, that probably would have been what we got. However, the last two lines of Sidney's poem self-consciously violate this expectation; the poet suddenly doffs his Neoplatonic mask to reveal the anti-Petrarchan beneath, contemptuously announcing that he's not interested in Stella's "soul," even if it is her true "self." Thus the poem ends with a sneering piece of proto-frat-boy wit: "Let virtue have that Stella's self; yet thus, / That Virtue but that body grant to us"—that is, "As long as I can have access to that body, you can keep her soul."

Despite the fact that the names Sidney and Donne are often casually linked in discussions of poetry and/as misogyny, Donne is rarely a "simple anti-Petrarchan" in this Sidneyan sense[55]—indeed, few poets are capable of Sidney's brilliant (if disturbing) succinctness and playful ease within this (anti) tradition. Nevertheless, many of Donne's most controversial and complex poems can and have been read as attempts to complicate or revise the hierarchical distinctions that dominate the Petrarchan and Neoplatonic traditions, between body and soul, or flesh and spirit. Perhaps the most famous and commonly adduced example of Donne's investment in embodied, physicalized (and thus anti-Platonic) love occurs in the final lines of "The Extasie":

> But O alas, so long, so farre
> Our bodies why doe we forbeare?
> They are ours, though not wee, Wee are
> The intelligences, they the spheres . . .

However, even in this poem, Donne's return to the body is no simple inversion of the Neoplatonic ladder. Instead, the poet wants to affirm *and* deny the body, and this produces the central paradox of "The Extasie." For the emotion that the two lovers feel has already been described as transcending biology, in the fundamental sense of "sexe":

> This Extasie doth unperplex
> (We said) and tell us what we love
> We see by this it was not sexe
> We see, we saw not what did move . . .

Here attraction of the most ecstatic kind is not based on gendered difference—that is, not based on the mutual recognition and attraction of differently sexed bodies—but precisely on something that is not amenable to the senses, something that "moves" us but that we cannot see. In short, for Donne, the knot that is "unperplexed" (here a Latinate neologism meaning "unweave") by the experience of the highest form of love is the knot of sexual difference itself.[56]

Now, as is well known, every dominant discourse in Donne's culture—the theological, the legal, and medical—asserts the essential inferiority of women; indeed, James Turner has written that "the need to make women 'naturally' inferior simply hangs in isolation" throughout the period, "beyond logic and beyond even the Logos, as a pure ideological imperative."[57] However, as we can see from the example of "The Extasie," in its most refined form, Neoplatonic idealism held out the possibility (or perhaps I should say the fantasy) of a desire that transcended the body, a desire that could therefore also potentially transcend notions of gendered hierarchy grounded in the "facts" of the sexed body, rendering men and women not just complementary beings (as the humanist ideology of the companionate marriage might have it) but, precisely, equal. (This spiritual equality, though still figured in terms of an antagonism, is actually rendered explicit early in the poem: "As . . . two *equall* Armies . . . [so] Our soules.")[58] I believe that Donne was unable to let go of this aspect of Neoplatonism entirely, despite his obvious investment in embodied desire, because he saw in it a way to justify his love of women before the gaze of what Lacan would call the big Other—that is, within the misogynistic symbolic order in which he could not help but be immersed. However, he was acutely conscious of the risk attending such Neoplatonic logic, the risk of backsliding (or, in the Neoplatonist's own terms, ascending) into an entirely disembodied, spiritualized realm. These conflicting impulses—to transcend gender and yet also to hold on to the body—not only lie behind the famous paradoxical relation of body to spirit in "The Extasie" (a relation that dozens of critical essays have attempted to explicate) but may also explain the obscurity of a lesser-known lyric such as the following:

The Undertaking

I have done one braver thing
  Then all the Worthies did,
And yet a braver thence doth spring
  Which is, to keepe that hid.

It were but madnes now t'impart
  The skill of specular stone,
When he which can have learn'd the art
  To cut it can finde none.

So, if I now should utter this,
  Others (because no more
 Such stuffe to worke upon, there is)
  Would love but as before.
But he who lovelinesse within
  Hath found, all outward loathes,
For he who colour loves, and skinne,
  Loves but their oldest clothes.

If as I have you also doe
  Vertue'attir'd in woman see
And dare love that and say so too
  And forget the Hee and Shee;

And if this love, though placed so
  From prophane men you hide,
Which will no faith on this bestow,
  Or if they doe, deride:

> Then you have done a braver thing
> Then all the Worthies did.
> And a braver thence will spring
> Which is, to keepe that hid.

This poem is titled "Platonique Love" in some manuscripts—which gives some idea of how easily Donne's position could on occasion be elided with or mistaken for that of conventional Neoplatonism. However, the poem seems less than straightforwardly "platonique" in its insistence that the kind of love-beyond-sex it advocates must be kept hidden from the eyes of "prophane men." It is almost as if Donne recognizes that such a love violates rather than confirms patriarchal ideology, so strong is his (twice repeated) insistence that it must be kept out of sight. In an interesting corollary of my arguments in my second chapter, it seems that, in the Renaissance, the love that dare not speak its name is not homosexuality but rather any love that dares to posit a woman as worthy of a man's complete devotion. The crucial line for my purposes, however, is that injunction to "forget the Hee and Shee." Michael Schoenfeldt has traced the origins of this sentiment to the Pauline argument that "there is no male and female for we are all one in Christ"; I agree with Schoenfeldt that this Pauline commonplace is precisely to the point, because while sexual difference is apparently rejected here, in Paul's theology the body will nevertheless be resurrected (and Donne's own belief in the resurrection of the body is well attested in the sermons and the critical literature).[59]

In summary, then, the two strains of thought regarding sexual difference that I have identified in Donne's work—that of reinscription, traditionally read as indicative of his misogyny, and that of indistinction, traditionally read as indicative of his protofeminism—are in fact the two distinct symptoms of two conflicting desires: the first being the desire to refuse the Neoplatonic tendency to denigrate the role of the body in love ("our bodies why do we forbeare?"); the second being the desire to detach one's object cathexis from any notion of the sex of the object ("forget the Hee and Shee") in order to escape essentialized notions of gendered hierarchy. We might say that in philosophical terms Donne wants to have his cake and eat it, to possess his lover's body *and* to leave it, to embrace physicality and at the same time to transcend the limitations apparently imposed by biology.

Donne's double fantasy is one that criticism has insistently reduced to an either/or, because each half of his doubled desire can be assimilated to the two opposed critical fantasies of the present day that I have explicated here: the fantasy of sexual difference as an essential condition fundamentally circumscribing the processes of representation and interpretation, and the fantasy of sexual difference as always already a matter of representation and interpretation. Although our reasoning and our reasons are not Donne's, we, too, would often like to "forget the Hee and Shee" by repudiating essentialist notions of difference; and yet, equally often, we feel that we cannot afford to "forbeare" the lived experience of the body. Before repudiating *or* defending Donne's fantasies of gender, then, perhaps we should first acknowledge our own—and acknowledge, too, that sometimes those fantasies may not be more sophisticated than Donne's. At the very least, poems like "Womans constancy" can be productively reread in the light of such inquiries; but perhaps more important, if we can come to recognize that in our critical fantasies of gender, we have not left the utopian dreams of a seventeenth-century "masculinist" like Donne so very far behind, we may learn a still rarer intellectual lesson: generosity.

CHAPTER FIVE

All or Nothing

The Possibility of Love

Throughout this book I have attended to the nexus of relations between knowledge, fantasy, and desire in critical interpretations of Donne's texts; but knowledge, fantasy, and desire are obviously also thematic concerns of those texts themselves. While I would not claim that a single consistent philosophical position can be extracted from Donne's various meditations on these themes, many of his individual poems can be read as self-reflexive theorizations of desire. In this chapter, then, I will reread Donne's poetic attempts to theorize desire through and against the work of perhaps the most influential theorist of the desiring subject to have emerged in contemporary academic discourse: Jacques Lacan. I will resist the temptation to "explain" Donne through Lacan— a practice that begs obvious questions of methodology—and instead juxtapose their ideas in what I hope is a mutually illuminating fashion. In the process, I hope to demonstrate that Donne's theorizations of desire are at least as sophisticated as those of the twentieth century, and may even show up some of the limitations of Lacanian orthodoxy (insofar as orthodoxies can be extracted from work as challenging and opaque as Lacan's) regarding the condition we call "love."

Although I explicate Lacan's key terms where necessary, and indicate (in notes) the ways in which some of his ideas would change over the course of his long career, I do not pretend to offer a fully comprehensive analysis of Lacan's thought. Some Lacanians may therefore find my account self-servingly piecemeal (since, for example, I make use of his "three orders" of the Imaginary, the Symbolic, and the Real, but judiciously avoid discussing notoriously problematic concepts like the signification of the phallus). I cannot entirely deny this charge, although I would prefer to characterize my approach as justifiably selective; I would add that to read Lacan selectively, rather than as a scientist or philosopher whose system must be absorbed and applied in toto, is to respond to his texts in a way that they implicitly (that is, stylistically) invite. I find support for this claim in the remarks of one of Lacan's most talented translators, Bruce Fink. For Fink, Lacan's thought does not simply resist systematic reformulation—it resists translation into *any* idiom other than "Lacanian French." Thus, speaking of the collected *Ecrits*, Fink declares that "translation into other languages is obviously impossible, at one level, when not altogether ridiculous"; but, in a disarmingly ingenuous acknowledgment of Lacan's difficulty, he goes on to express the hope that readers will find in his translations "an inexhaustible source of provocative formulations that stick with them *even if they aren't the least bit sure what they mean.*"[1] If Fink's Lacan sounds more like a modernist (or metaphysical) poet than an analyst at such moments, this is surely all the more reason to read Donne alongside him, rather than simply through him.

I

> The truest poetry is most feigning . . .
>
> —WILLIAM SHAKESPEARE, *AS YOU LIKE IT*

Like Lacan, Donne is notorious for his resonant, oracular formulations, for his vast learning, and for the extreme syntactic compression, intellectual difficulty, and outright obscurity of his writing. I believe that the rhetorical resemblances between the two figures are more than superficial and are highly instructive. It is not simply that both writers can be at once memorable and hard to understand, but that even when they do appear to make perfect sense on one level, they may make no sense at all at another level—and, moreover, these unusual disjunctions between sense and nonsense are often essential to the overall effect of their rhetoric.

Consider, for example, the following well-known poem:

> *The Flea*
> Marke but this flea, and marke in this,
> How little that which thou deny'st me is;

It suck'd me first, and now sucks thee,
And in this flea, our two bloods mingled bee;
Thou know'st that this cannot be said
A sinne, nor shame, nor loss of maidenhead,
    Yet this enjoyes before it wooe,
    And pamper'd swells with one blood made of two
    And this, alas, is more than wee would doe.

Oh stay, three lives in one flea spare,
Where wee almost, yea more than maryed are.
This flea is you and I, and this
Our marriage bed, and marriage temple is;
Though parents grudge, and you, w'are met,
And cloystered in these living walls of Jet.
    Though use make you apt to kill mee,
    Let not to that, selfe murder added bee,
    And sacrilege, three sinnes in killing three.

Cruell and sodiane, hast thou since
Purpled thy naile, in blood of innocence?
Wherein could this flea guilty bee,
Except in that drop which it suckt from thee?
Yet thou triumph'st, and saist that thou
Find'st not thy selfe, nor mee the weaker now;
    'Tis true, then learne how false, feares bee;
    Just so much honor, when thou yeeld'st to mee,
    Will wast, as this flea's death tooke life from thee.

(DONNE, *THE COMPLETE ENGLISH POEMS*, 2. SUBSEQUENT REFERENCES WILL
APPEAR IN THE TEXT AS "DONNE.")

The first poem in the 1635 edition of Donne's works, and often the
first in many modern editions, "The Flea" is also one of a small handful
that the reader is certain to discover in any anthologized selection of
Donne's verse; it is therefore fair to describe it as one of the most
popular and successful of all Donne's amorous lyrics. And yet it seems
unlikely that the success of the poem has anything to do with the logic
of Donne's reasoning. In fact, Donne makes clear that even the (entirely
fictitious?) woman addressed by the poem doesn't take his arguments
seriously, by having her kill the hapless flea around which his entire
performance is constructed between stanzas two and three.

The charm of this perennial favorite poem might be said to persist
not in spite of its failure as a convincing justification for premarital
sex, then, but precisely because of it. Its persuasive force, such as it is,
is directly proportional to its refusal of what we generally mean by

commonsense, and its reversal of conventional values: the rendering of a banally familiar lusty impulse in terms drawn from scholastic discussions of the theological mystery of the Trinity, the elevation of the trivial and the repulsive to the monumental, and so on. To deploy a vulgar but, I think, entirely appropriate idiomatic expression, the poem offers us a brilliantly self-conscious line of seductive bullshit—which is to say that the speaker takes a series of ever more elaborate rhetorical risks on the understanding that arguments don't always have to be received as literally true in order to do the job required. Indeed, the long-standing popularity of this poem would indicate that sometimes bullshit is exactly what we want, while its own internal logic implies that, at times, bullshit is the *only* thing that will persuade, where other more sincere forms of argument, exhortation, and protestation have failed.

To be clear: I am not saying that a reader who finds this poem successful *believes* Donne's bullshit but, rather, that he or she must accept the poet's implicit invitation to go along with it—that is, he or she accepts the invitation to be complicit in the generation of productive (or perhaps simply pleasurable) fantasies. To this extent, the poem perfectly illustrates the discourse of seduction as defined by Jean Baudrillard; seduction involves the knowing manipulation of the symbolic rather than the actual, and ultimately undermines the difference between seducer and seducee, since, for Baudrillard, one always has to *allow* oneself to be seduced.[2] To put the same point slightly differently: if we imagine that a woman could be persuaded to "yeeld" to Donne as a result of the argument of the "The Flea," as the poem invites us to do, then we must also imagine that same woman as at some level already persuaded, already sharing the desire of the speaker (even if not consciously or openly)—since it is self-evident that the argument of "The Flea" couldn't possibly convince someone who wasn't ready to be convinced (unless that person was astonishingly gullible).[3]

The rhetorical operation of "The Flea" bears comparison with the rhetorical operation of Lacan's textual voice, in one of his dominant modes. In making such a claim, I am of course also suggesting that we are sometimes justified in thinking of Lacan as a brilliantly seductive bullshitter. But as I hope my brief reading of Donne's poem indicates, such a description does not have to signify entirely negatively. To call someone a brilliantly seductive bullshitter may be to offer them a backhanded compliment, but it *is* a compliment, nonetheless. Moreover, when I call Lacan a seductive bullshitter I actually mean something rather less backhanded; I mean that, like Donne in "The Flea," Lacan recognizes that the discourse of the seductive bullshitter is a vital one, capable of a kind of persuasive work that more putatively direct and "honest" discursive modes cannot perform.[4]

Certainly, it is easy to demonstrate Lacan's investment in the rhetorical posture of the seducer, à la Baudrillard; he is constantly foregrounding his mastery over language, while at the same time either implicitly or explicitly insisting on our lack of control over the world beyond words (where human mastery is never more than imaginary). Witness his awful puns ("linguistricks," "extimacy," "l'hommelette," and so on), which often take on a life of their own, producing wild and sometimes entirely irrelevant associations quite independent of any point that Lacan is making.[5] Similarly, and despite Lacan's occasional claims to the contrary, it is tempting to read some of the anecdotal meanderings of his seminars as seductively exuberant displays of oratorical mastery rather than as conventionally didactic. This digressive style can also function in a more conventionally seductive fashion, as a kind of deliberate intellectual teasing.

But Lacan's flirtatiousness can be more overt. It is another interesting point of parallel or rather symmetry between the two authors that where Donne famously deploys all kinds of arcane knowledge (theological, alchemical, philosophical, scientific) in order (ostensibly) to lead us to the pleasures of the bedroom, Lacan will often adopt an overtly sexy register in order (ostensibly) to lead us to the pleasures of arcane knowledge (theological, alchemical, philosophical, scientific). "Honey is what I am trying to bring you," he purrs at the opening of the second session of Seminar VII; introducing Seminar XI *(The Four Fundamental Concepts of Psychoanalysis)* he punningly insinuates that "the fundamentals would take the form of the *bottom* parts, were it not that those parts were already . . . exposed"; and at the first meeting of Seminar XX he coos that "I am first of all going to assume that you are in bed . . . a bed employed to its fullest."[6]

In the case of both authors, the aim of such mixed modes of address is sometimes hard to discern. It's as if they can't quite decide if they are going for the head or the heart, the mind or the genitals. Indeed, an Augustan mistrust of such rhetorical and generic confusion lies behind Dryden's famous criticism that Donne "perplexes the minds of the fair sex" when he launches into elaborate philosophical speculations in the middle of what is supposed to be a love poem, after all. But then again, for thinkers for whom desire and knowledge are inextricably linked, such confusions of register are precisely to the point and must be embraced rather than eschewed.

The central role of bullshit within Lacan's thought is no less obvious than his investment in seduction, when we consider the complex significations of terms like "truth" and "knowledge" in his teaching and writing. Truth, for Lacan, is less a matter of objective observation but refers, rather, to the truth of the patient's desire. In Lacan's words: "If the truth we are seeking is a truth that frees, it is a truth that we will look for in a hiding place in our subject. It is a particular truth."[7] Which is to say that this particular truth might well be empirically false; only its truth status for the patient counts. Moreover, Lacan insists elsewhere on the "profound ambiguity of any assertion on the part of the patient, and the fact that it [the assertion] is, of itself, double-sided."[8] Indeed, the analysand not only never quite tells the truth, but is perhaps least interesting when making the effort (for it is then that we are most likely to be offered empty clichés: "I feel hollow inside"; "I love him more than anything"; "I know I should be happy, but . . ."; and so on). For Lacan, it is the *false* beliefs of the patient that are the most intimate and authentic. Thus, Slavoj Žižek writes apropos of the "early" Lacan that "the aim of psychoanalytic treatment is . . . to re-focus attention from factual accuracy to hysterical lies, *which unknowingly articulate the truth,* and then to progress to a new knowledge . . . what the Lacan of the 1950s called 'full speech' . . . in which *subjective truth reverberates.*"[9] Like the reader who takes pleasure in "The Flea," the Lacanian is asked to prize bullshit more highly than inevitably failed attempts at honesty. That Lacan recognized and relished this irony is evident from his claim that the central psychoanalytic method of free association essentially involves telling the patient: "Come on, say anything, it will all be marvelous!"[10]

Lacan also attributes a tremendously powerful seductive force to bullshit in his account of transference—Freud's name for the over-determined relationship that develops between patient and analyst, which must be "worked through" in any successful treatment. For Lacan, transference has not occurred until the patient gives the analyst the place of "the subject supposed to know." But what is the analyst supposed to know? "He is supposed to know that from which no one can escape, as soon as he formulates it—quite simply, signification."[11] In other words, for the transference to begin, the patient must attribute to the analyst the ability to hear the secret messages contained in the patient's speech and to bring the patient to knowledge of himself or herself that would otherwise remain hidden. At the same time, Lacan emphasizes that the analyst does not actually possess this knowledge and must not give in to the temptation to believe that he does. He must not fall for his own bullshit, and he must encourage the patient to move beyond his or her misrecognition of the analyst as the-subject-supposed-to-know if psychoanalysis is to escape the charge that it works primarily by suggestion. Thus, in a manner that again seems resonant of the mode of seductive bullshitter adopted by the speaker of "The Flea," the Lacanian "discourse of the analyst" constitutes a complicated form of autosubversion. It is a discourse that attempts to engage the patient's desire while simultaneously refusing any claim to "real" mastery, any relation to the realm of the actual. (In Lacanese, the analyst attempts to become the "object-cause" of the patient's desire.) Through this seductive self-subversion on the part of the analyst, it is supposed, the patient eventually comes to recognize that the transformational power of analysis derives not from the analyst's superior knowledge but rather from the extent to which his discourse reflects the patient's own desire back to the patient.[12] With the eventual recognition that the analyst is not really the-subject-supposed-to-know, but only a discursive function or cipher by which the patient comes to acknowledge his or her own disavowed desires, the analysis is considered complete.

Thus we might say for Lacan, as for Donne in "The Flea," the road of bullshit leads to the truth of desire and, from thence, it is hoped, to freedom to live according to that truth: that is, freedom from the neuroses brought on by shame, denial, disavowal, and repression—or, at least, freedom from ignorance as to the cause of those neuroses.[13] The free country of Lacanian psychoanalysis is not a moral vacuum, however, but runs according to ethical principles. Lacan is always enough of a Kantian to know that the only freedom that really makes sense is the freedom to obey the law. In fact, Lacan's ethics can be reduced to a single (admittedly tricky) sentence, one that builds on the Freudian maxim "Where Id was, I shall be"; "the true duty" of the "I" who emerges from the "Id," Lacan insists, is to oppose the fearful injunctions of the superego by refusing to give way on his or her desire.[14] The conclusion of "The Flea" similarly extols the truth of human desire over and above the social "superego" of traditional sexual moralism ("just so much honor") and expresses a similar faith that freedom from neurotic guilt will follow; in obeying the "truth" of our desire, Donne insists, we can also "learne how false, feares bee."

That's the theory, at any rate. "But is that the whole of our discovery?" Lacan asks himself in 1959. "Is that the whole of our morality? That attenuation, that exposure to the light of day, that discovery of the thought of desire, of the truth of that thought? Do we expect that as a result of its mere disclosure the area will be swept clean for a different thought?" The answer is yes: "In one way, it is indeed so, it is as simple as that."[15]

But, of course, it cannot remain so simple. Lacan continues, "Yet at the same time if we formulate things thus, then everything remains veiled for us." Indeed, there is a very real sense in which the next twenty years of Lacan's career can be read as a continuous attempt to pierce that veil in order to better understand the basic operation of psychoanalysis, by means of such "discoveries" as the Thing; the Big Other; the agency of the letter; the Three Orders of Being; the *objet petit a;* the stain of *jouissance;* the logic of the Symptom; the Real of the *sinthome;* the lamella; the command to "Enjoy!"; the Borromean knot; and numerous other, ever more elaborate and challenging concepts. But perhaps it would be more accurate to write that each of these strange and fascinating ideas constitutes a different attempt to *paint* rather than to pierce the veil in question, a veil that Lacan already knows can actually never be pierced, because the veil of which he speaks is a necessary veil, cast by thought itself over the chaos of being: it is the veil of perception.

We must commit some knowledge to obscurity in order to know anything at all—this is perhaps the single most important message that Lacan deciphers in the writings of Freud. The lesson of the unconscious is that the bright torch of the human mind cannot help but throw some shadows, too. Fascinatingly, Lacan at his most Freudian bears a curious resemblance to Donne at his most mystical. For Donne, too, recognizes that the inevitable failure of reason is part of the price of being human: that the condition of not knowing is, in fact, *evidence* of one's humanity. In the first of his *Essays in Divinity* he writes:

Men which seek God by reason, and naturall strength . . . are like Mariners which voyaged before the invention of the Compass, which were but Costers, and unwillingly left the sight of the land. Such are they which would arrive at God by this world, and contemplate him onely in his Creatures, and seeming Demonstration. Certainly, every Creature shewes God, as a glass, but glimmeringly and transitorily, by the frailty both of the receiver, and beholder . . . [and] by these meditations we get no further, than to know what he *doth,* not what he *is.* But as by the use of the

Compass, men safely dispatch *Ulysses* dangerous ten years travell in so many dayes . . . so doth Faith, as soon as our hearts are touched with it, direct and inform us in that great search of the discovery of Gods Essence . . . which Reason durst not attempt. . . . By this faith, as by reason, I know, that God is all that which all men can say of all Good; I beleeve he is [also] somewhat which no man can say or know. For, *si scirem quid Deus esset, Deus essem* [If I knew the being of God, I should be God]. For all acquired knowledg is by degrees, and successive; but God is impartible, and only faith which can receive it all at once, can comprehend him.[16]

"Reason," we should note, is not something that Donne simply rejects here. Nor does he merely insist, with any number of theologians, that the greatest knowledge lies beyond reason's reach; reason *does* provide access to "that which all men can *say* of all Good," to knowledge that can be verbalized. The point is not so much that reason fails, then, but that its most positive value is, paradoxically, negative. It is only in the *failure* of reason that we are afforded a glimpse of Divine totality; moreover, it is only in knowing that we *don't* know that we come to know ourselves for what we are.

In both Donne's negative theology and Lacanian psychoanalysis, then, the human being is defined by a failure to comprehend: defined, precisely, as the subject *not* supposed to know. Indeed, Lacan gestures toward an explicitly religious formulation of the epistemological challenge he is trying to negotiate in the introduction to Seminar XI, when he attempts to distinguish the production of psychoanalytic knowledge from "research" in the scientific sense.

Personally, I have never regarded myself as a researcher. As Picasso once said, to the shocked surprise of those around him—I do not seek, I find. . . . Furthermore, there is no doubt some affinity between the research that seeks and the religious register. In the religious register the phrase is often used—You would not seek me if you had not already found me. The already found is already behind, but stricken by something like oblivion. Is it not, then, a complaisant, endless search that is then opened up?[17]

Of course, where Donne finds some comfort in the compass of his faith, which at least points toward the horizon beyond which he cannot think, Lacan's analogous notion of the *already found* flickers for only the briefest of moments and then is gone again, "stricken by something like oblivion." Where Donne's reasoning seeker after God is at least engaged in a heroic sea quest, Lacan sounds more like the nihilistic protagonist of a Beckett novel, compelled to seek the truth but simultaneously (always already) condemned to ignorance—and indeed, this is precisely the difference of emphasis that one might expect to find between a seventeenth-century metaphysical poet and a modernist "antiphilosopher."[18] But that is part of my point—the difference we expect; the surprise is in the similarity.

For the remainder of this chapter, I will elaborate on the parallel forms of negative reasoning that I find in both Donne and Lacan, tracing their strangely similar attempts to catch a glimpse of the Beyond at the limits of thought and to find knowledge of the self in the very gaps of self-knowledge. I will explore their shared emphasis on the concepts of "nothing" (a key word in Donne's oeuvre, figured as the central concept of absence or lack in Lacan's work), "all" (another key word for Donne, as we can already see in the passage above, and one that figured as Imaginary plenitude in Lacan), and the relation of those terms to "knowing." Finally, I will employ Donne's work to question and to critique the value that Lacan attributes to the confrontation with the truth of one's desire, the necessary destitution of the subject that he associates with the traversing of one's own fantasy structures; and I will venture to suggest that a seventeenth-century poet, at least in some modes, may be less of a traditionalist in his vision of the (inevitably incomplete) satisfactions of human love than a modern scholar and doctor of the mind.

II

God made everything out of nothing. But the nothing shows through.

—PAUL VALÉRY, *OEUVRES II*

In *James I and the Politics of Literature,* Jonathan Goldberg compares Donne not only to James, but to the most arbitrary, solipsistic, foolish, and destructive king in Shakespeare's canon: Lear. In Goldberg's words "Donne's self-constitution is absolutist; like Lear, his concern is who's in and who's out, and there seems to be no alternative to that either/or situation."[19] I strongly disagree with Goldberg's general analysis of Donne as an "absolutist" of this tyrannical kind; however, his arguments have been much critiqued, and so I will resist the temptation to add my voice to the general chorus of disapproval.[20] Instead, I want to play devil's advocate for a moment and suggest that there may in fact be something suggestive about Goldberg's association of the Donnean ego with Shakespeare's most tragically wrongheaded king, despite the humorless interpretation of the poet that it entails.

In psychoanalytic terms, Lear's fantasies of omnipotence are most obviously legible as manifestations of a desire to return to the happiest days of infancy; that is, to a condition of blissful dependence on the unceasing ministrations of a nurturing maternal body (a dependence that is itself fantasized as evidence of the child's total power over that body). This is part of what the Fool is getting at when he chides his master: "thou mad'st thy daughters thy mother" (as Coppelia Kahn noted, some years ago, the Fool is a brilliant psychoanalytic critic).[21] In Lacanian terms, Lear's impulse to control the maternal body and its reproductive capacities—an impulse to which so many of his speeches bear eloquent witness—is itself the consequence of a primal identification that Lacan gives the name of "Imaginary." The fragmentary, plural, fluctuating self initially "imagines" itself as whole, singular and fixed, in the mirroring gaze of a loving other (usually but not necessarily the mother), a condition that it then attempts to recreate in subsequent relationships. While the case for Donne's "absolutism" remains unproven, then, I think that he might indeed be "like Lear" to the extent that many of his love poems demonstrate a similar investment in identifications of an "Imaginary" kind. I will offer some further explication of this key term in Lacan's vocabulary (along with some other terms), before elaborating on their Donnean parallels.

The Imaginary is the first of three nominally distinct but mutually constitutive and overlapping "orders" of experience into which Lacan divides the psychic life of the individual. As I have said, Imaginary identifications arise out of the subject's earliest (primal) identification with an ideal image of itself (an event known as "the mirror stage"). In the words of Malcolm Bowie: "The Imaginary is the order of mirror-images, identifications and reciprocities. It is the dimension of experience in which the individual seeks not simply to placate the Other but to dissolve his [sic] otherness by becoming his counterpart. By way of the Imaginary, the original identificatory procedures which brought the ego into being are repeated and reinforced."[22] Importantly, then, in Lacan's retelling of the birth of the subject, it is not so much "the mother" that the child desires but an idealized version of the self, a (mis)recognized reflection in the (m)other's eye.[23]

If the Imaginary order reinforces the ego by enabling identification with idealized images of the self, the second of Lacan's two orders—the Symbolic—might be said also to reinforce the ego, but by the opposite means: that is, by drawing a line between the self and the rest of the world. Lacan intends many things by his often melodramatic descriptions of the subject's "entry into the Symbolic," but primarily he is referring to the effects of language acquisition upon individual consciousness. Language is a tool that establishes an (uncrossable) boundary between self and world, even as it provides the means of describing and accounting for that world. As critic and clinician John P. Muller notes: "The signifying function of language enables us to have perspective on experience and provides a zone of mediation so we are not wholly captured by the immediate."[24]

However, Muller continues, "this taming . . . function of language is limited."[25] Beyond the Symbolic lies Lacan's third "order," that of the undifferentiated Real. In a fashion that reflects his propensity for paradox, Lacan calls this order the Real precisely to distinguish it from reality, "which is a differentiated social construction, a collection built of images and language [that is, a commingling of Imaginary and Symbolic registers]."[26] Of course, the obvious question raised by the concept of the Real, if it is that which resists "symbolization," is, How can we know anything of it? Lacan argues that indeed we cannot truly "know" the Real, except from its effects, which makes it sound rather similar to the unconscious, but placed as much "outside" the self as within (a fact that helps to explain another of Lacan's epigrammatic rewritings of Freud, that "the unconscious is the discourse of the Other"). In short, we only know the Real by breakdowns in the significatory system. Another way of characterizing the Real, therefore, is as a failure or rupture of the Symbolic, and not so much a third "order" of experience as a negation of the second. As Muller writes: "Usually we go through our day without attending to the limits of our consensually validated reality, but now and again we encounter the Real in the form of danger, catastrophe, death."[27] Thus we might say, in echo of Paul Valery, that if we make everything by *fiat,* out of nothing, like gods (or kings), then the Real is the nothing that shows through.

Donne's poetry contains many elements that resonate with the worldview projected by Lacan; indeed, the degree of crossover between their two registers of description is sometimes uncanny. To take the Imaginary order first: as may be implicit from the above account, Imaginary identifications in the Lacanian schema are associated primarily with the visual realm. To quote Muller again: "The ego is narcissistically sustained in its cohesion by reflections of itself such as photographs, automobiles, monuments, and in the interpersonal field, admiration, imitation, and especially the glow that comes from being found desirable as glimpsed in the eyes of another."[28] Or, as Lacan says unequivocally in his first seminar, "Love is a phenomenon which takes place on the imaginary level."[29] Love is therefore an experience that evokes the Imaginary register of the reflected and reflexive gaze, the ideal "I" that is (re)discovered in the meeting of lovers' eyes. Turning to Donne's lyrics, we find them filled with such reflexive interlocked gazes. To cite only some of the most memorable examples:

> Our hands were firmly cimented
>> With a fast balme, which thence did spring,
> Our eye-beames twisted, and did thred
>> Our eyes, upon one double string.

"THE EXTASIE" (DONNE, 48)

> I fixe mine eye on thine, and there
>> Pitty my picture burning in thine eye.

"WITCHCRAFT BY A PICTURE" (DONNE, 42)

> My face in thine eye, thine in mine appeares,
> And true plaine hearts do in the faces rest,
> Where can we find too better hemispheres
> Without sharpe North, without declining West?

"THE GOOD MORROW" (DONNE, 3)

Importantly, Donne's loving speaker is not concerned merely to recount the delights of looking upon the loved object. Perhaps surprisingly, the relation of sight to sexual desire in Donne's work is often not purely scopophillic. Instead, as Lacan's schema would lead us to expect, we are presented with something that goes far beyond the pleasure of voyeurism; Donne understands the interlocked gaze of the lovers to be constitutive of a mutually sustaining self-other relation. This understanding can result in tour de force displays of poetic pronoun juggling that match Lacan at his most elliptically inscrutable. For example, in "A Valediction of my name, in the window," Donne first identifies himself with his scratched name upon his lover's windowpane (a surface that can also serve as a mirror for her image), then produces the following head-spinning reflection upon loving reflections:

> 'Tis much that glasse should bee
> As all confessing, and through-shine as I
>> 'Tis more that it shewes thee to thee,
>> And cleare reflects thee to thine eye.
> But all such rules, loves magique can undoe,
>> Here you see me, and I am you.

(DONNE, 22)

Where is this "here" that will allow a "you" and an "I" simultaneously to emerge and fold together in a perfectly symmetrical structure, a dyadic relation that evokes a Romantic Hegelian synthesis, an act of negation (of the "I") that is also an act of affirmation (an "I am")? What is this place that makes possible an absolute unity of subject and object, a form of being-as-copula, an "I-am-you"? According to Lacan, at least, "here" can only be the Imaginary realm, with its primary mode of mirroring; here, love at once provokes "a sort of annihilation" and at the same time "reopens the door . . . to perfection."[30] Or as Muller notes, rather less cryptically: "[M]irroring reflects back the illusion of sameness and is almost always found in a dyadic relationship wherein one seeks to be affirmed as idealized by the other, to be found iconically in the consciousness of the other just as one is found in one's own narcissistic consciousness."[31]

It is worth recalling in this context that Lacan gives a twofold significance to the term "Other," often without specifying which signification he intends, in order to further underscore the complex combination of intersubjective and symbolic processes that produce our sense of subjecthood.[32] Thus, the term "Other" can refer "now [to] one member of the dialectical 'Subject-Other' relationship and now [to] the limitless field and overriding condition in which both members find themselves—'alterity,' 'otherness.' "[33] The second of these senses of the Other, which Lacan sometimes specifies as the "Big Other," is associated with the Symbolic order itself—the space of differences in which subject-other (lowercase) interaction takes place. Or as Lacan says, with typical compression: "The Other is, therefore, the locus in which is constituted the I who speaks *with* him who hears."[34]

The double meaning works as a reminder that if the other becomes a flattering mirror for the self in Imaginary identifications, then the most extreme examples of Imaginary identification can transform the Big Other—all alterity, all otherness—into such a mirror. Of course, this Imaginary identification of the self with all Otherness is, in clinical terms, a narcissistic form of psychosis; but Donne offers us no less an identificatory vision in the final stanza of "The Canonization," one of the most significant of his love lyrics for twentieth-century criticism. Famously, in these last lines, Donne envisions a glorious future time in which he and his beloved are invoked by subsequent lovers as a kind of secular Saint in a new earthly "religion" of love:

> . . . You whom reverend love
> Made one anothers hermitage;
> You, to whom love was peace, that now is rage,

Who did the whole worlds soule contract, and drove
    Into the glasses of your eyes
    So made such mirrors and such spies
That they did all to you epitomize,
    Countries, Townes, Courts: Beg from above
    A patterne of your love.

(DONNE, 12)

These lines are some of the most difficult in the poem, in part because
the notion that the lovers' interlocked gaze can provide access to a
mystical totality has been given another reflexive (and reflective) turn.
The act of making the eyes of another into a magical mirror that epit-
omizes the "all"—a (contracted) vision of "the whole worlds soule"—
is itself configured as an iconic ideal image (a "patterne") that will
function as a model to be imitated. In short, the lovers' act of mirroring
the all for one another will itself be imitated—mirrored—by all sub-
sequent lovers, who will in turn become mirrors of the all for one
another. In Lacánian terms, Donne doesn't only present the loving
couple in an Imaginary, mutually constitutive and reaffirming relation;
instead, the lovers themselves have become an ideal image with which
all other "subject-others" will identify in an Imaginary relation. This
is the *myse en abyme* of affection; spinning in circles of infinite regres-
sion, it is an endless love indeed.

Donne's capacity to recover an idealized Imaginary scenario defies
even the event of physical separation—a circumstance that might
generally be thought more likely to confirm the final inescapability of
difference and distinction, and hence the phantasmatic nature of the
Imaginary identification, than the ultimate unity of the lovers. In "A
Valediction of Weeping," Donne does initially acknowledge that the
physical separation of the lovers undermines the ego-enhancing work
of Imaginary identification, exposing "I" and "you" as mutually sus-
taining fictions and potentially reducing them to nothing ("So thou and
I are nothing then, when on a divers shore"); but, in the final stanza
of the poem, Donne nevertheless manages to bring the entire world
back into an Imaginary relationship with the two lovers. Addressing
his weeping companion he asks her to:

               . . . forbeare
To teach the sea, what it may doe too soon
    Let not the winde
    Example finde,
To doe me more harme, then it purposeth,
Since thou and I sigh one anothers breath,

> Who e'r sighes most, is cruellest, and hastes the others
> death.

(DONNE, 36)

Again, as at the conclusion of "The Canonization," the point is not simply that the two lovers are like one being, breathing together, but that events in the natural world—the Big Other beyond the subject-other dialectic of the two lovers—are here represented as imitating their sighs and tears of parting and as quite literally copying their "example." It is as if the forces of nature were locked in an Imaginary identification with Donne and his lover. A more grandiose version of what later criticism would term the pathetic fallacy would prove hard to find.

The desire for the circular, specular and spectacular comforts of Imaginary identification—attaining the point of connection where two can become the One that contains All in a climactic moment of proto-Hegelian synthesis—is clearly a desire that many people recognize and share, since simpler versions of the concept are a repeated element in countless popular representations of idealized love (examples from contemporary movies and song are so plentiful that I leave it to the reader to recall his/her own favorites); indeed, I would go so far as to say that it is in part his skill at evoking the experience of Imaginary identification—and in the case of "The Canonization," of encouraging Imaginary identifications with his own subject position on the part of the reader—that lies at the root of Donne's continued appeal over so many generations. Nevertheless, however seductive Imaginary identifications may be, as the term itself suggests, they are essentially illusory. As a good post-structuralist (at least some of the time), Lacan is skeptical about the possibility that the absolute unity of ostensible opposites can be achieved; he speaks scornfully of the "linkage by phantasmatic synthesis" that mars Romantic Hegelianism and argues that Hegel is most productively read against himself (as "correcting" himself) in such contexts.[35]

But Donne, too, has anticipated this position in several poems, and to this degree his work is often a poignant reminder that one does not need to have read Lacan (or Hegel against himself) to know that the metaphysical synthesis of subject and object experienced in the ecstasy of love proves unsustainable. For example, the muted, anxious ending of "A Valediction of my name, in the window" is a far cry from the Imaginary triumphalism of its beginnings:

> But glasse and lines must bee
> No meanes our firme substantiall love to keepe;

> Neere death inflicts this lethargie,
>   And this I murmure in my sleepe;
> Impute this idle talk to that I goe,
>   For dying men talke often so.

(DONNE, 25)

The tone of mild self-recrimination evoked in this final stanza is particularly interesting, for it suggests that Donne's speaker has come to see as "idle" the ecstatic, Imaginary identification of earlier stanzas. The deliberately paradoxical flip-flopping of pronouns, the reflexive game of mirroring gazes, become something that the speaker dismisses as "lethargic" ramblings, excusable only on the grounds of the stress he is feeling at an impending separation (which is itself figured metaphorically as a kind of death). It is as if the speaker of "The Canonization" or of "A Valediction of Weeping" had been forced to undergo therapy with a rather strict Lacanian analyst and had come to be suspicious of his own Imaginary fantasies of absolute unity. Remember, for the Lacanian, "the Imaginary is the scene of a desperate and delusional attempt to be and remain 'what one is' by gathering to oneself ever more instances of sameness, resemblance and self-replication."[36] In Lacan's early teaching in particular, "the term has a strong pejorative force and suggests that the subject is seeking, in a willful and blameworthy fashion, to remove himself from the flux of becoming."[37] The Imaginary produces a glimpse of the transcendent on the basis of an impossible fixity. It may make a heaven, but as in David Byrne's song, the "heaven" of the Imaginary is "a place where nothing ever happens."[38] On this point, Lacan, like Freud, also reveals a concerned moralism; the Imaginary realm is not a place where the healthy subject should be encouraged to reside.

According to Lacan, Imaginary fantasies not only require acts of denial and even violent repression in order to sustain themselves; they can also have terribly destructive consequences for the psyche of the individual who cannot relinquish his or her fantasy of complete identification with the other, in the face of the inevitability of separation. Donne's numerous poems that figure parting as a kind of death—and I have already alluded to two, but many others might be adduced—illustrate the same Lacanian point: the hyperbolic reaction to separation is an inevitable consequence of an equally hyperbolic fantasy of unity. Thus, Donne's figuration of separation as death can be read as a necessary result of his attempts to achieve coherence, fixity, and unity through Imaginary identifications, even as it marks the failure of those identifications. As Lacan puts it: "The illusion of unity, in which a human being is always looking forward to self-mastery, entails a constant danger of sliding back into the chaos from which he started."[39] In short, Donne's description of himself as a dying man, his reduction of "thou" and "I" to "nothing" in the face of separation, represents a kind of uncontrolled regression into a condition of incoherence and fragmentation—the inevitability of this regression being built into the very Imaginary identifications that were intended to ward it off.[40]

If mere physical separation can feel like death to a lover captivated by the Imaginary realm, what happens when death is no longer a metaphor for parting but has literally intervened to separate the lovers permanently? For one answer, we can turn to a poem that Peter DeSa Wiggins has recently described as "one of the greatest of the English Renaissance," Donne's "A nocturnall upon *S. Lucies* day."[41] Upon the final loss of his beloved, Donne's Imaginary experience of the all doesn't simply collapse into nothing; instead, nothing begins to acquire the weight of the all, becoming a new and paradoxical essence of negativity. Let us consider this extraordinary poem in full.

> *A nocturnall upon* S. Lucies *day,*
> *Being the shortest day*
> Tis the yeares midnight, and it is the dayes,
> Lucies, who scarce seaven houres herself unmaskes,
>   The Sunne is spent, and now his flasks
>   Send forth light squibs, no constant rayes;
>   The worlds whole sap is sunke:
> The generall balm th' hydroptique earth hath drunk,
> Whither, as to the beds-feet life is shrunke,
> Dead and enterr'd, yet all these seeme to laugh,
> Compar'd with me, who am their Epitaph.
>
> Study me then, you who shall lovers bee
> At the next world, that is, at the next Spring:
>   For I am every dead thing,
>   In whom Love wrought new Alchemie.
>   For his art did expresse
> A quintessence even from nothingnesse,
> From dull privations, and leane emptinesse
> He ruin'd mee, and I am re-begot
> Of absence, darknesse, death; things which are not.
>
> All others, from all things, draw all that's good,
> Life, soule, forme, spirit, whence they beeing have,
>   I, by loves limbecke, am the grave

Of all, that's nothing. Oft a flood
    Have we two wept, and so
Drownd the whole world, us two; oft did we grow,
To be two Chaosses, when we did show
Care to ought else; and often absences
Withdrew our soules, and made us carcasses.

But I am by her death, (which word wrongs her)
Of the first nothing, the Elixir grown;
    Were I a man, that I were one
    I needs must know, I should preferre,
        If I were any beast,
Some ends, some means; Yea plants, yea stones detest,
And love, all, all some properties invest.
If I an ordinary nothing were,
As shadow, a light, and body must be here.

But I am None; nor will my Sunne renew.
You lovers, for whose sake the lesser Sunne
    At this time to the Goat is runne
    To fetch new lust, and give it you,
        Enjoy your summer all,
Since she enjoyes her long night's festivall
Let mee prepare towards her, and let me call
This hour her Vigill, and her eve, since this
Both the yeares, and the dayes deep midnight is.

(DONNE, 40)

The rapid rhetorical movement of the remarkable first stanza sends me groping in the direction of the contemporary medium of cinema for an appropriately vivid descriptive vocabulary. We have a kind of textual version of the longest of long shots—the earth seen from the universe of space—and then the camera eye swoops past the sun and tracks down to earth, zooming in for the uncomfortable proximity of a tight close-up; we end up literally in bed with a corpse. This deathbed is itself more like a sponge, or the plughole of a modern bath, a vortex drawing in and draining the "balme" of life with an almost audible gurgle. But perhaps a better analogy for this sudden contraction of the forces of life from a space the size of a solar system into a space the size of a bed would be that of the black hole; in anticipation of modern physics, the weight of Donne's misery seems to pull everything into itself, absorbing light and distorting time. However, even this is not quite accurate, for strictly speaking the process takes place in reverse; it is not the massive concentration of matter that distorts time but,

rather, the concentration of the units of time into a single weighty mo-
ment ("Tis the yeares midnight, and it is the dayes") that creates the
condition of a more general, universal heaviness, a sinking of every-
thing toward a zero point of darkness and death. And yet the death of
the entire universe is as nothing, or so we are told in the last lines of
the stanza, compared to the nothingness that Donne's speaker em-
bodies. He is now the signifier of the death of death itself, the impos-
sible epitaph written after the end of everything. His paradoxical status
as the negative of the negative will generate similar paradoxical for-
mulations as the poem progresses ("I am re-begot / Of absence"; "I . . .
am the grave / Of all, that's nothing"; and so on).

The second stanza is the symmetrical inverse of the final stanza of
"The Canonization," a poem that ends, as I've noted, by proclaiming
that the relationship between Donne and his lover can serve as a pos-
itive example or "patterne" for generations of future lovers. Here,
Donne steps forward to offer himself up as a negative example to be
studied by all "you who shall lovers be." His suffering is thereby pre-
sented as the grim fate of all those foolish enough to succumb to the
temptations of Imaginary captivation, in Lacan's terms; or, to use the
terms of the Platonic/Christian tradition with which Donne would have
been familiar, his is the fate of all those who foolishly mistake the
beauty of the creaturely for that of the Creator. At the same time, we
might also note the dogged persistence of an Imaginary fantasy in the
third stanza of the poem, where the tears of previous partings are said
to have "Drownd the whole world, us two." Despite the pain of loss
and the sense in the second stanza of the poem that Donne recognizes
that his suffering could serve as a warning of the dangers of love, he
still doesn't want to let go of the Imaginary identifications that equate
possession of the beloved with the experience of all-encompassing unity
and wholeness.

In the fourth and fifth stanzas, however, Donne describes more am-
biguous feelings that may begin to signal what Lacan sometimes calls
the traversing of the fantasy: that is, a reorientation of the very struc-
ture of his desire for the lost object. Apparently no longer tormented
by the pain of separation and loss, or by overpowering sensations of
yearning for reunion, or even by feelings of anger and bitterness (as in
a poem such as "Twicknam Garden"), Donne instead characterizes
himself by a total *absence* of feeling, an absence that more perfectly
corresponds to the absence of his lost love. In other words, the depri-
vation he has experienced is so complete and pervasive that he seems

to have lost even the capacity to feel loss itself. The key passage in question bears closer scrutiny:

> Were I a man, that I were one
> I needs must know, I should preferre,
>   If I were any beast,
> Some ends, some means; Yea plants, yea stones detest,
> And love, all, all some properties invest.

We might read this little moment as, among other things, John Donne's anticipatory revision of Descartes's famous proof of subjective being. Here, existence is demonstrated not by the capacity for abstract thought but, rather, by one's specifically *emotional* orientation toward that which lies beyond the boundaries of the self: in short, "I feel; therefore, I am." But even this intriguing alternative to the conventional Cartesian formula is expressed negatively; for what Donne effectively says here is, "I do not feel; therefore, I am not."

Is this the beginning of the process of detachment and acceptance, and a first sign of emotional recovery, or only the deepest kind of depression? Predictably, commentators have disagreed as to whether the mood of this poem is "finally" despairing or hopeful, but I'm inclined to let the reader make up his or her own mind according to his or her psychological temper and mood. Suffice it to say that while an older generation of critics may have preferred the Imaginary triumphalism of "The Canonization" to the negative constructions of "A nocturnall . . . ," or the enervated, self-canceling ending of "A Valediction of my name, in the window," the strict Lacanian might be inclined to applaud the speakers of these latter poems for at least beginning to recognize the responsibility that they bear for their own suffering, as a consequence of their willing embrace of the false plenitude of Imaginary identification.[42]

Revealingly, it turns out that one doesn't actually have to have read Lacan to arrive at thoroughly Lacanian sounding-conclusions about "A nocturnall upon *S. Lucies* day." In a recent, loosely "historicist" critical study that is primarily concerned to locate Donne's poems in the literary-intellectual contexts of courtly culture, Peter DeSa Wiggins describes the spirit of the poem as one of "bitter self-mockery, because with the beloved woman's death the speaker realizes that the religious and cosmological meanings he lent their love are false. He was using language to tissue over the void."[43] I think Wiggins is too emphatic; the last lines of the poem do not seem to me so straightforwardly to repudiate the speaker for "false" love but, rather, to resist this dubiously comforting Christian "insight" (even though the poet clearly recognizes that this is indeed one possible lesson that can be gleaned from his experience). But regardless of whether the familiar seventeenth-century moral that Wiggins finds in the poem is one we finally choose to emphasize, it is a moral that reinscribes the Lacanian repudiation of Imaginary love in theological terms. To put the point the other way round, in deference to considerations of chronological priority: Wiggins's reading of the poem helps us to see that Lacan's critique of love as Imaginary "captivation" is itself a secular rewriting of the traditional Christian/Platonic mistrust of all earthly love.[44]

But obviously a Lacanian would not applaud the subject's recognition of his/her erroneous Imaginary identifications for precisely the same reasons as a Christian-Platonist—for whom God remains as the only appropriate and truly transcendent object of love. By contrast, for the Lacanian, suspicion of Imaginary identification is simply a necessary step on the road to understanding our immersion in the Symbolic order—to understanding, in other words, the insuperable distance between the self and the other, the inevitability of difference even from oneself, the absence of absolutes except by acts of reification, the always already of fantasy, even in those experiences that seem most "true," and so on.

To summarize then: in many poems, such as "The Good Morrow," "The Canonization," and "The Sunne Rising," Donne performs acts of negation and synthesis ("she is all states; and all princes I / Nothing else is") that Lacan associates with Imaginary identifications; less prosaically, he transforms the loving gaze into a mirrored shield against the petrifying Medusas of the Symbolic-Real. But elsewhere in his work, he cannot sustain these Imaginary identifications, and as a result, his own sense of self can become threatened, as in the evocation of death at the conclusion of "A Valediction of my name, in the window," or give way entirely, as in "A nocturnall upon S. Lucies day." Perhaps even in "The Canonization" the violence of the repression required to sustain the Imaginary fantasy can be detected in the language with which that fantasy is evoked: Donne's idealism cannot quite disguise the brutal force with which the contracted world is "driven" into the eyes of the two lovers—an image with horrific potential that almost works to suggest that, like *Lear*'s Gloucester, these lovers, too, must suffer a blinding before they can really learn to see. And as we also know from so many figures of Greek myth and legend, literally blind but gifted with second sight, seeing the All is often only the other side of seeing Nothing. This grim paradox is equally familiar to Donne and Lacan. Love is the means whereby the fragmented self can become whole. Love provides the magic by which we can transform ourselves into the everything that will serve as a stay against the nothing. But for both thinkers, the Imaginary fantasy cannot quite cover the abyssal gap upon which it is founded. The nothing shows through.

III

> I love talking about nothing. It's the only subject I
> know anything about.
>
> —OSCAR WILDE, *AN IDEAL HUSBAND*

Love, at least as conventionally understood, does not come off well in Lacan's world picture. In fact, his remarks on love become increasingly sarcastic as his career progresses. In the extraordinary, over-the-top, offensive, frustrating, wildly scattershot but occasionally lucid text of Seminar XX he remarks with casual scorn: "Everyone knows, of course, that two have never become but one, but nevertheless 'we are but one.' The idea of love begins with that."[45] In other words, according to Lacan, the "idea of love" is founded on a denial of its impossibility, an impossibility so obvious that "everyone knows" it already, even if they prefer not to say it. Unusually, Lacan prefers not to take the credit for this unsentimental insight: "in that respect . . . old father Freud broke new ground [when he realized] . . . that love, while it is true that it has a relationship with the One, never makes anyone leave himself behind. If that, all of that and nothing but that, is what Freud said by introducing the function of narcissistic love . . . the problem is how there can be love for another."[46] Lacan's answer to this problem—at least some of the time—is simply to say that, strictly speaking, there in fact *cannot* be love for another. In a gleefully balloon-bursting quip he declares that "the One everyone talks about all the time is, first of all, a kind of mirage of the One you believe yourself to be."[47] Or, as he puts it twenty years earlier, and rather more clearly: "It's one's own ego that one loves in love, one's own ego made real on the imaginary level."[48] Love so defined is not only narcissistic. It is an aggressively incorporative impulse, exactly parallel to an emotion like hate in this respect. Thus, in his first seminar, he declares:

"Love, the love of the person who desires to be loved, is essentially an attempt to capture the other in oneself, in oneself as object. . . . With hate it is the same thing. There is an imaginary dimension of hate. . . . That is what makes hate a career with no limit, just as love is."[49]

One might be tempted to ask why Lacan insists so strongly, even cruelly, on this point. After all, despite his protestations, his particular emphasis on the impossibility of love is not exactly Freudian. The narcissistic origin of any powerful act of transference, including love, was indeed famously and compellingly articulated by the "old father."[50] But Freud also wrote that "sexual love is one of the chief things in life, and [that] the union of mental and bodily satisfaction in the enjoyment of love is one of its culminating peaks."[51] It is hard to imagine Lacan making an equivalent statement; he is far more likely to speak contemptuously of sexual love as mere "oblational genitality"—a phrase that redolently reveals a typical aspect of Lacan's derogatory wit, conveying the emptiness of the experience named by means of an obviously absurdly contrived vocabulary.[52]

I believe the answer to this question lies in the fact that Lacan must posit the essential impossibility of love (at least, as conventionally understood), because this impossibility is the ground of one of his most fundamental revisions of Freud: his account of the origins and nature of desire. To use an epigrammatic formulation of the kind that Lacan himself was so fond—Lacan would have us abandon Imaginary love for Symbolic desire. More explicitly, and as we started to see in my earlier reading of Donne's "A nocturnall upon S. Lucies day," it might be reasonable to say that one of Lacan's central projects is to divert us from the delusory pursuit of fixed, immutable, Imaginary fantasies of satisfaction through a recognition of the fluid, the partial, the incomplete: the endless signifying chains of the Symbolic order.

The developmental etiology that allows Lacan to characterize love as a fundamentally narcissistic and even aggressive impulse can be traced back to what is sometimes called the "primary love" of the infant: that is, the acute need that the infant feels in its state of absolute dependence on the (m)other or chief caregiver in earliest life. The anxiety that results from a (nascent) awareness of this dependence links love to the most basic kinds of need. Lacan goes so far as to suggest that once the subject has come to understand that the mother is indeed an other, separate from the subject, each demand made of the mother (for food, warmth, comfort) conceals or is contiguous with a further demand for unconditional love as a promise of permanent presence—

a demand made in the face of an anxious realization that the subject doesn't actually control the other's movements. This demand-beyond-need comes to operate in all subsequent love relations. It is for this reason that

> [t]he desire to be loved is the desire that the loving object should be taken as such, caught up, enslaved to the absolute particularity of oneself as an object. The person who aspires to be loved is not at all satisfied, as is well known, with being loved for his attributes. He demands to be loved as far as the complete subversion of the subject into a particularity can go. . . . One wants to be loved for everything—not only for one's ego. . . . but for the colour of one's hair, for one's idiosyncrasies, for one's weaknesses, for everything.[53]

In short, our earliest anxieties create in us a demand for an impossible love alongside every need that *can* be satisfied—or as Lacan writes, "[D]emand in itself bears on something other than the satisfactions it calls for."[54] In this space between demand and need—opened up, let us recall, by the impossibility of securing love as permanent presence—the crucial Lacanian notion of "desire" appears.[55] Or as Lacan puts it in one of his most famous pronouncements: "Desire is neither the appetite for satisfaction, nor the demand for love, but the difference that results from the subtraction of the first from the second, the phenomenon of their splitting."[56]

This is a frustrating statement, in part because it borrows from the rhetoric of the mathematical equation to present a complex idea as if it were a relatively simple and graspable formula. When it comes to saying exactly what this formula means, and to teasing out its implications, it becomes difficult to render the concepts clearly without sounding too much like Lacan himself. But perhaps the first thing to emphasize is the careful insistence with which "desire" is defined only negatively in this conception. The departure from Freud's thinking is again obvious. Lacan's desire "is not an instinct, not a quasi-biological libido, not a variable flow of neural energy or excitation, not an appetite, not the concealed source from which appetites derive and not . . . the life principle itself."[57] To return to the terms that have preoccupied so much of this chapter, strictly speaking, desire is not really "something" at all. Instead, it is the ever present nothing that all our demands, ambitions, wishes, and fantasies are designed to conceal. It is a space that comes into being at the very moment the subject constitutes itself by addressing itself to another, a space produced by the subject's implicit "recognition" in that act of addressing another that there are, in fact, others "out there," and that it is not of itself complete and entire. Bowie describes the process less abstractly when he writes:

> Something else is always going on in dealings between the need-driven subject and the other who may or may not provide satisfaction. A demand for love is being made. The desiring subject, haunted by absence and lack, looks to the other not simply to provide his needs but to pay him the compliment of an unconditional yes. . . . [T]he paradox and the perversity to be found in any recourse to persons is that the other to whom the appeal is addressed is never in a position to answer it unconditionally.[58]

However, this is a fact that the subject cannot bear to face, according to Lacan, and for this reason, we allow (potentially realizable) demands to "cover" the unsealable gap of desire; that is, we live *as if* the demands we make could be entirely satisfied; or, more accurately still, we live as if we could be entirely satisfied *if only all our demands were met.*

For Lacan, then, the primary purpose of analysis is to bring the subject to the understanding that his or her desire will never be satisfied by any empirical object, in order that the "truth" of the subject's desire can be recognized.[59] In his words, analysis is "not a question of the satisfaction of desire, nor of I know not what primary love, but, quite precisely, of the recognition of desire."[60] This is still a potentially misleading way of putting things, however, for what we must recognize in desire, in some sense, is the impossibility of ever recognizing our desire within conventional systems of representation and signification. For again, Lacan insists: "There is . . . something radically unassimilable to the signifier. It's quite simply the subject's singular existence."[61] In other words, Lacan insists that the *real* truth of the subject, the ineffable "something missing" that ultimately shapes his or her relationship to *jouissance,* cannot actually be captured in language: it exists beyond representation but is nevertheless the condition of that subject's individuality. Or, as Henry Staten has written: "The beyond of the subject that constitutes its ownmost propriety is not to be comprehended within the dialectic of self and Other; it is rather what is always left over from any such entanglement." Therefore, recognizing the truth of one's desire means in some sense recognizing a blank or nothing, because that truth cannot be symbolized; but this nothing remains "an absolutely determinate nothing," in Staten's words, "because it is the nothing of this particular destiny. [The] Particularity [of the individual's desire] . . . is necessarily nothing because it is outside of both the identifications of the Imaginary and the significations of the Symbolic; yet this nothingness is not the mere negativity of the void, but the affirmation of an absolute self-proximity and self-propriety."[62]

We might say that Lacan wants to bestow upon his pupils and patients alike the perspective of Wallace Stevens's "Snow Man." He wants us to look upon the landscape of our desires and to see, with a new kind of detachment, "nothing that is not there *and* the nothing that is." We must learn to see "nothing that is not there" to the extent that we must abandon the illusion that there could ever be "something" out there that could finally satisfy us; and we must learn to see "the nothing that is" to the extent that we must recognize the negativity that is fundamental and constitutive of our very beings but that lies beyond the realm of symbolization. We must come to see the paradoxical nothing-that-determines-all, the nothing that lies behind all our quests for something.

The question of whether this ambition has any demonstrable therapeutic value is one that I expect would occur quickly in the mind of the skeptic, and I shall return to it in the final section of this chapter. But for now I simply want to draw attention to the ways in which Lacan's most advanced and sophisticated conceptions of desire as structured by and oriented toward a representational blank or absence are anticipated by Donne in some of his more complex theorizations of love. Indeed, when it comes to riddling metaphysical abstractions on this score, Donne once again proves worthy of Lacan at his most abstruse. Consider, for example, the following brief and relatively unnoticed poem, generally known as "Negative Love" but also titled "The Nothing" in several manuscript versions:

> I never stoop'd so low, as they
> Which on an eye, cheeke, lip, can prey,
>> Seldome to them, which soare no higher
>> Then vertue or the minde to'admire
> For sense and understanding may
>> Know what gives fuell to their fire:
> My love, though silly, is more brave,
> For may I misse, when ere I crave
> If I know yet, what I would have.
>
> If that be simply perfectest
> Which can by no way be exprest
>> But Negatives, my love is so.

> To All, which all love, I say no
> If any who deciphers best
>   What we know not, our selves, can know
> Let him teach me that nothing; This
> As yet my ease, and comfort is
> Though I speed not I cannot misse.
>
> (DONNE, 63)

The poem begins with an allusion to Neoplatonism. I have explored Donne's vexed relationship to Neoplatonic and Petrarchan theories of desire in my previous chapter, and in many ways the argument of this poem is of a piece with those that I have traced there; once again, by dismissing the mere sensualist in his first couplet, the poet sets us up to believe that we are to be offered a typically Neoplatonic argument praising inner virtue over the exterior elements of physical attraction. However, as the second couplet makes abruptly clear, in refusing to pay poetic homage to an individual "eye, cheeke [or] lip," Donne's speaker is not to be confused with any conventional Neoplatonist. The idea that admiring "vertue or the minde" is somehow a "higher" aspiration or form of love than admiring the body is also rather scornfully dismissed. As far as *this* desiring subject is concerned, such Neoplatonists do not climb a metaphysical ladder to some more elevated perspective, but are as "stoop'd" as the sensualists they superciliously condemn. With the fifth and sixth lines the speaker seems to suggest that, in any case, people who make such arguments are kidding themselves. What gave "fuell to their fire" of admiration, after all? Donne's speaker declares that we know the answer to this question from "sense and under-standing"—in other words, the means by which we know the answer is also the answer itself: "sense and understanding" together give "fuell" to the Neoplatonic fire. This is the central argument of "The Extasie" offered in a highly compressed form and turned against the naive Neo-platonist: "You could hardly have access to the virtue or to the mind of your loved object if you didn't use your (bodily) senses," Donne seems to be saying, "so perhaps you aren't being quite as Platonic as you think when you praise someone for those 'inner' qualities."

In the final triplet of the first verse, the poet seems about to offer us a description of his alternative to the (anti-Petrarchan and Petrarchan) forms of desire that he has described. It is all the more striking, then, that his object of desire ("my love") turns out not to be an object at all but, rather, a refusal of any knowledge about that object. What Donne seems to be declaring is that he would deserve to be frustrated and dissatisfied ("may I misse, when ere I crave") if he were to make the intellectually naive error of thinking he knows what he wants. In short, Donne has reached the point of "recognition of desire" that is one end product of Lacanian analysis. What he knows is that thinking that you know what you want is a mistake. Worse than a mistake, it is form of evasion, a way of concealing the impossibility of attaining one's desire by hiding its unsealable gap behind a substitute object. To express the point in the appropriate vocabulary once again: to say you know what you would have is to commit yourself to a false way of knowing that obscures the Nothing of desire by pretending that something—anything—could somehow stand for the All.

In the second stanza, Donne seems to locate this insight in a recognition of his own inevitable lack. The ultimate blindspot, the reason we are mistaken in thinking we could "know . . . what [we] would have," is because we don't know ourselves. It is tempting to read Donne's wry and rueful casting around in this stanza for advice from one who "deciphers . . . our selves" as an address to the as yet unborn professional analyst, but Donne indicates that he has already learned the lesson that analyst would teach him (at least, if he or she were a Lacanian); or perhaps, to evoke Freud, Donne has already recognized that psychoanalysis—the science of deciphering selves—is "the impossible profession." In fact, the final three lines of the poem suggest that he has taken that insight and applied it in precisely the way that the therapist would hope. Donne is able to declare that even if he doesn't attain his desire, this cannot be interpreted as a personal failure ("though I speed not I cannot misse"). What this surely means is that, having recognized that the attainment of any specific want will not satisfy the impossible demand of desire, Donne now knows that he lives in a world where, at some level, it is nonsensical to speak of getting what you want; however, by the same token, it is also nonsensical to speak of failing to attain one's desire—since no one can ever *succeed* at this task, it hardly makes sense to think of oneself as *failing*. Thus, we cannot miss our desire precisely because we cannot hit it. To accuse someone of failing in such circumstances would be like accusing someone who jumps off a cliff of "failing" to fly. The "failure" inheres in the belief that one could attain flight, not in the act of falling.

IV

> Can you make no use of nothing, nuncle?
>
> —WILLIAM SHAKESPEARE, *KING LEAR*

The air of optimism with which "Negative Love" closes is precisely the hoped-for therapeutic consequence of bringing a patient to a Lacanian "recognition of desire," at least as described by psychologist Joseph H. Smith: "Since any human unity is always marked by dividedness, always under siege, always lacking, concern and desire are constant. But at the point of recognizing desire as manifesting an indestructible want of unity [within the subject], anxiety in response to specific dangers is rendered less blind and less driven, by virtue of being coordinated with the detachment achieved in acknowledging concern as constant."[63] For Lacan, this insight was so fundamental that in a passage in the essay titled "The Direction of treatment and principles of its power" he makes it the central goal of all training analyses—that is, the analysis that the analyst is supposed to undergo before he or she can practice:

> Whoever cannot carry his training analyses to the turning-point at which it is proved with fear and trembling that all the demands that have been articulated in the analysis, and more than any other the original demand to become analyst, which is now about to be fulfilled, were merely transferences intend to maintain in place a desire that was unstable or dubious in its problematic—such a person knows nothing of what must be obtained from the subject if he is to be able to assume the direction of an analysis, or merely offer an accurate impression of it.[64]

In short, one can't do one's job properly as an analyst until one acknowledges that even the ambition to do one's job properly as an analyst is at bottom a way of covering over the void of desire, of representing to oneself the unrepresentable particularity of being. With a rigor that here seems to undermine the very discipline he is attempting to advance, Lacan returns again and again to the divided nature of the human subject as the knowledge upon which all other knowledge must be grounded. This is the ontology of the void—the bottom line turns out to be not a bedrock assertion but the discovery of a fissure at the base of everything and, below the fissure, nothing, nothing all the way down.

Stated so baldly, it is perhaps harder to square Lacan's almost Nietzschean glee in the face of this void with Smith's more moderate concept of "detachment" or even Donne's wry optimism at the end of "Negative Love"—although the difference may be a mere matter of degree. When, we might ask, does "healthy" detachment become a disturbing lack of affect? Lacan himself would probably dismiss the question, on the grounds that even to ask it is to presuppose the possibility of some absolute knowledge regarding what might be said to constitute psychic wellness, as well to assume that the ultimate goal of analysis is the happiness of the subject. "To make oneself the guarantor of the possibility that a subject will in some way be able to find happiness even in analysis is a form of fraud," Lacan insists; and, furthermore, the "ethics" of psychoanalysis reside beyond the naive altruism of other so-called caregiving professions, operating on what he clearly implies is a higher ontological plane: "The question I ask is this: shouldn't the true termination of an analysis—and by that I mean the kind that prepare you to become an analyst—in the end confront the one who undergoes it with the reality of the human condition?"[65]

But at moments like this, Lacan's so-called ethical position strikes me as being at least as arrogant as it is epistemologically rigorous. After all, is it *really* more morally responsible to assume that one's professional role is to bring subjects to an awareness of the "reality of the human condition" than to presume that one's professional role is to try to make people happy? And doesn't Lacan's breathtakingly casual implication that he in fact knows "the reality of the human condition" resound with false portentousness, not to mention gross intellectual conceit? To put the point slightly differently: if we are supposed to learn to see "nothing that is not there and the nothing that is," as I have suggested, it might be worth recalling that Wallace Stevens's famous metaphysical meditation is cloaked in a quite traditional seasonal metaphor; to see in such a way, one "must have a mind of winter." It is by no means obvious to me that we should always valorize this chilly perspective at the expense of human illusions of wholeness. In fact, when I encounter these moments in Lacan, I am often reminded of a sequence from the beginning of the animated movie *Antz*. We discover a depressed and neurotic anthropomorphic ant, voice supplied (appropriately enough) by Woody Allen, in the midst of an analytic session. The problem, as the ant says to his shrink—a magnificently superior and distant centipede—is that "I feel so insignificant." The centipede responds by saying, "Congratulations. You have made great progress." The ant is confused: "I have?" "Yes," replies the centipede. "You *are* insignificant."

As this last example may also help us see, a form of traditional truth value reemerges in Lacan's schema, despite his commitment to such potentially relativizing and antifoundationalist notions as the mediated nature of "reality." The truths of the Symbolic—the truth that all knowledge is mediated, the truth that desire cannot finally be satisfied (except, perhaps, in death), the truth that the subject is irrevocably split and unknown even to itself—at times this truth seems to become for Lacan the Truth that will set you free.[66] Thus, while his diagnoses of Imaginary identifications as delusory may well be accurate, his implicit insistence that these identifications must be abandoned for the sake of the "truth" of the Symbolic order displays a residual commitment to the "truth" of nihilism that is more modernist than poststructuralist. The point is not only, as Bowie notes, that "the moral qualities associated with the two orders [Imaginary and Symbolic] are themselves polarized, and often seem to rest on a categorical separation of virtue from vice that is of doubtful worth to psychoanalysis either as a mental science or as a therapeutic method."[67] The point, for my purposes here, is that a stricter antifoundationalism than the kind Lacan applies would not necessarily denigrate an Imaginary identification in favor of a Symbolic one, at least not on the basis that one is somehow "truer" and therefore "better" than the other. To put it another way, why should we force the choice between the "illusion" of love and the "truth" of the void, in the way that Lacan (sometimes) seems to require, when both positions are ones that we could only temporarily inhabit?

To this extent, the experience of Donne's love lyrics, taken as a whole, may be more instructive (not to say therapeutic, whatever *that* might now be thought to mean) than the work of Lacan. Now, I am aware that, if only because the profession of literary studies is perpetually crippled by a crisis of confidence, such a claim will seem outrageous. Moreover, given the horror with which Donne's sexual politics is generally regarded, the suggestion that we might learn something about love from him may seem positively retrograde. Even if this were not the case, the idea that "the literary" teaches us about life has been so often exposed as a false, sentimental sanctimony designed to license and enable a conservative program of cultural colonialism that it has become increasingly difficult to suggest that one of the reasons we read is to learn something about ourselves and our lives, without sounding like a hangover from the bad old days before we "knew" theory.

Let me say first: if Donne appears to me to be not only as intellectually sophisticated but also less proscriptive than Lacan in providing an understanding of the dialectic of subject-other relations, particularly as that dialectic emerges in the emotional condition that we give the name of "love," this is not a simple matter of intentionality. We may find evocations of the Imaginary register in some poems, and we may find insights into the impossibility of desire that suggest a more Symbolic investment in identification in other poems; but the reader of Donne is not obliged to prioritize, precisely because he or she is reading a collected body of discrete poetic works rather than a consistent linear thesis. If in the experience of reading Donne we are invited to take up any number of positions in turn within the dialectic of desire, this positive refusal to prioritize one position over another is perhaps an accident of genre rather than the result of authorial intent.

At the same time, Donne's treatment of the topic of love may provide some potential sources of comfort and solace for those of us who have experienced the joy of imaginary identification in a loving relationship, and the anxiety and despair that those same relationships produce, precisely because he takes the Lacanian insight into the impossibility of love seriously and goes beyond it. For, unlike the analyst, Donne does not generally advise us to adopt a posture of cold "detachment"—à la Wallace Stevens's "Snow Man"—in the face of the Lacanian insight. Instead, confronted with the impossibility of permanent satisfaction—a recognition, as he puts it in one poem, that "all our joyes are but fantasticall"—Donne advises a more active approach. At its most basic, he advocates creativity, and particularly the creativity of fantasy.

Again, let me be clear: the notion of fantasy to which I am appealing is not that of a "fake" substitute for "real" disappointments. Instead, as I described in my chapter on Donne and gender, fantasy is a structuring principle that underwrites that which is experienced as reality, and that organizes (rather than simply provides fictitious substitutes for) one's desire. Although this notion of fantasy is a psychoanalytic one, it derives less from the work of Lacan than from the speculations of two of his contemporaries, Jean Laplanche and Jean-Bertrand Pontalis, and has been given a clear and helpful reformulation in recent years by Slavoj Žižek:

> [F]antasy does not simply realize a desire in a hallucinatory way[;] . . . a fantasy constitutes our desire[—] . . . it literally teaches us how to desire. . . . To put it in somewhat simplified terms: fantasy does not mean that when I desire a strawberry cake and cannot get it in reality, I fantasize about eating it; the problem is, rather: *how do I know that I desire a strawberry cake in the first place?* This is what fantasy tells me. This role

of fantasy hinges on the fact that "there is no sexual relationship," no universal formula guaranteeing a harmonious sexual relationship with one's partner: because of the lack of this universal formula, every subject has to invent a fantasy of his or her own.[68]

We could turn to a number of Donne poems to support the claim that fantasy structures desire (for example, either of the two poems bearing the title of "The Dreame"). However, perhaps the boldest example of fantasy as a structure that "teaches" the subject how and what to desire can be found in a lengthy and quite extraordinary poem titled "The Expostulation." With a reading of this poem, I shall attempt to bring my comparison and contrast of these two great theorists of desire, Donne and Lacan, to a close.

"The Expostulation" begins by articulating the fear and hostility of a desiring masculine subject, gripped by anxiety as to the "truth"— that is, the fidelity—of his female love object.

> To make the doubt cleare, that noe woman's true
> $\quad$ Was it my fate to prove it stronge in you?
> Thought I but one had breathed purest ayre,
> $\quad$ And must she needes be false because shee's faire?
> Is it your beauties marke, or of your youth
> $\quad$ Or your perfection, not to studie truth? . . .
> Are vowes soe cheape with women, or the matter
> $\quad$ Whereof they are made, that they are writt in water
> And blowne away with winde?[69]

With his head full of cultural clichés and misogynistic projections about the dishonesty of attractive women, the speaker works himself up into a frenzy of uncertainty and doubt (rather like the protagonist of that horribly catchy 1970s hit by Dr. Hook, "When You're in Love with a Beautiful Woman"). But then, at the climax of this crisis, something remarkable happens: though he may indeed be inclined to think of women as untrustworthy (for this is the message that he has received, over and over, from the Big Other of the culture at large), he simply decides not to think of this particular woman in this way any more: "O I prophane; though most of women be / This kind of beast, my thought shall except thee." The decision to trust is presented as something that can have no basis in empirical evidence, in previous experience, in the acceptance or rejection of misogynistic cultural myths— indeed, in any obviously testable external "reality" whatsoever. Instead, Donne's speaker suggests that trusting and desiring his partner again is simply something he has to decide he wants to do.

If the poem ended here, then we would indeed have been left with a conventional definition of fantasy as a retreat from disappointing realities: "I don't know if you are the person I want you to be, but I'll pretend that you are and hope that you won't let me down." However, this is only the middle of the poem. Having recognized that his continued desire is in some sense dependent on a structure of fantasy, Donne also recognizes that he needs to encourage himself to enter into that structure. In other words, after having decided to decide that he wants this particular woman after all, after having expressed the desire to desire her, he goes on to invent a fantasy scenario precisely in order to produce that desire, so that he can really *know* that he desires her:

> My dearest Loue, though Froward Iealousie,
>   With circumstance, might vrge thy inconstancy,
> Sooner Ile thinke the Sun will cease to cheare
>   The teeming earth. . . .
> Or Nature, by whose strength the world endures,
>   Would chaunge her course before you alter yours.
> But ô that treacherous breast, to whom weake you
>   Did trust our Councells, and wee both may rue,
> Hauing his falshood found too late, t'was hee
>   That made mee *cast* you guiltie, and you mee.
> Whil'st hee black, wretch betray'd each simple word
>   Wee spake, unto the cunning of a third.

Given the mood swings of the speaker, and the astonishing arbitrariness with which he decides to adopt one perspective rather than another, the figure of the "treacherous breast" who suddenly (and quite unexpectedly) appears with the thirtieth line of the poem has the aura of invention. But in a fashion that seems to underline the reflexive relationship to fantasy itself that this poem will now display through to its conclusion, the potentially fantasized "treacherous breast" is accused of making both Donne and his (now) loved one engage in mistaken fantasies about one another: " 'twas hee / That made mee *cast* you guiltie, and you mee." The verb "cast" (italicized in the earliest printed versions of the text) emphasizes the role-playing aspect of the scenario, while the displacement of agency begins to raise the question of who exactly wrote the script for this lurid fantasy of love, misrecognition, and betrayal. Again, the poem seems to court confusion on the matter, when the loose-tongued betrayer is described as telling "each simple word / Wee [that is, Donne and his lover] spake" to a genderless "third" party. Donne himself is having trouble keeping count: the third party is actually the fourth participant to be imagined in this scene, which has rapidly expanded from a lover's quarrel to a triangle and now perhaps a quadrangle, the points of which are no longer in any clearly discernible relation.

The "treacherous" figure then inspires Donne to a second torrent of invective more vitriolic than that with which the poem began.

> Curst may hee bee, that soe our loue hath slayne,
>   And wander on the earth, wretched as Cain,
> Wretched as hee, and not deserue least pittie;
>   In plaguing him, let misery be wittie,
> Let all eyes shunn him, and he shunn each eye,
>   Till hee be noisome as his infamie;
> May hee without remorce, deny God thrice,
>   And not bee trusted more on his soules price.
> And after all self-torment, when hee dyes,
>   May wolues teare out his heart, Vulturs his eyes:
> Swine eate his bowels, and his falser tongue
>   That vtter'd all, bee to some Rauen flunge,
> And let his carrion corss, bee a longer feast
>   To the kings doggs; then any other beast.

It is tempting to wonder what Freud or Lacan might have made of Donne's detailed depiction of a thoroughly discorporated "rival"; but certainly they would not have been surprised to learn that after cursing this treacherous betrayer of confidences Donne finds the spark of his desire rekindled and, indeed, more than rekindled:

> Nowe haue I curst, let vs our Loue reuiue;
>   In mee the flame was neuer more aliue.
> I could beginne againe to court, and praise,
>   And in that pleasure lengthen the short dayes
> Of my liues lease; like Painters that do take
>   Delight, not in made worke, but whiles they make.
> I could renew those tymes, when first I sawe
>   Loue in your eyes, that gaue my tongue the lawe
> To like what you lik'd, and at maskes and playes
>   Commend the selfe same Actors, the same wayes,
> Aske how you did, and often with intent
>   Of being officious, bee impertinent.
> All which were such softe pastimes, as in these
>   Loue was as subt'illy catch'd, as a disease;
> But being gott, it is a treasure sweete,
>   Which to defend is harder then to gett
> And ought not bee prophan'd on either part,
>   For though t'is gott by chance, t'is kept by art.

These astonishing lines are suggestive in many ways. First and foremost, Donne seems to have recognized—along with many modern relationship counselors and self-help guides—that rekindling the flame of an old desire is often a matter of recalling your feelings upon first meeting the beloved. At one level, this recommendation is the opposite of a Lacanian one; we are encouraged not to reject Imaginary identification but to return to it, to try to recreate it again. Thus, Donne seems to say here: "Do you remember when we first met, how we would mirror one another—right down to our taste in entertainments?" Again, like many relationship counselors, Donne is also sensitive to the romantic potential of flirtation: "Do you remember, before I could really be candidly sexual with you, how I would flirt in the guise of polite concern?" ("with intent / Of being officious bee impertinent"). "Perhaps," the poet suggests, "we can be that way again."

But the most powerful and, for me, the most moving moment of this poem comes in its final lines—lines that cast a retroactive light on all that has gone before and make one wonder again about the "reality" of the treacherous rival, of the woman's infidelity—indeed, of all the scenarios that have exercised the speaker's attention and that have been responsible for stirring his desire. When people first meet, the poem implies, Imaginary identifications and games of flirtation are easy to sustain. In the beginning of a relationship, one doesn't have to strain to enter this realm; it's as easy as catching a cold ("as subt'illy catch'd, as a disease"). But as time goes on, more effort is required. Importantly, Donne seems in no doubt that the effort is worth it—Love "being got . . . is a treasure sweete"—but the effort is real nonetheless. To defend love once you have fallen is much harder than falling.

The best defense that Donne knows to shore up love, then, is not "truth"—not even the Lacanian truth that recognizes the impossibility of sealing the gap of desire. Instead, Donne returns us to the comforts of Imaginary fantasy, albeit *self-consciously acknowledged as such*. Donne's name for these creative fantasies that restore desire is, happily enough, one that also describes the nature of the very poetic productions in which he has chosen to articulate these ideas. The word is "art."

In short, for Donne, while the narcissistic delusions of the Imaginary will not survive the course of a long-term relationship, this does not mean that all such relationships are necessarily a compromise of misery based on an erotically pessimistic acceptance of the inevitable recursive curse of unsatisfiable desire. Instead, in the view that ends "The Expostulation" at least, a sustained relationship is like a poem or a painting, the product of attentive and careful contrivance and, more, of careful and attentive contrivance practiced *for its own sake*. "Painters . . . take Delight, not in made worke, but whiles they make." In other words, Donne is saying: "If we want this relationship to work, we must make it work by acts of recollection and creation, by continuing to dream and fantasize about the other. We must take responsibility for our own desire and fashion it according to fantasies that would otherwise fashion us, and which are, finally, inescapable." It is, I think, a perfect response to the psychoanalytic account of love as narcissistic fantasy to say—without necessarily disagreeing—that in that case love is an art form: the supreme fiction, indeed. "Can you make no use of nothing, nuncle?" the Fool asks Lear; one way of answering this question might be to say that falling in love constitutes the most creative use of nothing that anyone can make.[70]

At the risk of reduction, and in order finally to sharpen the distinction between Donne and Lacan that I have been attempting to delineate throughout this chapter: Lacan, we might say, sings a variation on a popular song of the 1960s. For Lacan, it's not that you can't always get what you want; instead, you can *never* get what you want, and once you know this, you know all that you need to know. Donne's response, I think, is slightly closer to the Rolling Stones' original: "You can't always get what you want. But if you try sometimes you might just find you get what you need." And how should we "try sometimes"? Well, according to Donne, we can start by thinking creatively about the ones we love. Art may not be what we *think* we want, in our pursuit of the truths of human contact, but sometimes it's exactly what we need. Of course, the metaphor of artistic production may seem like a slender reed on which to hang our emotional lives. But it's surely better than nothing.

The Desire of Criticism and the Criticism of Desire (Part II)

My previous chapter begs several important questions. For example, it might be observed that the kinds of analysis my psychoanalytic reading strategies produce are all very well, but it's hardly the only interpretive game in town (as my own methodologically divergent previous chapters attest). So why choose these particular perspectives over any other of the many interpretive models available? A more aggressive version of the question would insist on the inevitable blindspots of a reading that so blatantly disregards the differences of historical context and authorial intention that separate figures like Donne and Lacan: given those differences, surely to compare their respective discussions of love and desire is to compare apples with oranges?

I have already attempted to foreclose some of these questions in my introduction. But a hostile interlocutor is unlikely to be satisfied by my appeal there to the notion of the inescapability of fantasy within critical explication, since this notion is in some sense only an elaboration of the (frustratingly elliptical sounding) theoretical "principle" that all readings are also misreadings; and since my work moves through a recognizable, if not obviously coherent, trajectory—roughly speaking, from the literary-historical and metacritical to the psychoanalytic registers—my recourse to the inevitability of misreading to justify an apparently cavalier attitude toward the concept of methodological consistency could start to look evasive. The questions can still come back: Why these particular readings in this way? Might there be an implicit valorization of one form of (acknowledged) misreading over another in my critical practice? And what unstated assumptions about literary and critical value drive readings like the one I have just performed? If I am proposing, like Donne, that in matters of interpretation "though I speed not I cannot misse," does that mean I also renounce any claims my particular (mis)readings of Donne might have upon future readers?

These specific inquiries can be answered by addressing a more general question that has also gone begging up to the present moment, but that my last chapter also implicitly raises, and that adds a new wrinkle to my basic insistence that the engines of interpretation are driven by unacknowledged or unexamined desires. For psychoanalysis, with its central concept of the unconscious, suggests that many desires *cannot* be acknowledged or recognized: that desire is *always* the desire of the Other, in Lacanian terms, or, more simply, that "the heart has reasons that reason knows not of," as Pascal once wrote. What does it mean to argue that interpretations are words "chosen" out of desire, if desire itself is not obviously or entirely a matter of choice? To frame the problem in terms of one of the most influential explications of professional literary hermeneutics of recent years: what does it mean to suggest that when we speak of the constraints imposed on meaning by an "interpretive community"[1] we are also speaking of the desire of the Other? What consequences might such an observation have, not simply for Donne studies, but for the wider discipline of literary criticism? If desire is what we read with, and yet also at some fundamental level always unknown to us, what does this mean for our many proscriptions and descriptions regarding what and how we should read? Can the notion of interpretive desire not only help us to understand how critics as differently talented as Rosemond Tuve and William Empson can disagree so spectacularly over the same Donne poem, but also help us to understand debates about the curriculum and canon, about pedagogical and critical practice, and even about the history and future of English studies itself?

In these last pages, I will consider in greater depth some of the implications that emerge from acknowledging the centrality of desire to interpretive practice. I will continue to make use of psychoanalysis— the professional discourse that has, after all, been most engaged with the problematic of desire during the last century—although again my intent is not simply to explain literary study by recourse to psychoanalytic concepts, but to illuminate the processes and procedures of the two hermeneutic systems through comparison.[2] Comparisons between literary criticism and psychoanalysis are, of course, nothing new; but in the process, I also hope to show that the history of literary criticism can be productively reread as an unfolding story about a changing relationship between intellectual inquiry and desire—that is, as a story about the effects of a gradual "recognition of desire" (in the Lacanian sense) on those who produce literary knowledge.

I

> Where the story-teller is loyal, eternally and unswerv-
> ingly loyal to the story, there, in the end, silence will
> speak. Where the story has been betrayed silence is
> but emptiness. But we, the faithful, when we have
> spoken our last word, will hear the voice of silence.
>
> —ISAK DINESEN, *THE BLANK PAGE*

What makes a good literary critic? A commonsense answer would be to say that a good literary critic is a person who knows how to interpret texts correctly. But "given the complexities of texts, the reversibility of tropes, the extendibility of context, and the necessity for a reading to select and organize, every reading can be shown to be partial."[3] Indeed, and as my earlier chapter on the long-standing arguments over Donne's irregularity perhaps most clearly showed, "the history of readings is a history of misreadings, though under certain circumstances those mis-readings can and may be accepted as readings."[4] Where does this leave our definition of the good critic? What is the nature of critical aspira-tion in the face of the insights of poststructuralism?

For some, to acknowledge the inevitability of misreading is to put the entire literary critical enterprise in jeopardy. As M. H. Abrams asked, some years ago now: "If all interpretation is misinterpretation, and if all criticism (like all history) of texts can engage only with a critic's own misconstruction, why bother to carry on the activities of interpretation and criticism?"[5] One might respond that, if anything, deconstruction and other forms of nontraditional literary interpretation have resulted in more, rather than less, interpretive activity and so could be said to have reenergized the field rather than destroyed it; but this would not answer Abrams's question so much as deepen the mys-tery.

Perhaps we can say that the goal of criticism after deconstruction is something other than interpretation, or something other than a "cor-rect" interpretation, at least—if by "correct" we mean an interpretation that is free of individual idiosyncrasy and local or institutional bias, or one that will definitively stand as the only necessary or true reading of a text. But does this mean that anything goes? Clearly not, since all readings—even deconstructive ones—involve the making of truth claims and often further claims regarding the omissions or blind-spots of earlier readings. Each subsequent interpreter (re)declares his or her faithfulness to the object, even when admitting, in the form of a disclaimer, that certain aspects of the text will of course escape consideration (so that even the newest readings are not *entirely* faithful). But although this observation does not exactly bring us back to where we started, it is not clear whether we have progressed: it seems that all readings are unfaithful, but some are more unfaithful than others. The question, then, is not so much, "Why bother?" as, "When and how are we to distinguish between different misreadings?" Or more accurately, When and how do we decide to "forget" that a reading is partial, to "miss" its misreadings? as Jonathan Culler might say. How does one measure faithfulness or loyalty to a text? And what might unswerving loyalty look like?

The old woman narrator of Isak Dinesen's short story "The Blank Page" offers a vision of "unswerving [interpretive] loyalty," the reward of which is paradoxical or unimaginable: "to hear silence speak."[6] Here an instructive parallel between literary criticism and psychoanalysis emerges: the analyst, too, is taught to attend to everything in the patient's discourse—especially the things that seem least important—in the hope that this unswerving attention will provide access to the silent speech of the unconscious. But one of the great dangers of the psychoanalytic situation as traditionally conceived is the phenomenon of countertransference: that is, the ways in which the analyst's own individual idiosyncrasies and institutional bias will taint his or her view of the patient, clouding his or her perception of the unconscious workings of the patient's mind. Thus, as in the traditional literary critical situation, the desires of the interpreter are conceived as a problem—but, it is to be hoped, not such a problem that steps cannot be taken, or that rules cannot be followed, to minimize the distortions that these desires impose.

However, as a famous debate in the postwar history of Anglo-American psychoanalysis demonstrated, the effort to eliminate the effects of countertransference can produce distortions of its own. In the 1970s Charles Brenner notoriously argued that if an analyst were to commit some action that would be considered rude or insulting in a "normal" speech situation (such as, for example, falling asleep during a session), he should not apologize or offer any explanation or assurance of interest to the patient. Instead, Brenner claimed that

> the better course to follow is the usual one of encouraging the patient to express his thoughts and feelings about what has happened. Only in that way can one learn whether a patient has taken his analyst's mistake as a slight that has offended him . . . or as a sign of weakness that allows him to feel superior or even triumphant, or as a welcome excuse for anger, etc . . . [The analyst] must not assume what it [his mistake] must mean to his patient without hearing what his patient has to say. . . . It is a technical lapse to be other than an analyst in one's relation with an analytic patient.[7]

Here, being a good interpreter involves an almost Foucauldian policing of oneself, in order to keep any traces of oneself from contaminating the pure waters of the analytic situation. But the problem with the demand that one entirely eliminate one's own personal feelings and inclinations—one's desires—from the interpretive process, no matter what information one has been presented with, or what situation one finds one's patient in, is that it postulates an analyst who has no feelings: an analyst who is not human. Indeed, this aspect of the problem of countertransference led Janet Malcolm (picking up on a phrase of Freud's) to designate psychoanalysis *The Impossible Profession*. Brenner does not shy away from the more extreme and even absurd consequences of his position. Returning to the issue in a later article titled "Working Alliance, Therapeutic Alliance, and Transference," he writes:

> It is true enough that it often does no harm for an analyst to be conventionally "human." Still, there are times when his being "human" . . . can be harmful and we cannot know in advance when those times will be. As an example, for his analyst to express sympathy for a patient who has just lost a close relative may make it more difficult than it otherwise would be for the patient to express pleasure or spite or exhibitionistic satisfaction over the loss.[8]

In short, don't commiserate with a patient who has just lost a parent or child or spouse in case this act of commiseration influences his or her expressions of feeling. Malcolm comments that "this is taking respect for individual human experience . . . very far indeed."[9]

But is this not the respect—the loyalty—that literary criticism has demanded we give to our texts? Hélène Cixous, to name just one among numerous possible authorities, has argued that we should consider acts of reading to be acts of "listening" in a state of "active receptivity," a notion that is clearly modeled on the analytic scene.[10] But if such listening requires the listener to become something other than conventionally human, as Brenner acknowledges, then is not literary criticism also an "impossible profession"? What, after all, would a literary critical version of Brenner's analytic situation look like? If we are straining to hear all the possible nuances and inflections of the text, uncontaminated by our wishes and desires, then isn't the best posture something like that of Cordelia's before Lear, to "love, and be silent"?[11] Is that what Dinesen's storyteller means by unswerving loyalty to the story? Is the silence that we will hear the silent "speech" of a text, unencumbered by interpretations, messy with desire as they are?

The difficulty of ever attaining objectivity in the face of the text thus leaves literary criticism in what Samuel Weber has termed a "delicate—perhaps even aporetic—situation: it must seek to affirm the nonaffirmable [that is "literature"], at the same time allowing the latter to speak for itself."[12] To speak for the text and to hear the text speak for itself—this is the impossible task of the critic. Indeed, one might argue that the methodological imperatives of New Historicism (not a reading strategy much noted for receptivity to psychoanalytic insight) derive at some profound level from a melancholic insistence on this basic "impossibility" of literary interpretation, conceived in terms of a kind of pure receptivity. The endlessly reiterated theoretical rub for the historicist concerns the fact that the past is only ever available from the perspective of the present. Historicists are therefore like Brenner's analyst, caught in a temporally dictated version of the countertransferential relationship but nonetheless *morally obligated* (in the name of the higher truths of scholarship) to attempt to transcend that relationship.[13]

Weber also comments that this problem—which we can perhaps most neutrally describe as the problem of the proper relation of literary criticism to its object—was one that could be fairly effectively bracketed "so long as certain founding conventions concerning the nature of that object were regarded as unproblematic. The most important of those conventions . . . was the conviction that literature did indeed constitute an object, which is to say something *self-identical* and *self-contained*, whether as an individual work or collective canon."[14] Thus, according to Weber, it is the disruption of this founding convention that has forced criticism to confront the problem of its desire.

II

> Pleasure is the only thing worth having a theory
> about.
>
> —OSCAR WILDE, *THE PICTURE OF DORIAN GRAY*

One of the more notorious embarrassments of literary criticism in re-
cent years is that it is an academic discipline without a clearly defined
object of study. The tension between the specialized sense and the more
generalized or inclusive sense of the term "literature" has become in-
creasingly difficult to ignore since the postwar era, and particularly
since the 1970s, when pragmatist-derived notions regarding the essen-
tial cultural contingency of value, including aesthetic value, began their
ascendancy within professional intellectual culture. Thus, the dominant
position within the profession at present is, as Terry Eagleton puts it,
that "[l]iterature, in the sense of a set of works of assured and unal-
terable value, distinguished by certain shared inherent properties, does
not exist."[15] The older position, that "literature" represents "the best
that has been thought and the best that has been said"[16] within the
great texts of the Western tradition, was undoubtedly fundamental to
the instantiation of the study of vernacular writings within the modern
project of mass education and has a residual rhetorical power in certain
contexts outside the academy; but such ideas are now so suspect *within*
the discipline of literary studies itself that merely invoking the concept
of a "great text" in the wrong company can be a risky—even career-
destroying—business. (Anyone who has attended graduate school in
literary studies at some point in the last fifteen to twenty years will
know that I do not exaggerate.) Absurd though it may seem to out-
siders, for much of the 1980s and early 1990s, one of the most reac-
tionary things a professor of English could do was declare a "Love for
Literature" (with two capital *L*s), let alone a belief in "Great Books"
(with a capital *G* and *B*). Indeed, although I personally make such naive
invocations of greatness all the time—about books, movies, musicians,
and even, very occasionally, about other literary critics—and although
in everyday speech such invocations are considered perfectly reason-
able, since we generally understand ordinary uses of the phrase "x is
a great book" to mean little more than "I like x" or "I think x is im-
portant," the members of the academic discipline that is literary study

have proved (understandably) resistant to the idea that they are little more than instructors in the cultivation of "proper" aesthetic taste. This resistance derives from the recognition (associated with the broader insights of theory) that the conventions of aesthetic taste that determined the shape of traditional answers to the question "What is literature?" could not be easily distinguished from a thoroughly repugnant (classist, nationalistic, racist, and sexist) politics of cultural colonialism—since the best that had been thought or said invariably turned out to have been thought or said by a dead white European male. In the wake of the necessary abandonment of traditional literary aesthetics, then, "the essence of literature is to have no essence, to be protean, undefinable, to encompass whatever might be situated outside it," to quote Jonathan Culler.[17]

But in the light of such a (non)definition, it is small wonder that literary critics have such difficulty saying what literary criticism is these days; while it is without doubt a writerly and pedagogical practice founded on the principal tenet that we can get something out of putting questions to written texts, it seems that we're no longer sure what questions we should be putting, nor what texts we should be putting them to, nor indeed from whence our authority to reward (and punish) the students who do (or don't) read the texts we assign to them consequently derives. In fact, in the light of the (non)definition of the literary that currently dominates the professional scene, it becomes extremely difficult even to explain (to students, parents, deans, politicians, and other fund-granting institutions) the educational benefit that we presumably still imagine inheres in the encounter with those texts. Sadly, literary critics are therefore often not the best people to call upon when it comes to justifying the practice of literary criticism; when asked to do so, they tend to adopt postures that can seem sweepingly polemical ("Yes, let's euthanize that irrelevant conservative beast called literary studies and replace it with cultural studies / communication studies / media studies!"), overly defensive ("Well, what's the point of studying anything?"), uncomfortably retrograde ("*Surely* you don't think a complete education can omit the works of Chaucer / Shakespeare / Dickens / Joyce / My Favorite Dead White Male Author?"), or, at best, self-deprecatingly humorous ("Of course literary criticism is important—just ask a literary critic!").

However, Culler's nondefinition of the literary strikes a note that may sound familiar from other contexts. For if "the essence of literature is to have no essence, to be protean, undefinable, to encompass whatever might be situated outside it," then it bears a remarkable resemblance to the concept that I have all along been arguing is central to any understanding of the processes that constitute literary interpretation. Although Culler does not say so, it would seem from his account (which I think it is fair to describe as, at this point, thoroughly or-thodox) that *the essence of "literature" is desire.*

Therefore, if we haven't answered the question of what makes a good critic yet, we can at least offer a new definition of what a literary critic is: a literary critic is first and foremost, always already, a desiring sub-ject. This observation might begin to address the question of why we bother to "do" criticism, even in the face of the inevitability of mis-reading; for if literary critics are desiring subjects, then their interpre-tations of texts are expressions of desire before they are "correct" or "incorrect." (As obvious as this conclusion may now seem to some readers, it is *not* something the profession has always known about itself, and the realization has proved traumatic, as I shall show.) Ques-tions about the principles and procedures of the discipline that seemed unanswerable in a positivistic form—such as, "What makes one reading more faithful to the text than another?" can therefore be re-configured, and perhaps even partially answered, once the a priori na-ture of critical desire is acknowledged; for while one may approve or disapprove of a person's desires, it would make little sense to speak of those desires as "inaccurate" or "untrue." The question "What makes one reading better than another?" thus becomes a kind of category error. It would be more appropriate to ask, "Why are some kinds of critical desire considered acceptable and some unacceptable? What are the conditions of their acceptability, and how do those conditions change?" In other words, the question of what makes a critic "good" is indistinguishable from the question of what that critic wants, or is seen to want, from the obscure objects of his or her passion.

III

> Enjoyment . . . is constitutively an "excess." If we sub-
> tract the surplus we lose enjoyment itself.
>
> —SLAVOJ ŽIŽEK, *THE SUBLIME OBJECT OF IDEOLOGY*

So, what does a literary critic want? By framing the question thus, I am suggesting that, despite the protean nature of the literary object of desire, there is something potentially transhistorical about the critical impulse. But before we can see what it is about critical desire that persists, or insists, we must acknowledge that the discipline has undergone some enormous transformations in the last thirty years or so and that the question must first be historicized before we can even begin to approach it in something like "universal" terms. So, what *did* literary critics want?

As numerous histories of the modern discipline note, what literary critics once wanted above all was to be taken seriously *as* literary critics: that is, to be recognized and intellectually respected as the practitioners of a "real" discipline with its own rules and procedures, and its own clearly defined objects, rather than as woolly minded dilettantes working in a subfield that was merely an outgrowth of more senior and respectable branches of knowledge such as history, philosophy, or theology. Indeed, the most ambitious literary critics from the 1930s through to the 1950s aspired to the disciplinary rigor associated with the natural sciences: conducting "cold" readings in laboratory-style conditions in order to isolate the elements that caused misinterpretations (as in the interpretive "experiments" of I. A. Richards) and disdaining mere "appreciation" in proscriptive theoretical essays with titles like "The Intentional Fallacy." The New Criticism, as this movement became generally known, has long been denigrated for inattention to elements such as "historical context"; but such facile dismissals overlook the fact that the motivation for this "inattention" sprang from the pursuit of disciplinary autonomy, a pursuit that was, by and large, tremendously successful. It is one of the many ironies of critical historiography that the institutional power and prestige of literary studies, insofar as it goes, rests to a great extent on the achievements of figures that have been so repeatedly and vociferously repudiated.[18] Nor were the New Critics unself-conscious about this pursuit of the "literary" as distinct from the "historical," as the preface to a standard New Critical text like Cleanth Brooks's *The Well Wrought Urn* indicates. Brooks's language provides many clues as to the precise nature of New Critical desire, when he proleptically anticipates the charge that his methodology is "unhistorical": "A . . . formidable objection to the plan of the book might be that I have taken too little into account the historical backgrounds of the poems I have discussed. . . . [But] if literary history has not been emphasized in the pages that follow, it is not because I discount its importance. . . . It is rather that I have been anxious to see what residuum, if any, is left after we have referred the poem to its cultural matrix."[19] Brooks's desire, interestingly figured here as an anxiety, is to get to grips with something that is already perceived as an excess or remainder. The purely "literary" content of a poem, once abstracted from its "cultural matrix" is, precisely, a "residuum": literature, in short, is what's left over. This notion of literature as an obscure, inadequately defined remainder once again brings us back, in an almost uncanny way, to the Lacanian notion of desire—which, as I have demonstrated in my previous chapter, is explicitly figured in such terms. In fact, the literary object in this classic New Critical text is perfectly analogous to another late Lacanian concept, central to his writings on desire: the *objet petit a*.

What is the *objet petit a?* Well, precisely. Irritating though such a reply may be, it is nevertheless apt, for as Stuart Schneiderman has pointed out, Lacan's definitions of the *objet petit a* tend to "leave something to be desired"—and that's exactly the point.[20] The *objet petit a* is introduced into Lacan's later seminars without ever being fully or concretely defined, the idea being that the reader or student will pursue the elusive concept and thereby mimetically reproduce in the movement of his or her thought the movement of desire that the *objet petit a* is said to inspire. It is therefore one of the most infuriating concepts in Lacan's work, because you've only completely got it when you know you haven't got it completely—that is, when you know that there's always a remainder that you will never "get."[21]

This desirable leftover can be figured in many ways; in fact, numerous cultural and poetic symbols could be considered versions of the concept, and many artistic texts spend time investing ordinary items with the aura of ineffable significance that the *objet petit a* represents (think, for example, of Van Gogh's attempts to monumentalize such objects as an old pair of work boots, or the role of the bowler hat in Milan Kundera's *The Unbearable Lightness of Being,* or even William Carlos Williams's suggestion that "So much depends upon a red wheelbarrow / glazed with rainwater / beside the white chickens."). But if asked to name a figure for the *objet a* of literary criticism itself—to suggest a metaphoric representation of the unnamable remainder that captures and inspires the desire of the critic—we could do worse than the one Brooks himself appropriates from John Donne for the title of his book and say that the *objet petit a* of literary criticism (or at least of New Criticism) was once "a well wrought urn."[22]

In one immediate and obvious sense, the urn emblematizes human creativity in the face of the void: not only is it literally built around an emptiness, an emptiness it simultaneously calls into being, but, functionally, the urn is the ornate, decorative, art object designed to hold the ashes of the dead. Moreover, as a museum piece, it is a resonant symbol for the lost society that produced it, the cultural leftover or remainder that is imagined as metonymically containing an idealized totality. It is therefore probably not a coincidence that one of the most famous attempts in canonical English literature to describe a world beyond the endless dialectic of desire and dissatisfaction turns upon an urn: I mean, of course, Keats's ode to his "unravished bride of quietness," an artifact that stands outside time and so provides a glimpse of a place where lovers are "forever panting and forever young." And as that poem suggests, it is only possible to attain a desire "far above [the kind] / That leaves a heart high sorrowful and cloyed," that is, a desire above what is scornfully termed "breathing human passion," if it is captured, frozen, stillborn, a passion that does not breathe.[23]

Keats suggests that one can only refuse the dialectic of desire and disappointment by refusing life itself; but this was an insight that Ben Jonson also recognized and, strikingly, chose to figure with the same object. In his "Cary-Morison Ode" the death of a child at birth is imagined as a self-conscious decision to (re)turn to the urn:

> Ere thou wert half got out
> Wise child, didst hastily return
> And mad'st thy mother's womb thine urn
> How summed a circle didst thou leave mankind
> Of deepest lore, could we the centre find![24]

As if anticipating the first law of psychoanalytic theory, Jonson's infant simply refuses to leave his mother's body and thereby avoids the originary act of renunciation and loss that initiates and instantiates human life as structured by a dialectic of desire and lack. Jonson presents this evocation of the womb/urn as a magic circle that excludes the world as a piece of profound lore, but this is also a lore that locates the end of desire in the return that is also a leave-taking, the final return of death itself.

As the example of Jonson's ode suggests, Keats's poem is only one of several literary turns to the urn to represent the idea of perfected (because stillborn) desire, turns that in turn endlessly evoke the desire of the critic, prompting still further rereadings or re-turnings of the literary artifact that are also retunings of its unheard melodies, sweeter because they are unheard. From the urns that hold the ashes of heroes and lovers in Homer, to the most famous modernist descendant of

Keats's urn, Wallace Stevens's jar—a jar that is again self-consciously located "outside" ("I placed a jar in Tennessee") and that is also a point around which everything seems to turn ("it made the slovenly wilderness surround that hill"), a self-contained container that "did not give of bird or bush," a jar that represents the opposition and the mutual implication of such ostensible binary terms as nature and culture, perception and actuality, creativity and sterility, desire and death— "like nothing else in Tennessee," these literary urns stand outside and beyond the critical anecdotes that we spin around them.[25]

When Brooks made the urn his central emblem of the literary, then, he was doing more than enshrining the poetic object as an iconic unity or whole. He was also marking the professional enterprise of literary criticism with desire. More specifically, by representing "literature" with the urn that could in turn represent both an object of desire and the final negation of desire in death, an urn that could represent desire outside the dialectic of satisfaction and disappointment, an urn that could represent, therefore, an impossible notion of desire undiminished even in its attainment, Brooks made "literature" itself into an *objet petit a;* he (and the like-minded critics of his generation) thereby provided the final seal of institutional legitimation to a process that began with Romanticism—the pursuit of art qua art. Perhaps his only mistake was to believe that he had found was he was looking for.

Where? Well, in his pursuit of the literary object beyond the matrices of history and culture, Brooks famously thought that he had found what he was looking for—literature qua literature, the ungraspable *objet petit a* of critical desire—in, among other things, Donne's "The Canonization." The precise location of this remainder turns out to be the moment of self-referentiality that closes the poem, with its invocation of text as urn. Having refused worldly achievements for the private world of love, the speaker comments that he and his beloved have, in one another, an adequate alternative to everything else they may have given up:

> Wee can dye by it, if not live by love,
>   And if unfit for tombes and hearse
> Our legend bee, it will be fit for verse;
>   And if no peece of Chronicle wee prove,
>   We'll build in sonnets pretty roomes;
>   As well a well wrought urne becomes
> The greatest ashes, as half acre tombes,
>   And by these hymnes, all shall approve
>   Us *Canoniz'd* for Love.[26]

In some ways the thought is already a commonplace—already a return, we might say—since we can recognize the notion that artistic production provides an immortal monument to the beloved from many lyrics of the period, including Shakespeare's sonnets. Brooks writes, "The poem is an instance of the doctrine which it asserts; it is both the assertion and the realization of the assertion. . . . [T]he poem itself is the well wrought urn which can hold the lovers' ashes and which will not suffer in comparison with the prince's half acre tomb."[27] But part of the compelling force of his interpretation derives from our already having recognized a commonplace—from our already having made that prior return. However, in a reading of Brooks's reading of Donne, Jonathan Culler has pointed out that by making "The Canonization" a literary monument, and therefore a monumental example of the literary, Brooks only "responds much as the poem predicts" its readers will.[28] The satisfactory sense of closure that Brooks's reading produces, in which this poem stands apart as the long sought after and irreducible remainder that is synonymous with "literature," an organic, iconic whole just like the very urn that it describes—this sense of closure depends on a repression of the logical problems of self-reference. As Culler writes:

> In celebrating itself as urn the poem incorporates a celebration of the urn and thus becomes something other than the urn; and if the urn is taken to include the response to the urn, then the responses it anticipates, such as Brooks's, become a part of it and prevent it from closing. Self-reference does not close in upon itself but leads to a proliferation of representations, a series of invocations and urns. . . . There is a neatness to this situation but it is the neatness of transference, in which the analyst finds himself caught up in and reenacting the drama he thought he was analyzing from the outside.[29]

In short, Brooks mistakes self-reference for self-presence. To quote Dayton Haskin's reading of Culler's reading of Brooks's reading of Donne, "Brooks succeeded chiefly in displaying his own entanglement in a never ending chain of discourses."[30] As the proliferation of names in that last sentence indicates, subsequent critics are of course no less entangled: it's just harder for us to forget that fact.

However, as Culler clearly implies by his move into the language of psychoanalysis, what Brooks has also managed to demonstrate (unintentionally, according to Culler) is the power of certain texts to produce uncanny transferential repetitions of their main dramas. Culler is content to show that this is all that Brooks has shown, but the point that

I would emphasize is that *neither* critic is quite able to say exactly where the uncanny power of the text resides, or why its words activate a form of repetitive compulsion in the reader. In short, the central question of why anyone should feel compelled to make this text their urn, so to speak—why it should be an object of critical desire—has not been answered. Of course, it is the burden of Culler's argument that such a question *cannot* be answered and that Brooks's mistake was to believe that it can; to be able to say categorically why the text is an object of desire would, after all, to be able to say *why* it is a "good" poem, that is, *why* it is "literature," and while this is indeed exactly Brooks's project, Culler clearly does not think that we can say so much.

But perhaps these two readers are not so far apart as recent critical historiography suggests. Both, finally, are compelled by the notion of the remainder—of the bit that is left over after a certain kind of analysis has taken place—and both finally associate that desirable remainder with "the essence of the literary." The only difference is that one thinks that remainder can finally be isolated, and the other does not. To use the metaphor of the urn as *objet a* of literary criticism: one sees the urn as whole, restored, as part of a display in a museum that he curates (indeed, in an unusual gesture even among New Critical texts, *The Well Wrought Urn* reproduces all the poems discussed in its chapters whole and without commentary, in a kind of gallery, at the end of the book); the other sees the urn as cracked and leaking desire, or as a partial reconstruction, with some pieces always missing. But whether they see it whole or complete, both critics are clearly gripped by a repetitive compulsion to return to the literary urn.

IV

> Writing about desire: compulsive, a challenge, self-indulgence, anxiety . . . above all a project that defies completion.
>
> —CATHERINE BELSEY, *DESIRE*

In sum: a good literary critic can be defined as someone who expresses what the profession considers proper desires for "literature" (proper to those within the profession, even if eccentric and perhaps a little unseemly to some outside it); and "literature" can be defined as that which literary critics desire. So far, so tautological. But the point of these definitions of the literary and literary criticism that I have offered is not that they are circular but that they are mutually implicated: more specifically, that the relation of criticism to literature is precisely analogous to the relationship of "subject" and "object" within a dialectic of desire; which means further that the relation of the critic to his/her object is one with implications for the self-identity of both terms within the dialectic. This insight suggests a way not only of rethinking the history of the literary critical enterprise, but also of rethinking, and perhaps reinvigorating, that enterprise in the future.

Thus, the story of literary criticism might be retold as follows: Once, our critical desire had to be denied because that desire was (mis)-recognized as threatening the "objectivity" toward which criticism aspired as a guarantee of its intellectual legitimacy. Then, as the notion of objectivity in literary study was itself exposed as a fiction, one often pressed into the service of prejudiced and intolerant ideologies, critics learned to embrace and advertise their interpretive desires—perhaps most obviously in the poststructuralist advocacy of the free play of the text, but I would argue no less in all modes of criticism that self-consciously base their heuristics in identity politics. Reader-response criticism even took the step of making the desires of the reader central to the production of meaning; although, fearful of being misunderstood as saying that this meant meanings could be willfully projected onto texts, the notion of the interpretive community was developed as a kind of institutional box capable of containing or at least constraining readerly desire. But the "return to psychoanalysis" that my own work performs, and that is also attested to in much current criticism by the popularity of a Lacanian explicator like Slavoj Žižek, has the effect of transforming that "interpretive community" from a clean, well-kept, institutional space, with proscribed rules of procedure and engagement, into an agonistic, violent, seething mass of competing impulses, many of which cannot even be precisely articulated or recognized as such until after the fact.[31] As I hope the example of this book suggests, we can learn something more and say something new about the texts that compel our endless returns, by attending to this agonistic struggle of obscure desires—even though something must remain left over.

Which brings me to the question of the future, of the effects that the "recognition of desire" might have for the criticism of tomorrow. This is a tricky issue, because to speculate on one's hopes for the future of criticism is to render it an object of desire as well as an expression of it. To address one recurring fantasy regarding the critical project: some have seen the attempt to "reroute the questions of symbolic actions and their effects through the dialectic of desire" that I am advocating as a way to produce (yet once more) a "socially engaged" or politically productive form of theorizing.[32] Indeed, the most obvious example here would be the aforementioned Žižek, whose rearticulations of Lacanian theories of desire are always offered in the service of a better understanding of the workings of ideology and hence as a tool in the service of politically engaged critique.

I have to say I think that this notion of "the politically productive reading" represents only the latest version of the *objet petit a* of literary criticism. To extend the metaphor of the urn: we used to pretend that it was a whole, a unity; then we saw that the urn was broken and that all our efforts to restore it would fail; now some of us like to pretend that by telling everyone that the urn is broken, that it was always broken, we will bring down the edifice of capitalism, promote racial and sexual tolerance, and so on. I do *not* mean to foreclose the possibility of political efficacy within literary studies altogether. But I do think the immodesty of the grandest aspirations of much of the political criticism of the 1980s and 1990s is now evident, if only in the utter failure of the turn to political criticism to change the living and working conditions of people *within* the academy, let alone those who work outside it. To this extent, at least, I am inclined to agree with Stanley Fish when he says that "what the profession really [always?] wants is the renewal of its energies, a new angle from which to exercise its skills."[33]

In other words, I advocate the attempt to read texts through the dialectic of desire not because this will bring us any of the things that, at different times, we've thought we wanted—for example, more faithful readings of the text, or readings that emphasize plurality and the irreducibility of language, or readings that inspire political change. Instead, and without saying that we cannot *sometimes* achieve those aims, I advocate attention to the role played by the dialectic of desire within interpretive acts because I think such attention will bring us what we *always* want, which is a reason to return to our urns, to contemplate them again, and to produce still more interpretive turns upon them—despite the fact that this activity won't bring us any *necessary* reward, beyond its own satisfactions. Those satisfactions might even be enough when we are talking about spending time in the company of texts that we love: and isn't that, finally, what we are talking about when we talk about "literature"? Like Donne, advocating a renewal of the flames of a relationship by creative fantasy, I argue that we are always seeking excuses for or ways to renew our critical passions, in the face of our recognition that whatever dream of desire drives us to the text, it will never be entirely satisfied. The turn to interpretive desire that my own work exhibits might provide one such means to renewal, but it needn't be the only one. As long as there is a remainder to excite our desire and make us forget that it won't (finally) be satisfied, we will continue to return to our literary urns and spin new interpretive tales; and the evidence suggests that there will always be a remainder.

V

> To tolerate life remains, after all, the first duty of all living beings. Illusion becomes valueless if it makes this harder for us.
>
> —SIGMUND FREUD, *THOUGHTS FOR THE TIMES ON WAR AND DEATH*

Literary critics know something of the compulsion to repeat. Freud saw such compulsions as evidence of the failure to forget properly: a memory, no longer present to the conscious mind, has lodged in the unconscious like a bone in the throat, causing the patient to act out, compulsively. The psychoanalytic patient is therefore like the protagonist of one of Elvis Presley's early hits, a person who has forgotten to remember to forget. Ironically, analysis helps you to remember precisely in order to forget properly.

If my arguments are correct, the literary critic, like the analysand, needs to remember to forget something or, perhaps, to forget to remember something. For whether the literary critic adopts the traditional role of cultural high priest and textual master, or the poststructuralist role of the subversive celebrant of free play, or the role of political activist "whose readings of Shakespeare or Spenser . . . participate in the reformation of our own [culture]"[34]—all of these roles ultimately serve the same phantasmatic function: they are all ways of forgetting that interpretation is motivated by desires that must remain obscure and unknown, and that those obscure desires will shape those interpretations in ways that render them disputable, displaceable, provisional. Literary criticism, in all its incarnations, thus becomes the staging or reproduction of desire itself—of the subject's relation to an object-cause (an *objet petit a*) that has no object proper.

I should therefore revise my statement that literature is the *objet petit a* of the critic (for all that it may once have been for Cleanth Brooks). Nowadays, I would suggest, literature is no longer the *object petit a* of the critic; that role is instead played by literary criticism itself. An analogy may help clarify this point: Henry Krips writes that "the relation between the *objet a*, the desiring subject, and the object of desire resembles the relation between the chaperone, the suitor, and the beloved. By functioning as a site at which the suitor exercises his or her skills in order to get access to the object of desire, the chaperone covertly provides him with an opportunity for gaining pleasure (perhaps his only pleasure). Although the chaperone is not herself an object of desire, by standing in the way of what the suitor wants she becomes part of the structure that sustains, that is, causes, his desire." In other words, criticism is to the critic as the chaperone is to the suitor: "covertly the object–cause of desire and a source of pleasure without [itself] being desired."[35]

Of course, in saying all this I could be accused of saying nothing more or less profound than that literary criticism is simply a highly particular and perhaps even peculiar way of coping with existence: just one rather specialized mode of being in a life structured by the dialectic of desire. Such a claim could appear at once grandiose and banal, more "immodest" than any of the claims for political criticism that I have argued against and, at the same time, of no real help to people who would do critical work. Thus, as Freud remarked toward the end of his career on the general nature of psychoanalytic insight: "I find myself for the moment in the interesting position of not knowing whether what I wish to impart should be regarded as something long familiar and obvious or as something entirely new and puzzling."[36] But then again, to be at once grandiose and banal, to express what is obvious and at the same time puzzling, is perhaps only appropriate in a discussion of desire, which itself represents a meeting of the sublime and the ordinary since it is surely "the commonest and yet the most singular condition we know."[37]

At the same time, I hope the idea that we can "reroute" the questions of symbolic actions and their effects through the dialectic of desire *is* potentially helpful to practitioners of criticism, of all kinds. Indeed, I would go so far as to say that by opening the question of the relationship between interpretation and desire we can problematize the basic commonsense distinction between representation and reality—a task that strikes me as having obvious intellectual value (even if no *necessary* politically progressive actions follow from it), and one that literary critics are admirably equipped to perform. The acknowledgment of critical desire also foregrounds the inevitable rhetoricity of all critical acts and allows us to feel less guilty about the fact that when we write criticism, we are trying to make people share our desires, dislike what we dislike, love what we love, see things our way. More specifically, the notion of critical desire raises further questions about what we might call critical identification, questions that complicate such concepts as "the author-function" (suggesting, among other things, that the reason the author refuses to lie down in the face of poststructuralist assertions of his/her death is because we can't stop desiring him/her). But perhaps the single most important claim I am making for the analysis of interpretive desire can be summed up in the words of L. O. Aranye Fradenburg, writing in the context of her own defense of psychoanalytic modes of analysis in medieval studies: "It is not . . . simply a matter of recognizing that the position of the observer will change the object of observation." Instead, the twofold point that must be grasped is that "the un/conscious desire of the observer changes the object of observation, and *that analysis of this desire can produce knowledge about the object.*"[38]

But these suggestions regarding the interpretive possibilities of attending to interpretive desire are just that: suggestions. For it may be the most attractive aspect of the notion of interpretive desire that it leaves so much left over for us to consider. Finally, in the wake of a "recognition of desire," perhaps the purpose of criticism can be at once challenging *and* humble: to combine and connect our partial, incomplete readings of the fictive with our partial, incomplete (and indeed, fictive) readings of "reality," for no higher purpose than sending readers (back) to their texts with renewed interest, with renewed pleasure, with renewed desire.

Never Donne

Throughout this work, my desire has been to persuade you to see things the way that I see them, and to see *Donne* in the way that I see him, because that is the way I like him best—the way he gives me greatest pleasure. But risks attend such a project. In Tennessee Williams's *The Glass Menagerie,* Amanda Wingfield wants her children to be happy—because she loves them—but she is notoriously unable to imagine that happiness for them may not be the same thing as it is for her. She imposes her idea of happiness—her desires—on them, out of her love for them, and so makes them miserable. Her most generous impulse, to love, is thus also her most destructive impulse. Criticism is like love in this way, too, managing to be at once the most generous and the most selfish of modes. On the one hand, it is coercive, a way of saying, "See my desire, share it, recognize that it should be your own"; and on the other hand, it is offered as a gift, a way of saying, "Look at things this way and see what it will bring you." We cannot be sure which impulse is at work when we write criticism, and even if we are certain of our motives, we cannot be sure they will be understood. Do my interpretations invite students and readers to take new pleasures, or are they just a form of imposition? The fact that it is not for me to decide is exactly the point.

But perhaps there is another reason, besides the inevitability of misreading, that a critic's work is never done. Reading, after all, can be a terribly lonely business, for all its pleasures, and maybe criticism is a way of coping with that loneliness, of sustaining desire in spite of it.

To illustrate: Imagine a man in love, separated from his beloved by some considerable distance. All day he has wanted to hear her voice, but when he finally gets a chance to call her, he only gets her answering machine. Ever hopeful, he then thinks to check his voice mail—perhaps she left a message earlier. But, no, tonight there are no messages. Disappointed, he hangs up—and is startled a moment later by the ringing of the phone. Is it her?! For a moment he is filled with joy that his desire to speak with her will be satisfied. Then, lifting the receiver, he hears nothing: dead air. Somehow he had failed to disconnect properly when checking his messages, and this caused his phone to ring. It was not his beloved that inspired his delight but the echo of his own desire coming back to haunt him in the guise of a call from outside. Realizing this, he is sad. But his sadness doesn't stop him from calling again, if only to leave a message saying, "Call me back."

The scene of readerly pleasure is a little like this. When I read, I activate the text, becoming the living conduit between language and the world of the unconscious. But the circuit I complete is a closed one. I cannot be sure that the bells I hear ringing aren't just the echoes of my own desire. But if I can't get through to the object of my desire, criticism at least provides me with a place to leave a message. Criticism is not just coercive, an injunction to "desire as I do"; it is also an invitation, a way of saying, "Call me back." What I seek in criticism is the response of the other, the response that will renew my desire, that will teach me how to desire the text again, endlessly. I don't ever want to be done desiring Donne; criticism is the given name of a structure of fantasy ensuring that I never have to be.

Notes

Index

Notes

Introduction: The Desire of Criticism
and the Criticism of Desire (Part I)

1. John Donne, *Selected Prose,* ed. Helen Gardner and Timothy Healy (Oxford: Clarendon Press, 1967), 129.
2. John Donne, "Elegie XI: The Bracelet," "Lovers' Infiniteness," and "Elegie X: The Dream" ("Image of her . . ."), cited from *The Complete English Poems,* ed. C. A. Patrides, rev. Robin Hamilton (London: Everyman, 1994), 101, 14, 96. The question of which edition of Donne's poems to cite is difficult; despite the wealth of choices, no satisfying single text is currently available. *The Variorum Edition of the Poetry of John Donne* (Bloomington: Indiana University Press, 1994–), a projected eight-volume series under the meticulous general editorship of Gary A. Stringer, will no doubt come to represent the standard scholarly resource for many generations, but as I write, this project is far from complete. Among significant editions of Donne from the last century, none really supersedes Herbert J. C. Grierson's monumental two-volume *The Poems of John Donne* (Oxford: Clarendon Press, 1912), but the most inclusive collections currently available to the modern reader are A. J. Smith's *The Complete English Poems* (London: Penguin, 1977), which somewhat irritatingly prints the "Songs and Sonnets" in alphabetical order; John Carey's *The Major Works* (Oxford: Oxford University Press, 1990, rev. 2000), valuable for its elegant introduction and the inclusion of excerpts from Donne's prose works but marred by its organization (an often dubious chronological sequence); and Patrides's edition, a modest, inexpensive volume that employs old spelling, prints annotations on the same page as the primary text, and follows the general format of Donne's seventeenth-century collections (Hamilton's revised text also contains an extensive critical bibliography). I have generally consulted all these

before citing a poem but most often refer to Patrides's edition when the *Variorum* is unavailable.

3. With apologies to Gary Taylor.

4. Isobel Armstrong writes that "the constitutive nature of affect has been ignored or bracketed in contemporary theory because of its seeming resistance to analysis." See Armstrong's *The Radical Aesthetic* (Oxford: Blackwell, 2000), 13.

5. Vincent Crapanzano, *Hermes' Dilemma and Hamlet's Desire: On the Epistemology of Interpretation* (Cambridge, MA: Harvard University Press, 1992), 1.

6. Donne, *The Complete English Poems*, 12.

7. Slavoj Žižek, *The Sublime Object of Ideology* (London: Verso, 1989), 169.

8. Barbara Everett, "Donne and Secrecy," *Essays in Criticism* 51.1 (2001), 51; Elizabeth D. Harvey and Katherine Eisaman Maus, eds. *Soliciting Interpretation: Literary Theory and Seventeenth-Century Poetry* (Chicago: University of Chicago Press, 1990), ix; Ronald Corthell, *Ideology and Desire in Renaissance Poetry: The Subject of Donne* (Detroit, MI: Wayne State University Press, 1997), 11.

9. Judith Butler, "Against Proper Objects," *Differences: A Journal of Feminist Cultural Studies,* 6. 2–3 (1994): 6.

10. John Dryden, "A Discourse concerning the Original and Progress of Satire" (1693), in *The Poems of John Dryden,* ed. James Kinsley (Oxford: Oxford University Press, 1958), 2:604.

11. Samuel Johnson, *Lives of the English Poets* (London: G. Bell & Sons, 1890), 1:48.

12. Deborah Aldrich Larson, *John Donne and Twentieth-Century Criticism* (London: Associated University Press, 1989), 31.

13. Palgrave's remarks are cited in ibid., 43.

14. Richard Garnett and Edmund Gosse, *English Literature: An Illustrated Record* (London: Heineman, 1903), 2:292; C. S. Lewis, "Donne and Love Poetry," in *Selected Literary Essays* (Cambridge: Cambridge University Press, 1969), 111; J. E. V. Crofts, "John Donne: A Reconsideration," in *John Donne: A Collection of Critical Essays,* ed. Helen Gardner (Englewood Cliffs, NJ: Prentice-Hall, 1962), 80 (reprints an essay originally published in 1937); A. E. Housman, *Name and Nature of Poetry* (New York: Macmillan, 1933), 10; Louis Untermeyer, *Play in Poetry* (New York: Harcourt Brace and Co., 1938), 15; Karl Shapiro, *In Defense of Ignorance* (New York: Random House, 1952), 43, also cited in Larson, *John Donne and Twentieth-Century Criticism,* 102.

15. See David Aers and Gunther Kress, " 'Darke Texts Need Notes': Versions of Self in Donne's Verse Epistles," *Literature and History,* no. 8 (1978): 138–158, reprinted in Arthur Marotti, ed., *Critical Essays on John Donne* (New York: Macmillan, 1994), 102–123; Thomas Docherty, *John Donne, Undone* (London: Methuen, 1986); Stanley Fish, "Masculine Persuasive Force," in Harvey and Maus, *Soliciting Interpretation;* Arthur F. Marotti, *John Donne,*

Coterie Poet (Madison: University of Wisconsin Press, 1986); Jonathan Goldberg, *James I and the Politics of Literature* (Baltimore: Johns Hopkins University Press, 1998); Janel Mueller, "Women among the Metaphysicals: A Case, Mostly, of Being Donne for," *Modern Philology* 87 (1989): 142–151, reprinted in Marotti, *Critical Essays,* 37–48; Janet Halley, "Textual Intercourse: Anne Donne, John Donne, and the Sexual Politics of Textual Exchange," in *Seeking the Woman in Late Medieval and Renaissance Writings: Essays in Feminist Contextual Criticism,* ed. Sheila Fisher and Janet E. Halley (Knoxville: University of Tennessee Press, 1989), 187–206. I am acutely aware that within the vast professional structure of English studies many teachers and scholars have presented differently nuanced readings of Donne to their students and colleagues; and I do not mean to imply that this labor and commentary are less "important" in some absolute sense than that of the critics I have specifically cited. On the contrary, scholars who work outside the academic "star system" may be less subject to the vicissitudes of intellectual fashion than those within it (though they are perhaps more vulnerable to professional disillusionment). The list of scholars, past and present, who have produced "important" work on Donne in this wider sense is far longer than I could name, and I sincerely hope that no one will feel slighted if he or she is not directly acknowledged in these pages.

16. Ben Jonson, "Conversations with William Drummond," in *Ben Jonson: The Complete Poems,* ed. George Parfitt (London: Penguin, 1988), 466.

17. Indeed, Deborah Aldrich Larson describes twentieth-century Donne criticism as a "love-hate relationship" in *John Donne and Twentieth-Century Criticism,* 13. I would suggest it goes back quite a bit further (as Larson's own work shows). Should more evidence be required, see A. J. Smith, ed., *John Donne: The Critical Heritage* (London: Routledge, 1975).

18. William Kerrigan, "What Was Donne Doing?" *South Central Review* 4 (1987): 5.

19. Merritt Hughes, "Kidnapping Donne," in *Essential Articles for the Study of John Donne's Poetry,* ed. John R. Roberts (Hamden, CT: Shoe String Press, 1975), 44.

20. Donne, "The First Anniversarie," in *The Variorum Edition of the Poetry of John Donne,* vol. 6, *The Anniversaries and the Epicedes and Obsequies,* ed. Gary A. Stringer (Bloomington: Indiana University Press, 1995), 469.

21. Shoshana Felman, "Turning the Screw of Interpretation," in *Literature and Psychoanalysis—The Question of Reading: Otherwise,* ed. Shoshana Felman (Baltimore: Johns Hopkins University Press, 1982), 113.

22. Michael Morgan Holmes, *Early Modern Metaphysical Literature* (London: Palgrave, 2001), 2, 26, 28.

23. For a critique of New Historicism as inverted Romance, see Jonathan Crewe, *Hidden Designs: The Critical Profession and Renaissance Literature* (New York: Methuen, 1986), 74–75 et passim.

24. Kerrigan, "What Was Donne Doing?" 7.

25. Holmes, *Early Modern Metaphysical Literature,* 28.

26. William Empson, "Rescuing Donne," first published in *Just So Much Honor: Essays Commemorating the Four Hundredth Anniversary of the Birth of John Donne,* ed. Peter Fiore (University Park: Pennsylvania State University Press, 1972), 95–108, reprinted in *Essays on Renaissance Literature Volume One: Donne and the New Philosophy,* ed. John Haffenden (Cambridge: Cambridge University Press, 1993), 159–199. All citations from Empson's work on Donne are taken from the Haffenden volume.

27. Empson, *Essays,* 86–87.

28. John Carey, "Creating Canon Fodder," *Sunday Times,* November 29, 1989, G3, cited by John Haffenden, Introduction to Empson, *Essays,* 1. Haffenden's exemplary introduction provides an invaluable account of the critical debate over Empson's heretical Donne; see esp. 1–15.

29. Richard Strier, *Resistant Structures: Particularity, Radicalism, and Renaissance Texts* (Berkeley: University of California Press, 1995), 6.

30. Terry Eagleton, *Literary Theory: An Introduction* (Minneapolis: University of Minnesota Press, 1983), 169.

31. Jonathan Dollimore, *Sex, Literature, and Censorship* (Cambridge: Polity Press, 2001), 96, 97. My final block quote links passages on pages 97 and 163.

32. The phrase appears in their introduction to Silvan Tomkins, *Shame and Its Sisters: A Silvan Tomkins Reader,* ed. Eve Kosofsky Sedgwick and Adam Frank (Durham, NC: Duke University Press, 1995).

33. L. O. Aranye Fradenburg, *Sacrifice Your Love: Psychoanalysis, Historicism, Chaucer* (Minneapolis: University of Minnesota Press, 2002), 64.

34. James R. Kincaid, *Annoying the Victorians* (New York: Routledge, 1995), 77, 258.

35. This formulation might appear to confuse the proposition that "truths are always mediated" (which I believe) with the proposition that "there are no truths" (which I consider philosophically incoherent). However, I am employing the word "fantasy" in a psychoanalytic sense, as an *inescapable* condition of cognition; in other words, fantasy here names a network of interpretations that structure our beliefs, rather than something that can be opposed to an easily available or measurable reality. I return to this concept in my chapter on Donne and gender.

36. T. S. Eliot, *The Varieties of Metaphysical Poetry,* ed. Ronald Schuchard (London: Faber and Faber, 1993), 44, emphasis mine.

37. I do not denigrate these activities nor suggest that one can't be both a "scholar" *and* a "critic" at different times. I am simply raising the question of what it might mean to reintroduce Eliot's distinction in the present intellectual climate.

38. This is not to say that the imbrication of desire and knowledge is not potentially vertiginous, disturbing, and destabilizing. It is to advocate a less reactionary response to that fact.

1. Donne's "Fore-Skinne": Desire and the Seventeenth-Century Reader

1. Though the collection is not entirely without internal coherence; most of Donne's elegies are grouped together, as are the epithelamia and a handful of prose letters. Nevertheless, unlike subsequent collections, the 1633 volume has no overarching structural principle.
2. Leah Marcus, *Unediting the Renaissance* (London: Routledge, 1996), 193.
3. Arthur F. Marotti, *Manuscript, Print and the English Renaissance Lyric* (Ithaca: Cornell University Press, 1995), 252.
4. Ibid., 251.
5. Richard Barnfield, *Poems, 1594–1598,* ed. E. Arber (Westminster, 1896), 44.
6. John Donne, *Selected Prose,* ed. Helen Gardner and Timothy Healy (Oxford: Clarendon Press, 1967), 111.
7. Marcus, *Unediting the Renaissance,* 196.
8. Walton initiated a long-standing interpretive trend whereby the more disturbing aspects of Donne's sexual representations are neutralized through an appeal to the biographical narrative. See Izaak Walton, *The Life and Death of Dr. Donne,* first published with Donne's *LXXX Sermons* in 1640 and reissued separately in variant forms from 1658 as the *Life of Donne.* Walton's influence persists through Edmund Gosse's *The Life and Letters of John Donne, Dean of St. Paul's* (London, 1899) to R. C. Bald's *John Donne: A Life,* ed. Wesley Milgate (London: Oxford University Press, 1970) and beyond.
9. Quoted by Marcus, *Unediting the Renaissance,* 196; see also Marotti, *Manuscript,* 255.
10. Grierson suggests that this is *the* Sir Thomas Browne, author of *Religio Medici,* which would make "To the Deceased Author" his first published work. See Sir Herbert J. C. Grierson, ed., *The Poems of John Donne,* 2 vols. (Oxford: Oxford University Press, 1912), 2:255. However, Keynes speculates that this is an older Thomas Browne, a student at Christ Church, Oxford, during the 1620s, who later served as domestic chaplain to Archbishop Laud. See Sir Geoffrey Keynes, *A Bibliography of Dr. John Donne, Dean of St. Paul's* (Oxford: Clarendon Press, 1973), 196. In the absence of further evidence, I prefer to leave the matter open.
11. The placement of the printer's epistle varies in some editions. Marcus gives "sig. [A2]v" for this reference (*Unediting the Renaissance,* 194).
12. The text is from a facsimile of Donne's 1633 *Poems* (Yorkshire: Scolar Press, 1969), 376.
13. The elegy is so obscure, in fact, that Marcus misreads it, confusing the perspective of the "sharper eye[d]" reader with the argument of the author (see Marcus, *Unediting the Renaissance,* 195–196). However, Marcus's misreading is instructive; her inability to imagine a seventeenth-century reader who might react to Donne's "loose verses" with anything other than silence or

a strong gesture of repudiation reveals the extent to which Walton's response has come to dominate our sense of Donne's reception among his peers.

14. Only two other elegists, Lucius Cary and Jasper Mayne, directly acknowledge Donne's troublesome habit of writing erotic verse. Both adopt Walton's strategy, dismissing the poems as the folly of youth. Other elegists avoid referring to the actual content of Donne's writings. However, Thomas Carew's famous poem is perhaps closer in spirit to Browne; and although he does not *specifically* refer to Donne's acts of sexual representation, Carew's imagery takes on a new resonance in the light of Browne's less well known text: "Since to the awe of thy imperious wit / Our stubborne language bends, made only fit / With her tough-thick-rib'd hoopes to gird about / Thy Giant phansie" (Donne, *Poems*, 387).

15. According to J. W. Saunders, the expansion of print culture in the 1580s contributed to anxiety about the potential of the medium to blur established class boundaries. See "The Stigma of Print: A Note on the Social Bases of Tudor Poetry," *Essays in Criticism* 1 (1951): 139–164. Building on Saunders's argument in her feminist-textualist study *The Imprint of Gender: Authorship and Publication in the English Renaissance* (Ithaca, NY: Cornell University Press, 1993), Wendy Wall argues that the so-called stigma of print resulted in new efforts to render print culture attractive. One consequence: "a pervasive cultural phenomenon in which writers and publishers ushered printed texts into the public eye by naming that entrance as a titillating and transgressive act" (*Imprint*, 172). According to Wall, the new textual apparatus of the printed book actively lent itself to the cultivation of a sexually transgressive aura.

16. Alexander Ross, *A View of All Religions in the World* (London, 1672), 51, cited in James Shapiro, *Shakespeare and the Jews* (New York: Columbia University Press, 1996), 38. I am everywhere indebted to Shapiro's meticulous study; see particularly his first chapter, "False Jews and Counterfeit Christians," 13–42.

17. Shapiro, *Shakespeare and the Jews*, 38.

18. "More than anything else in the late-sixteenth-century . . . Paul's ideas about circumcision saturated what Shakespeare's contemporaries thought, wrote, and heard about circumcision. At times confusing and even contradictory, Paul's remarks and the extraordinary commentary produced to explain and resolve various ambiguities contained in them had an immeasurable impact." Ibid., 117.

19. On this topic, see G. Howard, *Paul: Crisis in Galatia* (Cambridge: Cambridge University Press, 1979), 8–10; Peder Borgen, *Paul Preaches Circumcision and Pleases Men, and Other Essays on Christian Origins* (Trondheim, Norway: Tapir, 1983), 15–43; Daniel Boyarin, " 'This We Know to Be the Carnal Israel': Circumcision and the Erotic Life of God and Israel," *Critical Inquiry* 18 (1992): 472–505; and Robert G. Hamerton-Kelly, *Sacred Violence: Paul's Hermeneutic of the Cross* (Minneapolis, MN: Augsburg Fortress, 1992).

20. *Dictionary of National Biography,* s.v. "Robins, John" and "Tany, Thomas."

21. The first part of the quotation is actually a chapter title from John Bulwer's *A View of the People of the Whole World* (London, 1654); see 346 and 367 for the latter part. An earlier edition of the same text was published under the title of *Anthropometamorphosis* (1653).

22. Aquinas was reluctant to deny circumcision any sacramental power but also determined that it should not be thought equivalent to Christian baptism. He settles for a compromise: those who were circumcised "received forgiveness for original and even actual sin, but not in such a way that they were freed from every punishment due to sin, as is the case in baptism in which more abundant grace is bestowed." See Saint Thomas Aquinas, *Summa Theologiae,* vol. 57, *Baptism and Confirmation,* trans. James J. Cunningham (New York: Blackfriars, 1975), 171.

23. John Milton, *The Complete Shorter Poems,* ed. John Carey (London: Longman, 1981), 167.

24. Donne himself adopts the position that circumcision was a thing indifferent, in a sermon preached on Genesis 17:24: "Abraham himselfe was ninety nine yeares old, when the foreskin of his flesh was circumcised." See *The Sermons of John Donne,* ed. Evelyn M. Simpson and George R. Potter (Berkeley: University of California Press, 1953), 6:186–204. Although unequivocal in his opening gambit, declaring that "the vertue [of circumcision] . . . was extinguished in Christ," Donne also accepts it as a kind of placebo: "for, though Circumcision were admitted in a few cases, in the *Apostles* time, *after* Christ, yet that was *as dead herbs* are re-admitted into *medicines* in the *winter* when fresh and green herbs cannot be had of that kind" (6:186). Dead herbs—inefficacious, perhaps, but not destructive.

25. See Thomas H. Luxon's *Literal Figures: Puritan Allegory and the Reformation Crisis in Representation* (Chicago: University of Chicago Press, 1995), esp. chap. 3, " 'Which Things Are an Allegory': Being a Son of God," 77–101. See also Leo Steinberg's *The Sexuality of Christ in Renaissance Art and in Modern Oblivion* (Chicago: University of Chicago Press, 1996), 165–167.

26. Augustine, *Expositions on the Psalms* LVI.9, quoted and translated in Jill Robbins, *Prodigal Son/Elder Brother: Interpretation and Alterity in Augustine, Petrarch, Kafka, Levinas* (Chicago: University of Chicago Press, 1991), 6.

27. Milton, *The Complete Shorter Poems,* 167.

28. See Samuel Purchas, *Purchas His Pilgrimage* ([London], 1626), 152. Again, Shapiro's work is relevant, esp. his third chapter, "The Jewish Crime" (*Shakespeare and the Jews,* 89–113). See also Jeffery Richards, *Sex, Dissidence and Damnation: Minority Groups in the Middle Ages* (London: Routledge, 1990), esp. 103–106.

29. John Donne, *The Complete English Poems,* ed. A. Patrides, rev. Robin Hamilton (London: Everyman, 1994), 60. Another relevant example would be

"A Valediction: Of the Book," in which Donne argues that his poems will serve as a new Bible to future generations of lovers.

30. Ibid., 346.

31. *The Encyclopedia of Religion*, ed. Mircea Eliade et al., 16 vols. (New York: Macmillan, 1987), 12:279. For a history of the transmission and supposed provenance of such relics from Christ's own body, including the foreskin, umbilical cord, and milkteeth, see Jonathan Sumption, *Pilgrimage: An Image of Mediaeval Religion* (London: Faber and Faber, 1975), 44–51.

32. Quoted in Thomas Tentler, *Sin and Confession on the Eve of the Reformation* (Princeton, NJ: Princeton University Press, 1977), 358.

33. John Calvin, *Commentary on the Gospel according to John*, trans. William Pringle, 2 vols. (Grand Rapids, MI: Eerdmans, 1956), 2:259.

34. The phrase is Debora Shuger's, from "Saints and Lovers," in *The Renaissance Bible: Scholarship, Sacrifice, and Subjectivity* (Berkeley: University of California Press, 1998), 172. This portion of my discussion owes much to Shuger's work.

35. Ibid., 176.

36. Here I steer a middle course between the positions of Richard Rambuss and Caroline Walker Bynum on the question of devotional eroticism. Bynum has cautioned against anachronistically importing contemporary notions of the sexual into our readings of earlier periods, claiming that "medieval people" did not "understand as erotic or sexual a number of bodily sensations which we interpret that way." See Caroline Walker Bynum, *Fragmentation and Redemption: Essays on Gender and the Human Body* (New York: Zone Books, 1992), 86. Richard Rambuss has criticized Bynum for adopting chastening interpretive postures in the name of scrupulous historicism. See Rambuss, *Closet Devotions* (Durham, NC: Duke University Press, 1998).

37. Shuger, "Saints and Lovers," 177. Rambuss criticizes Shuger's analysis as "overly schematic" (*Closet Devotions*, 164n.47). He may be correct, but Shuger is at least attempting to refine distinctions that Rambuss is perhaps too willing to collapse and without which the transgressive frisson upon which much of his own work depends cannot be explained.

38. As my scare quotes indicate, my argument ultimately raises questions about the value of distinctions such as *medieval, Renaissance,* and *early modern* by exposing their potential generality and artificiality. It seems worth noting that even as Browne's poem forces us to confront the fact of historical transformation, it also serves as a reminder of cultural continuity within such transformations. It is the familiar but profound historical paradox of continuity within change (inadequately figured by me with the notion of the "cusp") that Browne's elegy demonstrates, at least, as I read it.

39. This is not to suggest that modern medicine evinces an entirely objective attitude toward circumcision, as articles with titles like "The Rape of the Phallus" and "Penile Plunder" indicate. The medical efficacy of circumcision remains disputed; the most vociferous opponent of the practice is probably Dr. Edward Wallerstein, author of *Circumcision: An American Health Fallacy* (New York: Springer, 1980).

40. See, for example, Thomas Lacquer's *Making Sex: Body and Gender from the Greeks to Freud* (Cambridge, MA: Harvard University Press, 1990). For a distillation of ancient and early modern materials relating exclusively to the female body, see Ian Maclean, *The Renaissance Notion of Woman* (Cambridge: Cambridge University Press, 1980).

41. Galen, *On the Usefulness of the Parts of the Body*, ed. and trans. Margaret Tallmadge May, 2 vols. (Ithaca, NY: Cornell University Press, 1968), 2:661. Versions of this idea persist through the medieval period into the seventeenth century. For one account of their influence, see Danielle Jacquart and Claude Thomasset, *Sexuality and Medicine in the Middle Ages*, trans. Matthew Adamson (Princeton, NJ: Princeton University Press, 1988), esp. 43–45.

42. Sir Thomas Browne, *Sir Thomas Browne's Pseudodoxia Epidemica*, ed. Robin Robbins, 2 vols. (Oxford: Clarendon Press, 1981), 1:326.

43. Ibid., 2:923.

44. John Banister, *The Historie of Man: sucked from the sappe of the most approved anathomistes* (London, 1578), 88v. A similar example appears in H. Jackson's vernacular translation of Berengarius, *Mikrokosmographia* (London, 1664), 93, although it is unclear from this text which sex receives the pleasure of the foreskin: "The helps of the *Praeputium*, and of the aforesaid Pellicle fastning it to the *Glans*, are to yeeld some delight in Copulation, and to defend the *Glans* from outward hurts. . . . That *Praeputium* the *Jews* take away in Circumcisions, working contrary to the intent of Nature."

45. Quoted in Norman F. Cantor, *The Medieval Reader* (New York: Harper-Collins, 1994), 247.

46. See Andrew Taylor, "Reading the Dirty Bits," in *Desire and Discipline: Sex and Sexuality in the Premodern West*, ed. Jaqueline Murray (Toronto: University of Toronto Press, 1996), 286, emphasis mine. Taylor's essay explores the interrelation of religious individualism, erotic desire, and reading technology, a complex nexus of issues worthy of further examination. My own work here is intended as a small contribution to this emergent discussion.

47. On this topic, see Ian Frederick Moulton, *Before Pornography: Erotic Writing in Early Modern England* (Oxford: Oxford University Press, 2000), esp. 152–157.

2. Donne's "Frendship": Desire, Convention, and Transgression

1. Michel Foucault, *The History of Sexuality vol. 1, An Introduction*, trans. Robert Hurley (1976; New York: Vintage, 1980), 40–43 et passim.

2. By contrast, the second most famous proposition of Foucault's late work, that the structure of sexual knowledge is characterized by a historical movement "from acts to identities," has been variously challenged, qualified, and refined within medieval and early modern studies of sexuality. For one of the most historically wide-ranging oppositional accounts, see Allen J. Frantzen, *Before the Closet: Same-Sex Love from Beowulf to Angels in America* (Chicago: University of Chicago Press, 1998), esp. 1–29.

3. Studies of homoeroticism in the Renaissance that focus exclusively or pri-

marily on dramatic texts include: Mary Bly, *Queer Virgins and Virgin Queans on the Early Modern Stage* (Oxford: Clarendon Press, 2000); Mario DiGangi, *The Homoerotics of Early Modern Drama* (Cambridge: Cambridge University Press, 1997); John Franceschina, *Homosexualities in the English Theater: Lily to Wilde* (Westport, CT: Greenwood Press, 1997); Laura Levine, *Men in Women's Clothing: Anti-Theatricality and Effeminization, 1579–1642* (Cambridge: Cambridge University Press, 1992); Michael Shapiro, *Gender in Play on the Shakespearean Stage* (Ann Arbor: University of Michigan Press, 1994); Susan Zimmerman, *Erotic Politics: Desire on the Renaissance* (London: Routledge, 1992).

4. The "early" chronological designation derives from R. C. Bald's article, "Donne's Early Verse Letters," *HLQ* 15 (1952): 283–289. Although much of Bald's original article remains plausible, the assignment of a significant number of poems is based entirely on his conviction that their conventionality indicates the inexperience of the author: that is, on what Bald later admits are "grounds of style" alone (287). The chronology can thus be regarded with suspicion, at least to the extent that it reinscribes a conservative Waltonesque narrative, wherein the frivolous productions of youth give way to a more explicitly moralized sensibility.

5. Herbert J. C. Grierson, ed., *The Poems of John Donne*, 2 vols. (London: Oxford University Press, 1912), 2:165.

6. R. C. Bald, *John Donne: A Life* (Oxford: Clarendon Press, 1986), 74, 75, 76.

7. See Gary P. Storhoff, "Social Mode and Poetic Strategies: Donne's Verse Letters to His Friends," *Essays in Literature* 4 (1977): 11–18; Barbara L. DeStefano, "Evolution of Extravagant Praise in Donne's Verse Epistles," *Studies in Philology* 81 (1984): 75–94.

8. Arthur F. Marotti, *John Donne, Coterie Poet* (Madison: University of Wisconsin Press, 1986), 37.

9. Ibid., 36; George Klawitter, *The Enigmatic Narrator* (New York: Peter Lang, 1994), 6. All subsequent citations to Klawitter appear parenthetically in the text.

10. Wesley Milgate, ed., *John Donne: The Satires, Epigrams and Verse Letters* (Oxford: Clarendon Press, 1967), 212. All references to Donne's verse letters are from this edition unless otherwise indicated. Subsequent references in the text appear parenthetically as "milgate."

11. See William Empson, "Rescuing Donne," in *Just So Much Honor,* ed. Peter A. Fiore (University Park: Pennsylvania State University Press, 1972), 132.

12. In fact, the real scandal surely centers around the critical repression of the homoerotic rather than its imputation; what hermeneutic structures incline R. C. Bald, for example, to dismiss this poem (which he does not quote) with *one sentence,* as "a sample of undergraduate wit." See Bald, *John Donne: A Life,* 75. For readings of the poem that do address the issue of female-female desire and its representation, see Janet Halley, "Textual Intercourse: Anne Donne, John Donne, and the Sexual Politics of Textual

Exchange," in *Seeking the Woman in Late Medieval and Renaissance Writings: Essays in Feminist Contextual Criticism,* ed. Sheila Fisher and Janet E. Halley, 187–206 (Knoxville: University of Tennessee Press, 1989), esp. 200; Elizabeth Harvey, *Ventriloquized Voices: Feminist Theory and English Renaissance Texts* (London: Routledge, 1992), 134–135; and H. L. Meakin, *John Donne's Articulations of the Feminine* (Oxford: Clarendon Press, 1998), 57–64. While Klawitter fails to address the poem as a representation of female-female desire, neither Halley nor Harvey displays any interest in the question of male-male desire. Meakin's account of "To Mr. J.D.," by far the most detailed to date, makes superb use of primary sources and addresses the oversights of Halley and Harvey but fails to consult any recent theoretical work on Renaissance sexuality. Of course, it is impossible to address every issue that poems as difficult as this one raise. Future discussions of these poems will certainly find insufficiencies of my own analyses; I can only hope that they are not too glaring.

13. Other examples include "To Mr. R.W." ("Kindly' I envy thy Songs . . ."), "To Mr. S.B." ("O thou which to search . . ."), and "To Mr. E.G." ("Even as lame things . . .").

14. Milgate, *The Satires,* 213.

15. John Donne, *The Sermons of John Donne,* ed. George R. Potter and Evelyn Simpson (Berkeley: University of California Press, 1959), 5:266–267.

16. This interpretation of "The Relique" was offered by William Empson. See Empson, "Donne in the New Edition," in *Essays on Renaissance Literature* (Cambridge: Cambridge University Press, 1993), 1:141–142.

17. The predominant strain of traditional criticism assumes some basic connection between life and art in Donne's heteroerotic verse, often utilizing biography to date the composition of individual poems. See Dayton Haskin, "On Trying to Make the Record Speak More about Donne's Love Poems," in *John Donne's "Desire of More": the Subject of Anne More Donne in His Poetry,* ed. M. Thomas Hester (Newark: University of Delaware Press, 1996), 39–66, for an excellent critical historiography of these processes with regard to "The Canonization."

18. The point ultimately derives from a Derridean conception of "ordinary language"—which is not that there are "no effect[s] of ordinary language" but "simply that those effects do not exclude what is generally opposed to them term by term." See Jacques Derrida, "Signature Event Context," in *Margins of Philosophy,* trans. Alan Bass (Chicago: University of Chicago Press, 1982), 327.

19. Forrest Tyler Stevens makes a version of this simple but profound point in a discussion of parallel case: Erasmus's letters to Servatius Rogerus. These letters also contain numerous emotional and perhaps erotically charged passages. Stevens exercises caution in his reading, acknowledging that the "true" nature of the relationship between Erasmus and Rogerus cannot be known (not, at least, if we insist on reducing the "truth" of any relationship to the question of whether or not genital contact took place); but, at the

same time, Stevens calls the bluff of those interpreters who would dismiss the homoeroticism of the Servatius letters as " 'simply' conventional." Importantly, Stevens does *not* dispute the formulaic quality of Erasmus's letters (the conventionality of their potential homoeroticism is precisely the point), but he does reject any recourse to that conventionality or "literary-ness" that would result in the *desexualization* of these texts, "as if the literary were the agent which would police the propriety of sexual content and connotation" (125). See Forrest Tyler Stevens, "Erasmus's Tigress," in *Queering the Renaissance,* ed. Jonathan Goldberg (Durham, NC: Duke University Press, 1994).

20. Jonathan Goldberg has offered the most far-reaching explication of this argument:

> If . . . sodomy named sexual acts only in particularly stigmatizing contexts, there is no reason not to believe that such acts went on all the time, unrecognized as sodomy, called, among other things, friendship or patronage, and facilitated by the beds shared, for instance, by servants or students, by teachers and pupils, by kings and their minions or queens and their ladies. . . . Hence the unlikelihood that those sexual acts called sodomy, when performed, would be recognized as sodomy, especially if, in other social contexts, they could be called something else, or nothing at all.

See Goldberg, *Sodometries: Renaissance Texts, Modern Sexualities* (Stanford, CA: Stanford University Press, 1992), 19. Goldberg's argument extends Alan Bray's pioneering study *Homosexuality in Renaissance England* (London: Gay Men's Press, 1982), esp. 75–80.

21. Dudley Carleton to John Chamberlain, quoted in Paul Hammond, *Figuring Sex between Men from Shakespeare to Rochester* (New York: Oxford University Press, 2002), 128.

22. Eve Kosofsky Sedgwick, "Swan in Love," in *Between Men: English Literature and Male Homosocial Desire* (New York: Columbia University Press, 1985), 35.

23. Alan Bray, "Homosexuality and the Signs of Male Friendship in Elizabethan England," in *Queering the Renaissance,* ed. Jonathan Goldberg (Durham, NC: Duke University Press, 1994), 47.

24. Ibid., 57, 50.

25. Jeffrey Masten, *Textual Intercourse: Collaboration, Authorship, and Sexualities in Renaissance Drama* (Cambridge: Cambridge University Press, 1997), 36.

26. DiGangi, *Homoerotics,* 11.

27. A similar interpretive principle was applied by at least one other man of letters during this period to the act of male-male anal intercourse. The example I have in mind is Josias Bodley's account of an episode that occurred during a journey through Ireland from 1602, as cited by Hammond in *Figuring Sex between Men,* 28–29. Bodley, sharing a bedroom with several male

traveling companions, notes that some of them greet one another in the morning "per viam de retro" (by the back passage). Bodley's recording of these events suggests that he is surprised by them; but his lack of outrage is also apparent. In his personal judgment, the practice is not "honestum," but he allows that it may be medically beneficial ("bonum pro lumbis," or good for the loins) and concludes that "nihil male fit quod non male accipitur" (nothing is amiss if it is not taken amiss).

28. John Donne, *The Divine Poems,* ed. Helen Gardner (Oxford: Clarendon Press, 1978), 11.

29. Richard Rambuss, *Closet Devotions* (Durham, NC: Duke University Press, 1998), 50.

30. George Knox, "Donne's holy sonnets, XIV" (1956), cited in ibid., 150n.54.

31. Ann Baynes Coiro, cited in ibid., 51.

32. But see Ronald Corthell, *Ideology and Desire in Renaissance Poetry: The Subject of Donne* (Detroit: Wayne State University Press, 1997), 154, and Elizabeth M. A. Hodgson, *Gender and the Sacred Self in John Donne* (London: Associated University Presses, 1999), 103–105, for two slightly different arguments.

33. Rambuss, *Closet Devotions,* 49.

34. John Donne, *Selected Prose,* ed. Helen Gardner and Timothy Healy (Oxford: Clarendon Press, 1967), 125.

35. Marotti, *John Donne, Coterie Poet,* 259–61.

36. Michael C. Schoenfeldt, *Prayer and Power: George Herbert and Renaissance Courtship* (Chicago: University of Chicago Press, 1991), esp. 21–113.

37. John Donne, *The Complete English Poems,* ed. C. A. Patrides, rev. Robin Hamilton (London: Everyman, 1994), 350.

38. The other poems unique to the Westmoreland manuscript are the verse letters "To Mr. E.G." and the Holy Sonnet "Oh to vex me." In addition, two lines of the poem "To Mr. I.L." ("Bless'd are your north parts") are only found in this collection, while two poems "To Mr. R.W." ("Muse not that by thy mind" and "Zealously my Muse") are found in only one other manuscript.

39. Helen Gardner, 123.

40. Ibid., 122.

41. As Lukas Erne has shown in "Donne and Christ's Spouse," *Essays in Criticism* 51.2 (2001): 208–229, Gardner's account remains influential despite strong critiques of her work by William Kerrigan and David Novarr. This influence persists in spite of what Erne describes as "flagrant" misreadings of the poem in her pages of annotation; among them, her assertion that Donne means us to understand "Mount Moriah, where Solomon built the temple," by the phrase "one hill." As Erne points out, the poem provides no hint regarding this identification, and the Genevan Calvinist Church is a more natural inference since "the greatest part of what constituted Geneva in the sixteenth century is situated on a conspicuous hill" (216). But Gardner cannot admit this interpretation; the Church on "no hill" must refer to Ge-

neva, rather than the more obvious candidate of Canterbury, because otherwise Donne might indeed seem to be expressing less than complete faith in the institution of the Church of England, a possibility that Gardner's entire interpretation is designed to foreclose. Erne cites no less than five editions of Donne's poems published within the last fifteen years that exactly reproduce her commentary in their own glosses. In Erne's words: "most annotations are . . . derivative, but it is surprising that an edition which first appeared as far back as the 1950s can still exert such a . . . powerful influence" (218). In my view, this puts it mildly. Let us be clear about what Gardner's reading of the poem does. While carefully avoiding a frank discussion of its eroticism, Gardner also obscures the single most intellectually bold aspect of the text: the skepticism shown by the speaker toward the institutions of three major branches of western European Christianity, including the Church of England. In short, Gardner's critical apparatus works to contain all the real challenges of the poem. The fact that her reading has been adopted unquestioningly by no less than five recent editors of Donne is less surprising than it is depressing—at least for those of us anxious to build a case for Donne's artistic and intellectual daring.

42. Rambuss, *Closet Devotions*, 59; Marotti, *John Donne, Coterie Poet*, 283; Janel Mueller, "Women among the Metaphysicals: A Case, Mostly, of Being Donne Fur," *Modern Philology* 87 (1989): 149. Other responses include that of D. M. De Silva, "John Donne—An Un-metaphysical Perspective," *Ceylon Journal in Humanities* 2 (1971): 3–14, who sees the sexual nature of the image and finds it "repulsive" (6); and David Novarr, who criticizes Gardner's reading in *The Disinterred Muse: Donne's Texts and Contexts* (Ithaca: Cornell University Press), 140. Perhaps the most brilliant reading the poem has yet received is in William Kerrigan's "The Fearful Accommodations of John Donne," *ELR* 4 (1974): 337–363, reprinted in the *New Casebook: John Donne*, ed. Andrew Mousley (London: Macmillan, 1999), 198–216. Kerrigan's argument turns on the problematic philosophical implications of anthropomorphism and has influenced my own thinking, although our conclusions differ.

43. F. L. Brownlow, "The Holy Sonnets," in *Donne and the Resources of Kind*, ed. A. D. Cousins and Damian Grace (London: Associated University Press, 2002), 102.

44. Hodgson, *Gender and the Sacred Self in John Donne* 108.

45. Ibid., 109; Kerrigan, "The Fearful Accommodations," 210–211, emphasis mine.

46. The theoretical problems here are quite profound, ultimately having to do with the vexed role of human agency in the production of history and culture. The philosopher-historian J. G. A. Pocock has observed that "language changes may appear as brought about by a concurrence or consensus of speech acts performed by so many actors, in so many language situations, that it is easier to think of the changes in language as occasioned than intended." But, Pocock goes on, it also cannot be denied that "conspicuous

actors do seem to occur in history; they acquire, sometimes quite rapidly, the status of authorities who are to be followed or of adversaries who are to be rebutted; and it is not at all impossible to imagine some kinds of language change as brought about by the utterance performed by identifiable actors and the responses of others not less identifiable to them." See Pocock, "The Concept of Language and the metier d'historien: Some Considerations on Practice," in *The Languages of Political Theory in Early Modern Europe*, ed. Anthony Pagden (Cambridge: Cambridge University Press, 1987), 32.

47. See Tom Webster's fascinating essay " 'Kiss Me with the Kisses of His Mouth': Gender Inversion and Canticles," in *Sodomy in Early Modern Europe*, ed. Tom Betteridge, 148–164 (Manchester: Manchester University Press, 2002), for several examples. Webster suggests that the social role of the clergyman was at odds with traditional conceptions of masculinity in medieval and early modern culture, creating some interestingly fluid conceptions of gender identification and producing complex defensive reactions among post-Reformation churchmen. His work provides another context in which to consider Donne's deployments of gender and sexuality in his religious lyrics.

48. For more on the catchall character of the accusation of sodomy, see Theo van der Meer, "The Persecutions of Sodomites in Eighteenth-Century Amsterdam: Changing Perceptions of Sodomy," in *The Pursuit of Sodomy: Male Homosexuality in Renaissance and Enlightenment Europe*, ed. Kent Gerard and Gert Hekma, 263–307 (New York: Harrington Park Press, 1989).

49. This quotation comes from the jacket of A. J. Smith's Penguin edition of Donne's poems; see *The Complete English Poems* (London: Penguin, 1977).

3. Donne's "Irregularity": Desire's Measure

1. Garrett Stewart, *Reading Voices: Literature and the Phonotext* (Berkeley: University of California Press, 1990), 1.

2. Seymour Chatman, *A Theory of Meter* (The Hague: Mouton, 1965), 103. Chatman wrote before the emergence of generative metrical theory, associated with linguistic rather than literary approaches and first outlined by M. Halle and S. J. Keyser in "Chaucer and the Study of Prosody," College English 28 (1966): 187–219. However, generative models have been no less contentiously received. Halle and Keyser famously offered a three-point definition of Chaucer's line; and as Gilbert Youmans has written, "every aspect of this original definition has been disputed not only by traditionalists but by generative metrists themselves." See Youmans, "Introduction: Rhythm and Meter," in *Phonetics and Phonology, vol. 1, Rhythm and Meter,* ed Paul Kiparsky and Gilbert Youmans (San Diego: Harcourt Brace Jovanovich, 1989), 2.

3. David Baker, ed., *Meter in English: A Critical Engagement* (Fayetteville: University of Arkansas Press, 1996), 3. The contributors to this volume are unable to reach unanimous agreement about even one of ten basic prosodic principles proposed at the outset by poet and critic Robert Wallace.

4. Derek Attridge, *The Rhythms of English Poetry* (London: Longman, 1982), 3.

5. T. V. F. Brogan, *English Versification, 1570–1980: A Reference Guide* (Baltimore: Johns Hopkins University Press, 1981), xix.

6. Cited in Alan Holder, *Rethinking Meter: A New Approach to the Verse Line* (Lewisburg, PA: Bucknell University Press, 1995), 21. For a more recent example, see Shira Wolosky's *The Art of Poetry* (Oxford: Oxford University Press, 2001), 135.

7. Richard D. Cureton, *Rhythmic Phrasing in English Verse* (London: Longman, 1992), 432.

8. See T. S Eliot, *Selected Prose* (London: Penguin Books, 1953), 90. For a more recent statement of the position that "free verse" is "really" metrical, with its allegiance to Eliot clearly indicated in the title, see Annie Finch, *The Ghost of Meter: Culture and Prosody in American Free Verse* (Ann Arbor: University of Michigan Press, 1993). For a very different understanding (one that problematizes Finch's entire project), see Lewis Putnam Turco's "Verse vs. Prose / Prosody vs. Meter," in Baker, *Meter in English*, 249–265.

9. Susanne Woods summarizes the problem as follows: "Commonly there are two questions asked, one way or another, about Donne's versifying: is Donne's verse generally metrical, and are his poetic rhythms effective? While the answer is usually conceded to be yes in both cases, the sense of unease remains." See Woods, *Natural Emphasis: English Versification from Chaucer to Dryden* (San Marino: Huntington Library, 1984), 253.

10. Ben Jonson, *The Complete Poems,* ed. George Parfitt (London: Penguin, 1988), 462.

11. Samuel Johnson, *Collected Writings,* ed. Patrick Cruttwell (London: Penguin Books, 1968), 403.

12. Deborah Aldrich Larson, *John Donne and Twentieth-Century Criticism* (London: Associated University Presses, 1989), 26.

13. See A. J. Smith, ed., *John Donne: The Critical Heritage* (London: Routledge, 1975), 234.

14. Joseph Warton's specific image is that of a "weighty bullion" that must be "melt[ed] down and cast anew": the image of "buried" wit also occurs in David Hume's comments on Donne from the same period; the language of "disguise" appears in Andrew Kippis's account of Donne's life (see ibid., 234, 212, 253).

15. Ibid., 235, 234.

16. Ibid., 236.

17. Ibid., 239, 243.

18. Ibid., 235, 249. Numerous examples praising the superiority of Pope's versions of the satires can be found during this period.

19. This account of meter as a barrier, or more accurately, a semipermeable membrane (letting pleasure through but keeping unpleasure out), resembles that which Adela Pinch discovers in Wordsworth's *Preface* to *Lyrical Ballads.* See "Female Chatter: Meter, Masochism, and the *Lyrical Ballads,*"

ELH 55 (1988): 835–852. In Pinch's analysis, the screen of meter enables enjoyment while preventing "sympathetic identification"(840) with an affective excess specifically designated as feminine; in short, meter maintains manliness. In the context of the larger history of "osmotic" meter that I am sketching here, the association of linguistic excess and the feminine that Pinch identifies looks like a constitutive rather than a marginal feature of Romantic aesthetics. As I will go on to show, it is an element of Coleridge's discussions of meter, as well as Wordsworth's.

20. Sigmund Freud, *The Standard Edition of the Complete Psychological Works,* ed. James Strachey (London: Hogarth Press, 1959), 9:172–173.

21. John Donne, *The Complete English Poems,* ed. C. A. Patrides, rev. Robin Hamilton (London: Everyman, 1994), 155.

22. Alexander Pope, *The Works of Alexander Pope,* ed. Elwin and Courthope (London: John Murray, 1881), 428.

23. Stanley Fish, "Masculine Persuasive Force: Donne and Verbal Power," in *Soliciting Interpretation: Literary Theory and Seventeenth-Century English Poetry,* ed. Elizabeth D. Harvey and Katherine Eisaman Maus (Chicago: University of Chicago Press, 1990), 223; Johnson, *Selected Writings,* 449.

24. Smith, *The Critical Heritage,* 276.

25. Ibid., 265, 266.

26. Ibid., 271.

27. Ibid., 266.

28. The Coleridgean leap into paradox is more explicable when we consider that other nineteenth-century critics sympathetic to Donne found themselves with almost no room to maneuver inside the demands of a metricentric aesthetic. For example, George Henry Lewes is forced to conclude, apparently against his better judgment, that whatever else Donne was, he was not "really" a poet. Lewes's comments are reproduced in ibid., 367–370.

29. Arnold Stein, "Meter and Meaning in Donne's Verse," *The Sewanee Review* 52 (1944): 288–301, reprinted in John R. Roberts, ed., *Essential Articles for the Study of John Donne's Poetry* (Hamden, CT: Archon Books, 1975), 162–177. All citations are from Roberts's text.

30. Ibid., 162.

31. Ibid., 163.

32. Donne, *The Complete English Poems,* 3.

33. Roberts, *Essential Articles,* 166, 167.

34. Graham Bradshaw, "Donne's Challenge to The Prosodists," *Essays in Criticism* 32.4 (1982): 340.

35. Donne, *The Complete English Poems,* 161.

36. Bradshaw, "Donne's Challenge," 340–341.

37. Ibid., 342. Bradshaw is somewhat peremptory in his attempt to clear up confusions he thinks he has identified in the prior work of Philip Hobsbaum and David Daiches, among others; that his own thesis depends on theoretical confusions that date back to the sixteenth century and that have been identified as such many times is ironic, to say the least. Harvey Gross and Robert

McDowell are even more patronizing than Bradshaw in their second edition of *Sound and Form in Modern Poetry* (Ann Arbor: University of Michigan Press, 1996). After informing us that we must "expect to find metrical ineptness in popular books of appreciation" (whatever they might be), they draw a distinction between phrasing and scanning that parallels Bradshaw's distinction between metrical and lexical stress, then remark that "this practical confusion is quite common . . . today, *especially among American poets and critics;* some no longer recognize meter, and some cannot adequately describe it"(4, emphasis mine). The implication seems to be that Europeans have "natural" poetic rhythm.

38. Holder, *Rethinking Meter,* 49. This portion of my argument has been powerfully influenced by Holder.

39. An extreme version of this Platonic conception of the relation between metrical and lexical stress can be found in Vladimir Nabokov's *Notes on Prosody* (New York: Bollingen Foundation, 1964), a small volume intended to accompany his translation of Pushkin's *Eugene Onegin*. With magisterial pride Nabokov announces that because English prosody has been "very imperfectly described" (unlike the Russian variety, apparently), he has been "forced to invent a little terminology." The pages that follow are filled with elaborate descriptions of "scuds" (Nabokov's name for a foot made up of an unaccented unstressed first syllable followed by what he calls an "unaccented stress"), "semiscuds," "tilts," "duplex tilts," and more. Bradshaw cites Nabokov at length to support his own claim that Donne is "regularly iambic" even when he doesn't seem to be; but even Bradshaw balks at Nabokov's suggestion that Lear's "Never, never, never, never, never" is an example of "iambic pentameter entirely consisting of five tilted scuds [!]"(Nabokov, 18). In embracing such counterintuitive conclusions so forthrightly, Nabokov at least has the courage of his convictions. Moreover, when faced with wonderful sentences describing "a certain teasing quality of rhythm, in the tentative emergence of an intonation that *seems* in total opposition to the dominant meter, but actually owes its subtle magic to the balance it tends to achieve between yielding and not yielding" (20), it seems positively churlish to cry intellectual foul. But perhaps that is not necessary; for when Nabokov claims, a few pages later, that "the beauty of English elision lies . . . in the delicate sensation of something being physically preserved by the voice at the very instant that it is metaphysically denied by the meter"(32), he could be said to have let the transcendental cat out of the pseudo-empirical bag. Such a sentence is, after all, an implicit admission that despite his recourse to "scientific" prosodic trappings (an elaborate vocabulary, detailed taxonomy, diagrams, etc.), Nabokov knows he is describing an event whose "objective" reality is dubious and finally undemonstrable: for what else can it mean, finally, to say that you can hear something being "metaphysically denied"?

40. Although metricentric prosodists have proved the most common and hardy of the species, other varieties have always existed. O. B Hardison Jr. dem-

onstrates in *Prosody and Purpose in the English Renaissance* (Baltimore: Johns Hopkins University Press, 1989) that Elizabethan prosodists drew not only on a classical system based on quantative meter but also on contemporary romance language traditions of syllabic verse that emphasized syntactic over metrical stress; and in the twentieth century, prosodists with an interest in language-in-performance, particularly those of a linguistic bent, began to express doubt about the principles upon which the cherished notions of "interplay" or "tension" are based. In the 1970s so-called phrasalists, such as D. W. Harding and David Crystal, argued against the metricentric approach in favor of one based on syntax; and more recently, metricentrism has again been subject to a variety of differently "accented" critiques in the work of scholars such as Richard D. Cureton, Donald Wesling, Garrett Strong, and Alan Holder. My own work here attempts to raise (and in part answer) the question of why traditional metricentric prosody continues to dominate the field, *despite* the powerful challenges that these and other critics have presented to it.

41. See, for example, Arthur Wayne Glowka, *A Guide to Chaucer's Meter* (London: University Press of America, 1991), a sprightly and clearly written book that nevertheless manages to insist that readings that do "justice to our ears" still somehow "obscure the meter of the poem"(22–23); or most of the essays in Baker's *Meter in English*.

42. This point was powerfully made by Paul de Man; it has been brilliantly restated in a prosodic context in an unpublished article by Aaron B. Kunin. I am grateful to Kunin for sharing his insights with me.

43. After Derek Attridge's initial groundbreaking work in the area, I would include under this rubric such diverse figures as Donald Wesling, Garrett Strong, Richard D. Cureton, and Alan Holder, whose works I have already cited at relevant points throughout this chapter. I would also consider certain essays by Jonathan Crewe, Wayne Koestenbaum, Adela Pinch, and Susan Stewart as falling into the "New Prosody" category.

44. Charles L. Stevenson, "The Rhythms of English Verse," *Journal of Aesthetics and Art Criticism* 28 (Spring 1970): 327.

45. See Handison, *Prosody and Purpose.*

46. Cureton proposes that "what has been perceived in the tradition as metrical segmentation and direction be dissolved back into the more basic facts of hierarchical patterning, phrasal relations, and associative 'marking.' " See *Rhythmic Phrasing,* 427.

47. If this is not clear from the argument over Donne, consider, as a final example, the following lines from Milton's "At a Solemn Musick": "Wed your divine sounds, and mixt power employ / Dead things with inbreath'd sense able to pierce / And to our high-rais'd phantasie present / That undisturbed Song of pure concent." The last line could be proffered—indeed, it has been so proffered—as about as perfect an example of iambic pentameter as one could hope to find; the preceding lines, on the other hand, must be subjected to closer scrutiny before they are admitted or excluded from that metrical

category, and I suspect disagreements would crop up among expert witnesses very quickly. But what kind of knowledge is required to "recognize" even the seemingly indisputable test case of the last line? Plainly, it is not enough to know only that the accent must fall on every second syllable, over ten syllables. We must also already have taken on board the fact that this poem is by John Milton, a poet of the seventeenth century, and that therefore we must pronounce the word "undisturbed" with four syllables. However, what if we had come upon the same line in a poem by, say, Philip Larkin? Then even this apparently secure test case would then cease to function as a pentameter line, because the archaism of a four-syllable "undisturbed" would have been quite unacceptable to a poet famous for his plain-spoken, deliberately antipoetic rhetoric. Instead, we would have to consider the line defective or irregular—one foot short. As this example proves, the meter of a line is no more inherent than its meaning; and the structure of belief required to identify that meter is far more complex than any model based on simple counting would suggest.

48. Fredric Jameson, "Metacommentary," *PMLA* 86 (1971): 9.

49. Ibid., 10.

4. Difference and Indifference: Fantasies of Gender

1. I am paraphrasing Elizabeth Cowie on "women and film." See "Woman as Sign," in *The Woman in Question*, ed. Parveen Adams and Elizabeth Cowie (Cambridge, MA: MIT Press, 1990), 117.

2. Elizabeth D. Harvey, *Ventriloquized Voices: Feminist Theory and English Renaissance Texts* (London: Routledge, 1992), 104. All further citations appear in parenthetical references in the text.

3. Ibid., 11.

4. The notion that fantasies are not so much mental objects but rather sequences or structures ultimately derives from Freud's "A child is being beaten." See *The Standard Edition of the Complete Psychological Works of Sigmund Freud*, ed. J. Strachey (London: Hogarth Press, 1955), 17:175–204. Jean Laplanche and Jean-Bertrand Pontalis have elaborated Freud's initial observations to emphasize the ways in which an individual may insert himself or herself into the structure of the fantasy in various places, identifying with numerous possible subject positions. See Laplanche and Pontalis, "Fantasy and the Origins of Sexuality," first translated in *The International Journal of Psychoanalysis* 49 (1968), reprinted, in *Formations of Fantasy,* ed. Victor Burgin, James Donald, and Cora Kaplan, 5–28 (London: Routledge, 1989).

5. For an elaborate account of this basic position, see Diana Fuss, *Essentially Speaking* (London: Routledge, 1990).

6. Judith Butler, *Gender Trouble* (London: Routledge, 1990), 6, 7.

7. Ibid., 33.

8. See Joan Copjec, *Read My Desire: Lacan against the Historicists* (Cambridge, MA: MIT Press, 1994), 202. I agree with Copjec that this is an

implication of Butler's argument in *Gender Trouble,* although, as Slavoj Žižek notes: "In her more recent writings, Butler . . . accepts the key [Lacanian] distinction between sexual difference and the 'social construction of gender': the status of sexual difference is not directly that of a contingent socio-symbolic formation: rather, sexual difference indicates the enigmatic domain which lies in between, no longer biology and not yet the space of socio-symbolic construction." See Slavoj Žižek, *The Ticklish Subject: The Absent Centre of Political Ontology* (London: Verso, 2000), 275.

9. Arthur Symons, *Figures of Several Centuries* (1899; New York: E. P. Dutton, 1916), 102. Cited in Deborah Aldrich Larson, *John Donne and Twentieth-Century Criticism* (London: Associated University Presses, 1989), 137.

10. Evelyn M. Simpson, *A Study of the Prose Works of John Donne* (Oxford: Clarendon Press, 1924), 71; also cited by Larson, *John Donne and Twentieth-Century Criticism,* 137.

11. Ilona Bell, "The Role of the Lady in Donne's Songs and Sonets," *SEL* 23. 1 (1983): 129.

12. Thomas Docherty, *John Donne, Undone* (London: Methuen, 1986), 57. All subsequent citations appear in parentheses in the text.

13. Eve Kosofsky Sedgwick, "Gender Criticism," in *Redrawing the Boundaries,* ed. Stephen Greenblatt and Giles Gunn (New York: MLA, 1992), 276.

14. Like so many other tendencies in Donne criticism, the tradition of praising poems "for" Anne has its origins in Walton's seventeenth-century hagio-biography, which contextualizes "A Valediction: Forbidding Mourning" within "real-life" events of Donne's marriage; for a more recent version of the tendency, see Camille Wells Slights, "A Pattern of Love: Representations of Anne Donne," in *John Donne's "Desire of More,"* ed. M. Thomas Hester (Newark: University of Delaware Press, 1996); conversely, John Carey's hostile reading of "Elegy XIX" in *John Donne: Life, Mind and Art* (London: Faber and Faber, 1981) proceeds from and even requires us to think that the woman in question *cannot* be Anne.

15. Michel Foucault, *The History of Sexuality,* vol. 1, *An Introduction,* trans. Robert Hurley (New York: Vintage, 1980), 108.

16. Bruce Woodcock, " 'Anxious to Amuse': Metaphysical Poetry and the Discourse of Renaissance Masculinity," in *Writing and the English Renaissance,* ed. William Zunder and Suzanne Trill (New York: Longman, 1996). All subsequent citations appear in parentheses in the text.

17. I am referring to Janel Mueller's close reading of this poem, titled "Troping Utopia: Donne's Brief for Lesbianism," published in *Sexuality and Gender in Early Modern Europe,* ed. James Grantham Turner, 182–207 (Cambridge: Cambridge University Press, 1993).

18. Ibid., 204.

19. The phrase "author function" derives, of course, from Foucault's "What Is an Author?" reprinted in Joseph V. Harari's translation in *Modern Criticism and Theory: A Reader,* ed. David Lodge, 196–210 (London: Longman, 1988).

20. Barbara Correll, "Symbolic Economies and Zero Sum Erotics: Donne's

'Sapho to Philaenis,' " *ELH* 62 (1995): 494. All subsequent citations appear in parentheses in the text. According to Correll, Donne conceives of lesbianism as a structure of desire based on sameness rather than difference; lesbianism therefore represents a possible escape for Donne from an anxiety-ridden heteroerotic poetic economy "based upon the principle of a loss that must always be made good . . . [through] the resecuring of difference"(501). However, the particular form of Donne's investment in lesbianism as a closed signifying economy also produces a "regression to self-referential collapse and signifying failure" (499).

21. Teresa De Lauretis, *Technologies of Gender: Essays on Theory, Film and Fiction* (Bloomington: Indiana University Press, 1987), 25.

22. The phrase is Richard Halpern's, from "The Lyric in the Field of Information: Autopoiesis and History in Donne's Songs and Sonnets," *Yale Journal of Criticism* 6.1 (1993): 200. The conception of women as blurring the lines of difference, and of Donne as a threatened masculinist who attempts to reinscribe that line or to control the threat of the feminine, also appears in Correll, "Symbolic Economies"; Ronald Corthell's book-length study *Ideology and Desire in Renaissance Poetry: The Subject of Donne* (Detroit, MI: Wayne State University Press, 1997, esp. 24–55; Acsah Guibbory, " 'Oh, let mee not serve so': The Politics of Love in Donne's Elegies," *ELH* 57 (1990): 811–833; Janet Halley, "Textual Intercourse: Ann Donne, John Donne, and the Sexual Politics of Textual Exchange," in *Seeking the Woman in Late Medieval and Renaissance Writings*, ed. Sheila Fisher and Janet E. Halley (Knoxville: University of Tennessee Press, 1989); Janel Mueller, "Women among the Metaphysicals: A Case, Mostly, of Being Donne For," *Modern Philology* 87 (1989): 142–151. Other examples could no doubt be produced.

23. Donne, "The Comparison," in *The Complete English Poems*, ed. C. A. Patrides, rev. Robin Hamilton (London: Everyman, 1994), 92.

24. Here the standard example is the elegy "Change." However, Barbara Estrin has challenged those who see that poem as typically representative of Donne's misogyny (she cites Fish, although Fish is not alone in interpreting "Change" as aggressively masculinist). Estrin sees the final lines of the poem as a positive imitation of a female voice—an expression of Donne's desire to be like, rather than to repudiate, the female. Estrin does not consider any of the poems in female "voices," but her work is in the spirit of my own and also runs counter to recent majority opinion. See Barbara L. Estrin, *Laura: Uncovering Gender and Genre in Wyatt, Donne and Marvell* (Durham, NC: Duke University Press, 1994).

25. Corthell, *Ideology and Desire in Renaissance Poetry*, 59.

26. Donne, *The Complete English Poems*, 8. All subsequent citations appear in the text.

27. Mueller, "Women among the Metaphysicals," 145.

28. Arthur Marotti, *John Donne, Coterie Poet* (Madison: University of Wisconsin Press, 1986), 76. Subsequent citations appear in the text. Ronald Corthell provides a lengthy and subtle reading of this poem, critically en-

gaging Marotti's work (see Corthell, *Ideology and Desire in Renaissance Poetry*, 59–65). My interpretation is at odds with Corthell's (the "fear of women and perhaps fear of turning into a woman" [61] that he attributes to Donne strikes me as owing more to recent critical discourse), but I admire the sustained attention he brings to bear and strongly agree with his more general claim that "poems like 'The Indifferent' disclose our culture's tendency to construct love or sexuality around oppositions like promiscuity and fidelity, sex and love, male and female"(64).

29. Victor Burgin, "Fantasy," in *Feminism and Psychoanalysis: A Critical Dictionary*, ed. Elizabeth Wright (London: Blackwell, 1992), 85. I don't mean to assume what Teresa De Lauretis calls "the optimistically silly notion of an unbounded mobility of identities for the spectator-subject." See De Lauretis, *The Practice of Love: Lesbian Sexuality and Perverse Desire* (Bloomington: Indiana University Press, 1994), 140. The capacity of different individuals to identify with different subject positions in any given fantasy scenario does not translate into a capacity to choose, willy-nilly, from those positions or to vary them whenever one feels like it.

30. Arthur Marotti, *Manuscript, Print, and the English Renaissance Lyric* (Ithaca, NY: Cornell University Press, 1995), 57.

31. Peter Beal, *Index of English Literary Manuscripts* (London: Mansell, 1980–), vol. 1.i.245.

32. These two manuscript collections were rediscovered by Peter Beal in 1977 and have been made available in a facsimile edition, *The First and Second Dalhousie Manuscripts: Poems and Prose by John Donne and Others*, ed. Ernest W. Sullivan II (Columbia: University of Missouri Press, 1988). The pairings of "Communitie" and "Womans constancy" appear at 106–107 and 179–180.

33. See, for example, Marotti. *John Donne, Coterie Poet*, 73. Docherty's elaborate reading (see *John Donne, Undone*, 222–225) represents an exception, but I find it largely incomprehensible.

34. The phrase occurs in R. C. Bald's brief reference to the poem in his *John Donne: A Life* (Oxford: Clarendon, 1986), 71.

35. See, for example, Horace Ainsworth Eaton, "The Songs and Sonnets of John Donne," *Sewanee Review* 22 (1914): 72.

36. Donald L. Guss's perspective in *John Donne, Petrarchist: Italianate Conceits and Love Theory in the Songs and Sonnets* (Detroit: Wayne State University Press, 1966), 115.

37. James S. Baumlin, *John Donne and the Rhetorics of Renaissance Discourse* (Columbia: University of Missouri Press, 1991), 232.

38. Lynn Hunt, "Introduction: Obscenity and the Origins of Modernity," in *The Invention of Pornography*, ed. Lynn Hunt (New York: Zone Books, 1993), 38.

39. Corthell, *Ideology and Desire in Renaissance Poetry*, 66.

40. The most well known antipornography feminists are of course Andrea Dworkin and Catherine MacKinnon, though other figures such as Robin

Morgan and Susan Kappeller might be cited; anticensorship feminists speak from an equally diverse variety of perspectives. For a good summary of the opposed positions, see Linda Williams's *Hard-Core: Power, Pleasure and the "Frenzy of the Visible"* (Berkeley: University of California Press, 1989), esp. 13–30.

41. Valerie Traub, *Desire and Anxiety: Circulations of Sexuality in Shake-spearean Drama* (London: Routledge, 1992), 114 et passim.

42. John Donne, *The Variorum Edition, Volume II: The Elegies,* ed. Gary A. Stringer (Bloomington: Indiana University Press, 2000), 409–410. I have modernized the letters "u" and "v" for the convenience of the reader.

43. The bibliography for this poem is considerable. For a detailed reading of this passage, which also addresses most prior interpretations, I refer readers to H. L. Meakin's *Donne's Articulations of the Feminine* (Oxford: Clarendon Press, 1998), 127–134.

44. Ibid., 410, emphasis mine.

45. I do not deny that Donne plays with notions of mirroring and sameness in his depiction of female-female desire ("mee in my glasse I call thee") but only that he reproduces that eroticism in hostile, heterosexist terms, as sterile or nonsignifying; that is the position of James Holstun in "Will You Rent Our Ancient Love Asunder: Lesbian Elegy in Donne, Marvell, and Milton," *ELH* 54 (1987): 835–867; Holstun's argument is echoed, with different inflections, by Harvey (*Ventriloquized Voices*) and Correll ("Symbolic Economies"). Paula Blank argues that it is in fact Holstun and not Donne who negatively projects narcissism onto lesbianism. See her "Comparing Sappho to Philaenis: John Donne's "Homopoetics," *PMLA* 110.3 (1995): 358–368. For a classic critique of the traditional psychoanalytic account of the relation between homosexuality and narcissism, see Michael Warner, "Homo-Narcissism; or, Heterosexuality," in *Engendering Men: The Question of Male Feminist Criticism,* ed. Joseph A. Boone and Michael Cadden, 190–206 (London: Routledge, 1990). For a reappropriation of the psychoanalytic arguments, see Steven Bruhm's *Reflecting Narcissus: A Queer Aesthetic* (Minneapolis: University of Minnesota Press, 2001).

46. Harvey, *Ventriloquized Voices,* 129.

47. On this topic see Julia M. Walker's "Anne More: A Name Not Written," in *John Donne's "Desire of More,"* ed. M. Thomas Hester, 89–105 (Newark: University of Delaware Press, 1996).

48. Harvey writes that it is "tempting—if sexually complicated—to read "restore / Me to me; thee, my half, my all, my more" as referring to Ann [*sic*] More" (*Ventriloquized Voices,* 131) but does not give in to this temptation. Ronald Corthell also acknowledges the possibility of this pun on Anne's name (Corthell, *Ideology and Desire in Renaissance Poetry,* 73) but curiously does not mention the first pun, on Donne's name.

49. Although I cannot help pointing out that even the relation of this particular poem to the politics of the traditional canon is rather more complex than

most interpreters have been inclined to acknowledge. Its own canonical status is actually less than secure; Helen Gardner consigned the poem to the ranks of *Dubia* (on the basis of nothing more substantive than personal distaste, as far as I can tell), and her opinion has been echoed by more recent authorities such as Marotti (who does not read the poem in his otherwise exhaustive book on the poet; he insists that Gardner had "good reasons" for excluding "Sapho to Philaenis," without telling us what those reasons were). The poem was also subject to censorship in seventeenth-century manuscript and print versions. On this topic, see Ted-Larry Pebworth, "The Early Censorship of John Donne's Elegies and 'Sapho to Philaenis' in Manuscript and Print," *Text: An Interdisciplinary Annual of Textual Studies* 13 (2000): 193–201.

50. See Meakin, *Donne's Articulations of the Feminine,* 86; Holstun, "Will You Rent," 843; Harvey, *Ventriloquized Voices,* 132; Woodcock, " 'Anxious to Amuse,' " 64; Correll, 'Symbolic Economies," 490; Corthell, *Ideology and Desire in Renaissance Poetry,* 71–72. Although it is more sympathetic, and more in keeping with the emotional spirit of the poem, Janel Mueller's claim that Donne "really undertakes to imagine the pleasures, sustenance, and ideological implications by which lesbianism, as a mode of loving and being, resists patria rchal disposition and diminution of women" ("Women among the Metaphysicals," 183) universalizes the notion of "lesbianism" and consequently fails to catch at the historical specificity and idiosyncrasy of Donne's radical imagination. Diana Terviño Benet is exceptional in stating that "Sapho to Philaenis" raises "the basic question of sexual difference: What differentiates her loving from his?" See Benet, "Sexual Transgression in Donne's Elegies," *Modern Philology* 92 (1994): 22.

51. To attempt to transcend gender at the level of desire is not *necessarily* to engage in a politically progressive (let alone a queer theoretical) project. Such fantasies of transcendence can also universalize what is in fact a normative male perspective; contemporary critics, historians, and philosophers who are concerned either to recover, discover, or theorize the specificity and differentness of female desire, homosexual desire, lesbian desire, and so on, may therefore be inclined to resist a criticism (or a poetics) that assimilates those desires within the (no doubt, compelling) fantasy of an originary "objectless" libido. Still, I believe Donne was attracted to the fantasy of sexual indifference at the level of desire for reasons that were ultimately more utopian than repressive (despite the inevitable failure of all utopian impulses). Moreover, while "Sapho to Philaenis" is not concerned in the way that, say, a modern lesbian critic might be, with "real" relations between women (on this topic, see Valerie Traub, The *Renaissance of Lesbianism in Early Modern England* (New York: Cambridge University Press, 2002), and esp. her comments on this poem and its criticism, at 337 and 463–464), in its refusal to "masculinize" Sappho's desire, the poem is more remarkable than most of its professional readers have allowed. As Teresa De Lauretis writes:

> [F]eminist theory has argued for well over two decades [that] sexuality
> in the dominant forms of Western culture is defined from the frame of
> reference of 'man,' the white man, who has enforced his claim to be
> the subject of knowing, and woman—all women—his object: object of
> both his knowledge and desire. Heterosexuality is therefore doubly en-
> forced on women . . . enforced as heterosexuality in the sense that
> women can and must feel sexually in relation to men, and enforced as
> heterosexuality in that sexual desire belongs to the other, originates in
> him. In this standard frame, amazingly simplistic and yet authoritative,
> and reaffirmed again and again, alas even in feminist theory, whatever
> women may feel toward other women cannot be sexual desire, unless
> it be a 'masculinization,' a usurpation or an imitation of man's desire.
> (*The Practice of Love*, 111).

Without being entirely sure that I have convinced myself, I want to suggest
the possibility that in "Sapho to Philaenis," at least, Donne may be doing
almost exactly the reverse.

52. Traub, *Desire and Anxiety*, 7.

53. As always with Donne, the reader will not be surprised to learn that the
reverse argument has also been made (in, for example, Guss's *John Donne,
Petrarchist*). The opposition is perhaps in any case a false one; the first "anti-
Petrarchist" of note was, of course, Petrarch. Discussions of Donne vis-à-
vis "Petrarchism" are legion, but I have greatly profited from reading
Heather Dubrow's *Echoes of Desire: English Petrarchism and Its Counter-
discourses* (Ithaca, NY: Cornell University Press, 1995).

54. My text is taken from *Silver Poets of the Sixteenth Century*, ed. Douglas
Brooks-Davies (London: Everyman, 1992), 251. Compare also Sonnet 21.

55. One might consider the abrupt and unexpected lewd joke at the end of
"Lovers Infiniteness" as similarly originating in anti-Petrachist impulses—
"But we will have a way more liberall, / Then [than] changing hearts to join
them." However, even here, Donne sounds more like a sexual enthusiast
than Sidney's dismissive misogynist.

56. It is intriguing that Donne's Latinism should implicitly define sexual differ-
ence as a knot, a favored psychoanalytic metaphor in discussions of sexual
difference (as in, for example, Lacan's "The Signification of the Phallus").
The knot is cinched in psychoanalysis by the Oedipus complex; it is undone,
in Donne, by ecstatic desire.

57. James Grantham Turner, *One Flesh: Paradisal Marriage and Sexual Rela-
tions in the Age of Milton* (Oxford: Clarendon, 1993), 100.

58. Here we might instructively compare Donne to Milton, whose Adam and
Eve are "Not equal, as their sex not equal seem'd" (Milton, *Paradise Lost*
4: 295–296); on this topic, see Meakin, *Donne's Anticulations of the Fem-
inine*, 128.

59. See Michael Schoenfeldt, "Patriarchal Assumptions and Egalitarian De-
signs," *JDJ* 9.1 (1990): 23–26. The impossible (or mystical) fantasy of tran-

scending sexual difference while retaining the body is not confined to "The Extasie" and "The Undertaking." The difficulty of the last stanzas of "The Relique" attests to the presence of this paradox. Even a poem like "Aire and Angells" (traditionally read as thoroughly anti-Petrarchan and therefore as insisting on embodied notions of difference) can be seen as attempting to transcend gendered difference in the very act of its assertion; indeed, this is the burden of Schoenfeldt's article, a brief but brilliantly original reading of the poem, which he interprets as rendering the "disparitie" between men and women as a distinction without difference.

5. All or Nothing: The Possibility of Love

1. Bruce Fink, Preface to *Reading Seminar XI,* ed. Richard Feldstein, Bruce Fink, and Maire Jaanus (Albany: SUNY Press, 1995), xiv, emphasis mine. Indirectly problematizing any claim to offer a "Lacanian reading" of a text, Fink also prefaces his translation of Seminar XX by declaring that "Lacan's French is . . . so polyvalent and ambiguous that some frame must be imposed to make any sense of it whatsoever." See his preface to *Encore: The Seminar of Jacques Lacan: Book XX. On Feminine Sexuality, The Limits of Love and Knowledge,* ed. Jacques-Alain Miller, trans. Bruce Fink (New York: Norton, 1998), vii. Hereafter cited as *Seminar XX.*

2. See Jean Baudrillard, *Seduction,* trans. Brian Singer (1979; London: Macmillan, 1990).

3. I make no claims about the relation of this poem to historical or biographical fact. The existence of an entire subgenre of parasite poems during the period, and of a classical Ovidian precedent for that subgenre, indicates that the poem is a witty exercise with no "real" addressee. At the same time, I would not rule out a scenario in which Donne might present a poem like this to a real woman to whom he was genuinely attracted. Some might think this suggestion naive, but we do not know enough about Donne's life or about male-female intimacy in the period to dismiss it out of hand; and Donne would hardly be the only poet to try getting someone into bed with a line of charming bullshit.

4. One might even say that, from a psychoanalytic point of view, bullshit has been integral ever since Freud decided that it didn't really matter if the memories his patients "recovered" were objectively real or only fantasized reconstructions.

5. For instance, he concludes an aside on Aristotle by proclaiming that the philosopher appeals to "Du bi, du bien, du benêt!" (Lacan, *Seminar XX,* 55; translated by Fink as: "The good, the bad, and the oafish!"). The phrase may recall the title of a spaghetti western, the slogan of a contemporary French commercial for Dubonet liquor, and (Fink speculates) the sounds of scat-singing, but the understanding of the student/reader is not deepened by any such references.

6. Jacques Lacan, *The Seminar of Jacques Lacan: Book VII. The Ethics of*

Psychoanalysis, trans. Dennis Potter (New York: Norton, 1992), 19 (hereafter cited as *Seminar VII*); *The Seminar of Jacques Lacan: Book XI. The Four Fundamental Concepts of Psychoanalysis,* trans. Alan Sheridan (New York: Norton, 1981), 5 (hereafter cited as *Seminar XI*); *Seminar XX,* 2.

7. Lacan, *Seminar VII,* 24.

8. Lacan, *Seminar XI,* 138.

9. Slavoj Žižek, *The Plague of Fantasies* (London: Verso, 1997), 37, emphasis mine. Žižek adds that the later Lacan is more concerned to bring the analysand to what he calls "knowledge" of the drive than to interpret the analysand's statements in order to arrive at the subjective truth of his/her desire. See 37–40.

10. Lacan, *Seminar XVII,* 59, cited by Dylan Evans in *An Introductory Dictionary of Lacanian Psychoanalysis* (New York: Brunner-Routledge, 1996), 198.

11. Lacan, *Seminar XI,* 253.

12. Or, as Lacan says in *Seminar XI,* the analyst acknowledges his "deception" of the analysand at "the point at which the analyst awaits the subject [analysand], and sends back to him, according to the formula, his own message in its true signification, that is to say, in an inverted form"(139–140).

13. Lacan clearly recognizes that the alleviation of suffering is one of the promises of psychoanalysis: "are we [analysts] simply, but it is already a lot, something that must respond . . . to the demand not to suffer, at least without understanding why?" (*Seminar VII,* 8).

14. Philosophically minded readers will note that this formulation renders the temporal paradox of the psychoanalytic developmental narrative particularly clear: what is the status of this desire that somehow preexists the self? Lacan's entire career is arguably an attempt to address this question, but it might be the case that desire is granted an ontological priority within his system that, strictly speaking, it has not earned.

15. Lacan, *Seminar VII,* 24.

16. John Donne, *Selected Prose,* ed. Helen Gardner and Timothy Healy (Oxford: Clarendon Press, 1967), 70.

17. Lacan, *Seminar XI,* 7.

18. Alain Badiou makes much of Lacan's claim to be "antiphilosophical," which he explicitly understands as a celebration of resistance to the limitations of explanation; adopting Lacan as one of his "masters," Badiou claims that "philosophy should always think as closely as possible to antiphilosophy." See Badiou, *Ethics,* trans. Peter Hallward (London: Verso, 2002), 122.

19. Jonathan Goldberg, *James I and the Politics of Literature* (Baltimore: Johns Hopkins University Press, 1998), 66, 219.

20. Goldberg's position here represents one of the more obvious versions of the "containment" thesis associated with New Historicism. For some counter-arguments, see Alan Sinfield, "Power and Ideology: An Outline Theory and Sidney's Arcadia," *ELH* 52 (1985): 259–277, reprinted in *Faultlines: Cultural Materialism and the Politics of Dissident Reading* (Berkeley: University

of California Press, 1990), 80–94; David Norbrook, "The Monarch of Wit and the Republic of Letters," in *Soliciting Interpretation: Literary Theory and Seventeenth Century English Poetry*, ed. Elizabeth D. Harvey and Katherine Eisaman Maus (Chicago: University of Chicago Press, 1990), 3–36; and Ronald Corthell, *Ideology and Desire in Renaissance Poetry: The Subject of Donne* (Detroit, MI: Wayne State University Press, 1997), 57. Still others could be listed.

21. William Shakespeare, *The Tragedy of King Lear,* ed. Jay Halio (Cambridge: Cambridge University Press, 1992), 128; Coppelia Kahn, "The Absent Mother In King Lear," in *Re-writing the Renaissance,* ed. Margaret W. Ferguson, Maureen Quilligan, and Nancy Vickers, 33–49 (Chicago: University of Chicago Press, 1986).

22. Malcolm Bowie, *Lacan* (Cambridge, Mass.: Harvard University Press, 1991), 92.

23. Thus, *King Lear* does not represent an inverted Electra complex or a repressed incest narrative (as a traditional Freudian analyst might be inclined to claim). Lear's demand for his daughters' love can be more precisely understood as a manifestation of the Lacanian Imaginary, to the degree that Lear wants to make his children into the vessels that will reconstitute him—or *reanoint* him—as his own ideal self (that is, as omnipotent, deserving of unconditional devotion, "kingly"), even as he divests himself of the official responsibilities of kingship. This is why Lear finds Cordelia's reply that she can say "Nothing" in response to his notorious demand so unbearable: she is not so much withholding something from him as she is turning him *into* nothing, negating his putative identity by denying his fantasy of omnipotent selfhood, and making him, in the words of the Fool, "an O without a figure"(Shakespeare, *Lear,* 129). As Lacan writes: "What I seek in speech is the response of the other. What constitutes me as subject is my question." See Jacques Lacan, *Ecrits: A Selection,* trans. Alan Sheridan (New York: Norton, 1977), 86. This demand for "self-constitution" through speech explains why audiences sense much more than the literal threat that Cordelia will not receive her "portion" of the kingdom lying behind Lear's response: "Nothing will come of nothing, speak again" (Shakespeare, *Lear,* 100).

24. John P. Muller, *Beyond the Psychoanalytic Dyad: Developmental Semiotics in Freud, Pierce and Lacan* (New York: Routledge, 1996), 3.

25. Ibid.

26. Ibid.

27. Ibid., 4.

28. Ibid.

29. Jacques Lacan, *Seminar of Jacques Lacan: Book I. Freud's Papers on Technique,* trans. John Forrester (New York: Norton, 1988) 142 (hereafter cited as *Seminar I*). Toward the end of Seminar I, Lacan gestures in the direction of a more valorized notion of love, conceived as an "active gift" rather than "imaginary passion"; somewhat contradictorily, this "active" love seems nevertheless to depend more on the authentic self-perception of the beloved

than on the perceptions of the lover (see *Seminar I*, 276). Moreover, in some late passages in *The Seminar of Jacques Lacan: Book II. The Ego in Freud's Theory and in the Technique of Psychoanalysis* [hereafter cited as *Seminar II*], trans. Sylvia Tomaselli (New York: Norton, 1988), Lacan contrasts imaginary love with the "symbolic pact" of married love (in some passages inspired by Levi-Strauss on the traffic in women) and suggests that the "primitive form" of marriage has a "universal function" lost to more civilized cultures (see *Seminar II*, 260–263). It is hard to take these claims entirely seriously, or even to know whether we are being asked to do so; and, as Henry Staten notes, such arguments are in any case difficult to reconcile with those of the previous seminar. See Staten, *Eros in Mourning* (Baltimore: Johns Hopkins University Press, 1995), 167–185, esp. 224n.15.

30. Lacan, *Seminar I*, 142.
31. Muller, *Beyond*, 120.
32. My phraseology may raise the hackles of those who prefer to follow Lacan *avant la lettre;* although in earlier essays (e.g., "The Function and Field of Speech and Language in Psychoanalysis") Lacan uses the term "intersubjective," he came to mistrust the concept as too evocative of the dyadic symmetries of the Imaginary and therefore detrimental to the aim of treatment. On this shift, see Evans, *Introductory Dictionary*, 90.
33. Bowie, *Lacan*, 83.
34. Lacan, *Ecrits: A Selection*, 141.
35. Cited in Bowie, *Lacan*, 97. Lacan's divergencies from poststructuralism have been emphasized by both critical and sympathetic commentators. One of Lacan's more skeptical readers, Henry Staten, writes that "Lacan seems to deny satisfaction to the nostalgia for presence in what might be taken as a most scrupulously deconstructive fashion. This aspect of his doctrine is well known and no doubt constitutes a crucial element in its attractiveness for post-structuralism. . . . [H]owever, through this movement of negativity Lacan preserves in a sophisticated new fashion the Christian/Platonic depreciation of the worldly libidinal object" (Staten, *Eros in Mourning*, 167). In a more positive vein, Žižek also insists on "the anti-post-structuralist emphasis" of Lacan's notion of "the substance of enjoyment, the real kernel around which . . . signifying interplay is structured." See Slavoj Žižek, *The Sublime Object of Ideology* (London: Verso, 1989), 72.
36. Bowie, *Lacan*, 92.
37. Ibid.
38. Talking Heads, "Heaven," *Fear of Music* (Sire, 1979).
39. Jacques Lacan, "Some Reflections on the Ego," *International Journal of Psycho-Analysis* 34 (1951): 15.
40. According to Lacan, the failure of Imaginary identifications is typically accompanied by dreams of bodily fragmentation, decapitation, ripping open, and so on. While clinical evidence for this remains disputed, we might note in this context Donne's interest in anatomized (and fragmented) bodies. Donne's imagery of fragmentation frequently occurs in poems describing the aftermath of a failed love relationship—that is, in Lacan's terms, a failed

imaginary identification. A further exploration of Donne's poetry as a manifestation of the Lacanian imaginary might therefore begin with those poems of ripping, cutting, and dissection, such as "The Dampe," "The Legacie," and "The Will."

41. Peter DeSa Wiggins, *Donne, Castiglione, and the Poetry of Courtliness* (Bloomington: Indiana University Press, 2000), 111.

42. Indeed, while "The Canonization" was a favorite poem of New Criticism, "A nocturnall" and "A Valediction of my name, in the window" both proved more popular with deconstructivist critics during the 1980s and 1990s.

43. Wiggins, *Donne*, 108–109.

44. Wiggins's reading thus underlines the accuracy of Henry Staten's argument regarding the basic continuity between some of Lacan's central conceptions and what Staten calls the "erotophobia" of the Christian-Platonic tradition. See Staten, *Eros in Mourning*, esp. 175–179.

45. Lacan, *Seminar XX*, 47.

46. Ibid.

47. Ibid.

48. Lacan, *Seminar I*, 142.

49. Ibid., 277. On this, at least, Lacan is consistent. On the last page of *Seminar XX* he is still insisting on the unhappy idea that "true love gives way to hatred"(146).

50. The primary text is, of course, Freud's paper "On Narcissism," in *The Standard Edition of the Complete Psychological Works,* ed. James Strachey (London: Hogarth Press, 1957), 14:67–104.

51. Freud, "Observations on Transference-Love," in *The Standard Edition* (1958), 12: 157–174. Indeed, according to Jonathan Lear, for Freud it is "the existence of love" rather than the irreducibility of language that "underlies the idea that the individual cannot be understood in isolation." See Lear, *Love and Its Place in Nature: A Philosophical Interpretation of Freudian Psychoanalysis* (New Haven: Yale University Press, 1998), 157n.2. Lear's book offers an important alternative to the Lacanian "return to Freud."

52. The notion of "genital oblativity" is first introduced in Lacan's early paper "Aggressivity in psychoanalysis," in *Ecrits: A Selection*, 8–29. Of particular relevance is the passage where Lacan claims that "one cannot stress too strongly the irreducible character of the narcissistic structure [in "liberated . . . genital libido"]. . . . [N]o notion of oblativity could produce altruism from that structure"(24). For related examples, see *Seminar VII*: "Do I need to emphasize the role we attribute to a certain idea of 'love fulfilled'? . . . That is the idea of genital love—a love that is supposed to be itself alone the model of a satisfying object relation: doctor-love, I would say if I wanted to emphasize in a comical way the tone of this ideology; love as hygiene, I would say, to suggest what analytical ambition seems to be limited to here"(8).

53. Lacan, *Seminar I*, 276.

54. Lacan, *Ecrits: A Selection*, 286.
55. "Desire begins to take shape in the margin in which demand becomes separated from need." Ibid., 311.
56. Ibid., 287.
57. Bowie, *Lacan*, 122.
58. Ibid., 136.
59. As I've noted, for the later Lacan, the "truth" of the subject is still derived from some deeper, unrepresentable, unconscious force or substance, but his emphasis is more on the blind imperatives of the drive than the multiplicity of desire.
60. Lacan, *Seminar I*, 183.
61. Lacan, *Seminar III*, 179, cited in Staten, *Eros in Mourning*, 168.
62. Staten, *Eros in Mourning*, 168. Staten adds that "the subject as pure desire cannot have the particularity of a thing in the world, but only that of a pure structure or form. . . . Yet structure is normally the element of transparticularity or universality, whereas the structure of Lacanian desire has to be understood as the structure of an *absolute particularity*, of individuation beyond that which matter can bestow"(171). In *The Plague of Fantasies*, Žižek explains all kinds of compulsive behaviors through this Lacanian insight: "*Jouissance* is . . . the ontological aberration, the disturbed balance (*clinamen*, to use the old philosophical term) which accounts for the passage from Nothing to Something; it designates the minimal *contraction* (in Schelling's sense of the term) which provides the density of the subject's reality. Someone can be happily married, with a good job and many friends, fully satisfied with his life, and yet absolutely hooked on some specific formation ('sinthom') of *jouissance*, ready to put everything at risk rather than renounce *that* (drugs, tobacco, drink, a particular sexual perversion . . .). Although his symbolic universe may be nicely set up, this absolutely meaningless intrusion, this *clinamen*, upsets everything, and there is nothing to be done, because it is only in this 'sinthom' that the subject encounters the density of being—when he is deprived of it, his universe is empty" (49). This passage explains why Lacan equates the particularity of a structure of desire with the essence of the subject; but it also potentially adds to the confusion by multiplying the rhetorical figures that describe that particularity (*jouissance*, *clinamen*, "sinthom," and so on). This, for me, is one of the most frustrating aspects of Lacan's thought; while these terms (and related concepts, such as the *objet a*, the drive, pleasure) are often distinguished from one another as different elements of the subject's structure of desire, at other times they seem like different names for the same thing: the unrepresentable Truth of the subject's being. Thus, one often gets the sensation, when reading Lacan (or Žižek), that one is being offered a new formulation or concept, only to find oneself returned to the same (non) place.
63. Joseph H. Smith, *Arguing with Lacan: Ego Psychology and Language* (New Haven: Yale University Press, 1991), 54.
64. Lacan, *Ecrits: A Selection*, 271.

65. Lacan, *Seminar VII,* 303.

66. As Staten writes: "Lacan, like other moralists of an absolutist stripe, seeks to make us feel that the lives we lead are a degraded version of the real thing. But isn't it a little late in the day for making such sharp divisions between darkness and light, such a clean break with the creaturely?" (*Eros in Mourning,* 184).

67. Bowie, *Lacan,* 93.

68. Žižek, *The Plague of Fantasies,* 7. For Jean Laplanche and Jean-Bertrand Pontalis's original essay "Fantasy and the Origins of Sexuality," see *Formations of Fantasy,* ed. Victor Burgin, James Donald, and Cora Kaplan (London: Methuen, 1986).

69. John Donne, *The Variorum Edition of the Poetry of John Donne,* vol. 2, *The Elegies,* ed. Gary A. Stringer (Bloomington: Indiana University Press, 2000), 369.

70. Tim Dean suggests that this valorization of the aesthetic as the "beyond" of desire/sexuality may be less incompatible with a Lacanian perspective than I've suggested. See his courageous and stimulating *Beyond Sexuality* (Chicago: University of Chicago Press, 2000), the last sentence of which reads: "Beyond sexuality lie the myriad possibilities of aesthetics."

Conclusion: The Desire of Criticism and the
Criticism of Desire (Part II)

1. The phrase is, of course, associated with the work of Stanley Fish, particularly *Is There a Text in This Class?* (Cambridge, MA: Harvard University Press, 1980).

2. My emphasis will be more literary-critical than psychoanalytic, but for an essay that reverses this direction, and inspired a good deal of my thinking, see Adam Phillips's "Poetry and Psychoanalysis," in *Promises, Promises* (London: Faber and Faber, 2000), 1–34.

3. Jonathan Culler, *On Deconstruction: Theory and Criticism after Structuralism* (Ithaca, NY: Cornell University Press, 1982), 176.

4. Ibid.

5. M. H. Abrams, "The Deconstructive Angel," *Critical Inquiry* 3 (1977): 434.

6. Isak Dinesen, *Last Tales* (New York: Random House, 1975), 126.

7. Charles Brenner, *Psychonanalytic Technique and Psychic Conflict* (New York: International Universities Press, 1976); quoted in Janet Malcolm, *Psychoanalysis: The Impossible Profession* (New York: Random House, 1982), 45.

8. Quoted in Malcolm, *Psychoanalysis,* 46.

9. Ibid., 47.

10. Hélène Cixous, "Conversations," in *Writing Differences: Readings from the Seminar of Hélène Cixous,* ed. Susan Sellers (New York: St. Martin's Press, 1988), 147.

11. William Shakespeare, *The Tragedy of King Lear,* ed. Jay L. Halio (Cambridge: Cambridge University Press, 1992), 98.

12. Samuel Weber, *Institution and Interpretation* (Minneapolis: University of Minnesota Press, 1987), 33–34.

13. For an insightful account of the many ironies attending the historicist resistance to psychoanalytic theory, see L. O. Aranye Fradenburg, *Sacrifice Your Love: Psychoanalysis, Historicism, Chaucer* (Minneapolis: University of Minnesota Press, 2002), esp. "Becoming Medieval," 44–78.

14. Weber, *Institution*, 34.

15. Terry Eagleton, *Literary Theory: An Introduction* (London: Blackwell, 1983), 11.

16. The phrase is, of course, Matthew Arnold's.

17. Culler, *On Deconstruction,* 182.

18. Richard Halpern comments with wry wit on the way in which New Critical notions of the autonomous lyric have presented an "almost hypnotically tempting target" to contemporary theorists: "Poetic closure has, indeed, been elevated to the uncomfortable and paradoxical status of most-favored victim; no one believes in it anymore, yet it is sustained in a kind of half-life, like a comatose patient, only in order to be wheeled out and beaten as occasion demands." See Halpern, "The Lyric in the Field of Information," *Yale Journal of Criticism* 6 (1993): 185.

19. Cleanth Brooks, *The Well Wrought Urn* (New York: Harvest, 1947), x.

20. Stuart Schneiderman, *Jacques Lacan: The Death of an Intellectual Hero* (Cambridge, MA: Harvard University Press, 1983), 69.

21. Famously, Lacan would not allow Alan Sheridan to include the *objet petit a* in his glossary of terms when he translated Seminar XI for an English audience, preferring to leave "the reader to develop an appreciation of the concept" over the course of the text. See Jacques Lacan, *The Seminar of Jacques Lacan: Book XI. The Four Fundamental Concepts of Psychoanalysis,* trans. Alan Sheridan (New York: Norton, 1981), 282.

22. Indeed, in his discussion of the concept of the Thing (generally read by Lacanians as an early incarnation of the *objet petit a*) in Seminar VII, Lacan offers the image of the vessel or "vase" as a paradigmatic emblem of creation. See Jacques Lacan, *The Seminar of Jacques Lacan: Book VII. The Ethics of Psychoanalysis,* trans. Dennis Potter (New York: Norton, 1992), esp. 120–121, 170–172. As Halpern has pointed out, "[T]he vase's physical emptiness, the void it creates by surrounding it, allegorizes its own status as an empty signifier, a signifier of nothing." Having drafted this chapter before reading this work, I was unable to take full advantage of Halpern's insights; however, I hope that the general tenor of my discussion conforms with his own lucid account. See Halpern, *Shakespeare's Perfume: Sodomy and Sublimity in the Sonnets, Wilde, Freud, and Lacan* (Philadelphia: University of Pennsylvania Press, 2002), esp. 87–101.

23. John Keats, "Ode on a Grecian Urn." The text is that provided in the two-volume *Norton Anthology of English Literature,* ed. M. H. Abrams (New York: Norton, 1986), 2:822–823.

24. Ben Jonson, "To the Immortal Memory and Friendship of That Noble Pair,

Sir Lucius Cary and Sir H. Morison," in *The Complete Poems,* ed. George Parfitt (London: Penguin, 1988), 212.

25. Wallace Stevens, "Anecdote of the Jar." I quote from the *Norton Anthology of Modern Poetry,* ed. Richard Ellmann and Robert O'Clair (New York: Norton, 1973), 249. For other significant urns in canonical American modernism, one could also cite Faulkner; see David Minter, *William Faulkner: His Life and Work* (Baltimore: Johns Hopkins University Press, 1980), esp. 99–103, and Gail L. Mortimer, "The Smooth, Suave Shape of Desire: Paradox in Faulknerian Imagery of Women," *Women's Studies* 13 (1986): 149–161, for critical discussions of "urn" imagery in his work.

26. John Donne, *The Complete English Poems,* ed. C. A. Patrides, rev. Robin Hamilton (London: Everyman, 1994), 11–12.

27. Brooks, *The Well Wrought Urn,* 17.

28. Culler, *On Deconstruction,* 204.

29. Ibid., 204–205.

30. Dayton Haskin, "On Trying to Make the Record Speak More about Donne's Love Poems," in *John Donne's "Desire of More": The Subject of Anne More Donne in His Poetry* (London: Associated University Presses, 1996), 42. Haskin sees Culler's disagreement with Brooks as an aggressive repudiation: "as Culler would have it, Brooks demonstrated both his presumptuousness, when he implied that his unified reading of the poem constituted a 'well wrought urn' in its own right, and his naïveté" (42).

31. I am not advocating a return to the kind of psychoanalytic criticism that analyzed characters or authors in simple Freudian terms. After feminism, after Foucault, after queer theory, after the linguistic turn of poststructuralism, and the ethical demand (or melancholic fascination) of historicism, any return to psychoanalysis as a discourse of desire must also be a revision and transformation. For an inspiring meditation on this topic, see the final pages of Tim Dean's *Beyond Sexuality* (Chicago: University of Chicago Press, 2000). By a return to psychoanalysis, perhaps all I am really advocating is an idea that I associate with the psychoanalytic tradition, that interpretation should be, insofar as possible, an act of love. See, for example, Jonathan Lear, *Love and Its Place in Nature* (New Haven, CT: Yale University Press, 1998), 10–16.

32. The phrase is Barbara A. Biesecker's, from a review of several critical texts that urge this "rerouting." See her "Rhetorical Studies and the 'New' Psychoanalysis: What's the Real Problem? or Framing the Problem of the Real," *Quarterly Journal of Speech* 84 (1998): 235.

33. Stanley Fish, *Professional Correctness: Literary Studies and Political Change* (Oxford: Clarendon, 1995), 50. Having said this, I strongly disagree with Fish's absolutist insistence that no political consequences ever follow from the practice of criticism. The impact of feminist criticism alone on the lives of countless English undergraduates seems to me to undermine Fish's point (although it is admittedly extremely hard to quantify such an impact). Perhaps the most thoughtful reply to *Professional Correctness* is that of Michael

Berube in *The Employment of English: Theory, Jobs and the Future of Literary Studies* (New York: New York University Press, 1998), 143–169, esp. 148–158. Berube's position echoes my own when he contends that "our skills *may* have political force, and that we should proceed . . . as if" they do (158); but this modestly worded proposal unquestionably involves a scaling back of the rhetoric of politic criticism from that of the previous ten to fifteen years.

34. Louis Montrose, "Professing the Renaissance: The Poetics and Politics of Culture," in *The New Historicism,* ed. H. Aram Veeser (New York: Routledge, 1989), 30.

35. Henry Krips, *Fetish: An Erotics of Culture* (Ithaca, NY: Cornell University Press, 1999), 10.

36. Sigmund Freud, *The Standard Edition of the Complete Psychological Works,* ed. James Strachey (London: Hogarth Press, 1964), 23:275.

37. Catherine Belsey, *Desire: Love Stories in Western Culture* (London: Blackwell, 1994), xii.

38. Fradenburg, *Sacrifice Your Love,* 48.

Index

Harvard University Press is a member of Green Press Initiative
(greenpressinitiative.org), a nonprofit organization working to
help publishers and printers increase their use of recycled paper
and decrease their use of fiber derived from endangered forests.
This book was printed on 100% recycled paper containing
50% post-consumer waste and processed chlorine free.